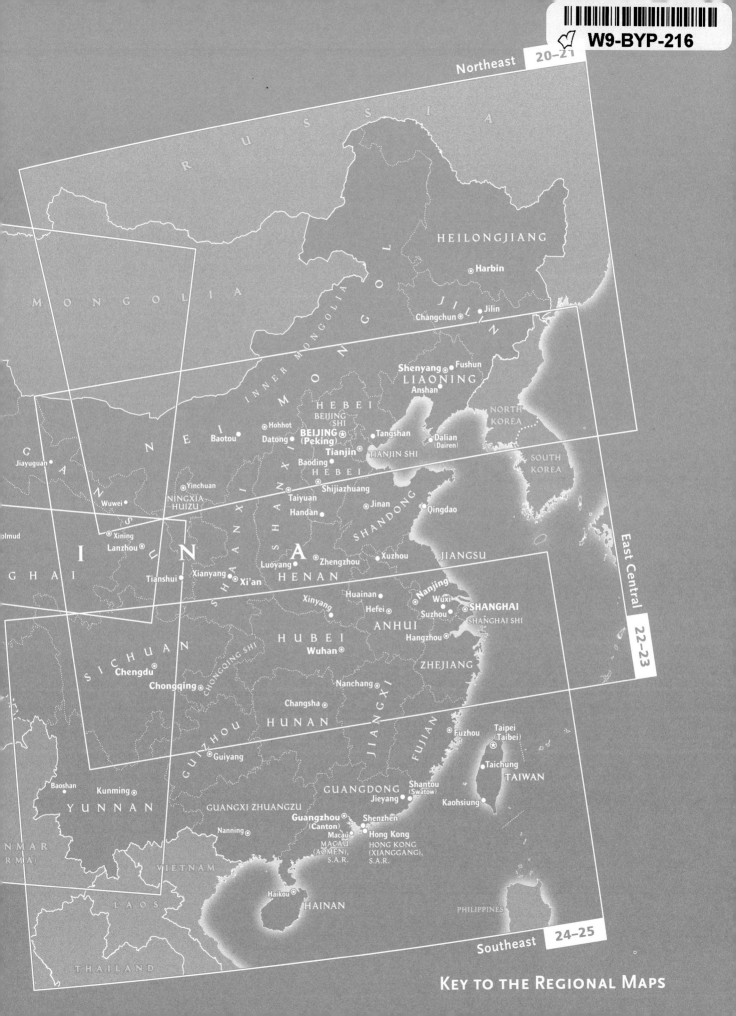

Northeast 20–21

East Central 22–23

Southeast 24–25

R U S S I A

HEILONGJIANG

⊙ Harbin

M O N G O L I A

MONGOLIA

JILIN

Changchun ⊙   ⊙ Jilin

Shenyang ⊙ ⊙ Fushun

LIAONING

Anshan ⊙

NORTH
KOREA

Hohhot ⊙

HEBEI

BEIJING
SHI

BEIJING
(Peking) ⊛

Tangshan ⊙

Dalian
(Dairen) ⊙

SOUTH
KOREA

I N N E R

M O N G O L

N E I

Baotou ⊙

Datong ⊙

Tianjin ⊙

TIANJIN SHI

Jiayuguan ⊙

Baoding ⊙

HEBEI

G A N

Yinchuan ⊙

Shijiazhuang ⊙

Wuwei ⊙

NINGXIA
HUIZU

Taiyuan ⊙

Jinan ⊙

Qingdao ⊙

olmud ⊙

Xining ⊙

S U

Handan ⊙

SHANDONG

S H A A N X I

S H A N X I

I

Lanzhou ⊙

C

N

A

Zhengzhou ⊙

Xuzhou ⊙

JIANGSU

G H A I

Tianshui ⊙

Xianyang ⊙

Luoyang ⊙

HENAN

Nanjing ⊙

Wuxi ⊙

Xi'an ⊙

Xinyang ⊙

Huaian ⊙

Hefei ⊙

Suzhou ⊙

SHANGHAI ⊛

SHANGHAI SHI

ANHUI

Hangzhou ⊙

HUBEI

CHONGQING SHI

Wuhan ⊙

ZHEJIANG

SICHUAN

Chengdu ⊙

Chongqing ⊙

Nanchang ⊙

Changsha ⊙

HUNAN

JIANGXI

Taipei
(Taibei) ⊛

GUIZHOU

Guiyang ⊙

FUJIAN

Fuzhou ⊙

Taichung ⊙

TAIWAN

Baoshan ⊙

Kunming ⊙

Y U N N A N

GUANGXI ZHUANGZU

Shantou
(Swatow) ⊙

Kaohsiung ⊙

GUANGDONG

Jieyang ⊙

Nanning ⊙

Guangzhou ⊙
(Canton)

Shenzhen ⊙

Macau ⊙

Hong Kong ⊙

NMAR
RMA)

MACAU
(AOMEN),
S.A.R.

HONG KONG
(XIANGGANG),
S.A.R.

VIETNAM

Haikou ⊙

LAOS

HAINAN

PHILIPPINES

THAILAND

KEY TO THE REGIONAL MAPS

NATIONAL
GEOGRAPHIC

Atlas
OF •
China

NATIONAL GEOGRAPHIC

Atlas
OF
China

NATIONAL GEOGRAPHIC

WASHINGTON, D.C.

Contents

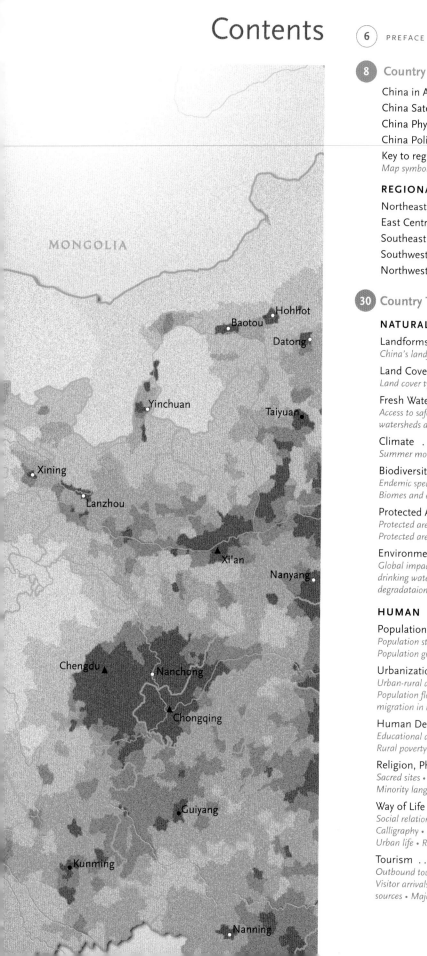

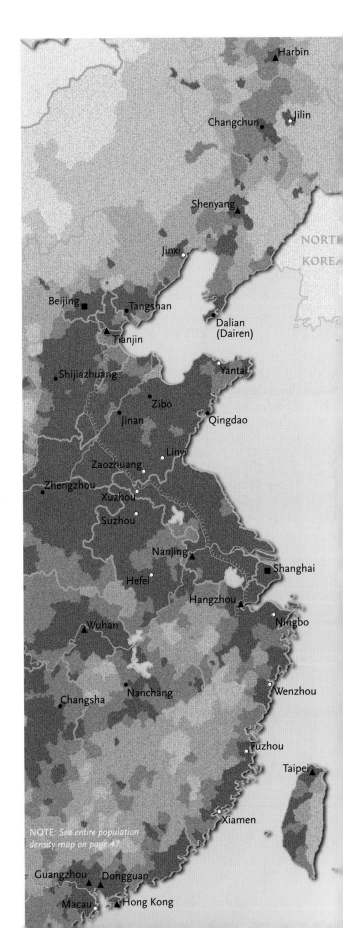

NOTE: *See entire population density map on page 47.*

Preface

A Startling Society During the span of its 4,000-year history, China became a cultural force, its influence extending throughout East and Southeast Asia. Now, as the 21st century unfolds, the impact of this great nation is rapidly extending beyond its Asian domain. "Made in China" labels pepper shelves in marts and malls everywhere. Almost any statistic attached to China is a large one. With a population of some 1.3 billion people—roughly a fifth of humanity—China now has 51 cities with a population of over a million people and is home to 55 ethnic minorities. More remarkable yet is China's emergence from a century and a half of foreign intervention, military occupation, civil war, dogma-driven policies with horrendous consequences, and competing economic theories to become a major global economic and political player. How China uses its enormous and growing potential will play a significant role in the future of the planet. To help understand

The night view from the Bund section of Shanghai—once the epicenter of European finance, influence, society, and architecture—across the Huangpu River was until the 1990s a gaze into darkness. Before then Pudong was farmland and swamp—no blazing towers, no new financial center of China, no 5,000 buildings more than 18 stories high, no prime example of a country that has packed three centuries of economic growth into three decades.

this often contradictory and endlessly fascinating nation, National Geographic's cartographers, writers, editors, researchers, and independent consultants have created this *Atlas of China*. Regional maps, compiled especially for this volume, present a detailed portrait of China's cities and towns, rivers, and roadways. Map notations address the politically charged Kashmir and Taiwan issues. Physical maps show the sweep of China's terrain, from the remote heights of the Tibetan plateau to the long, river-cut eastern coastline. Thematic maps trace China's diversity and its most pressing issues, from the strain on its natural resources to the growing divide between rich and poor to urbanization, Westernization, consumerism, military strength, and many more essential aspects of life in the modern "Middle Kingdom." We hope that this unique *Atlas of China* will engage you and provide the knowledge necessary to begin to comprehend the wonders and challenges of this vast, complex country.

—Terry B. Adamson

Terry B. Adamson *is Executive Vice President of the National Geographic Society.*
He is a Trustee of the Asia Foundation and served as its Chairman of the Board of Trustees
for more than four years.

Country and Regional Maps

"Made in China" is a ubiquitous tag, but for most consumers, China's geography is a mystery. The maps in the following section help illustrate China and its diverse landscape. The first map, China in Asia, presents the country from the Chinese point of view—at the center of Asia and the world. The satellite and physical maps use a multitude of colors and patterns to portray China's magnificent variety of physical features, where green plains contrast with rugged mountains and uplands that make up two-thirds of China's terrain. The political country map represents China's administrative divisions and a continuous border shared with 14 other countries—the most of any nation. The five regional maps—each uniquely compiled and drawn at the same scale—provide a roaming window of rich detail. These larger scale sections show thousands of cities and towns, and the roads and railways that connect them. A digital elevation model enhances the view of China's natural physical features.

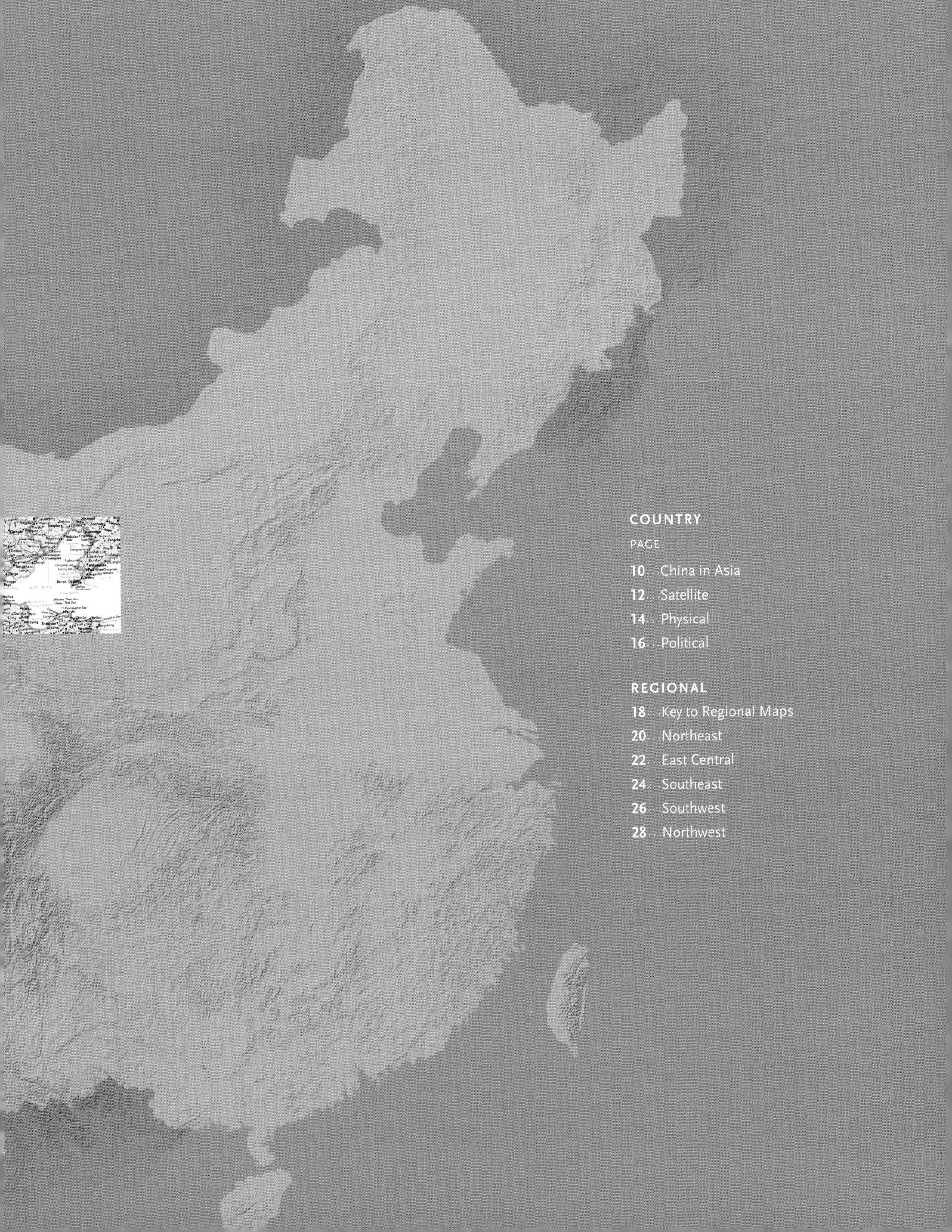

COUNTRY

PAGE

REGIONAL

110° 120° 130° 140° 150° 160° 60°

E R I A
Lena

Aldanskoye
Nagor'ye
Aldan

A

•Skovorodino

Ozero
Baykal
(Lake Baikal)

Vitim

•Chita
•Ulan Ude

I A

Heilong Jiang
Amur

•Komsomol'sk
na Amure

Amur

•Blagoveshchensk

OSTROV
SAKHALIN

Udskaya Guba

•Okha

SEA
OF
OKHOTSK

POLUOSTROV KAMCHATKA
(KAMCHATKA PENINSULA)

Zaliv
Shelikhova

•Magadan

BERING
SEA

•Petropavlovsk-
Kamchatskiy

50°

•Ulaanbaatar
(Ulan Bator)

Herlen

Hulun Nur

Songhua

•Qiqihar

D O N G B E I
(M A N C H U R I A)

•Harbin

Xingkai
Hu

Ozero
Khanka

•Khabarovsk

Tatarsky Proliv

•Yuzhno-
Sakhalinsk

Russia
Urup

KURIL'SKIYE OSTROVA
(KURIL ISLANDS)

Iturup
Kunashir

•zadgad
•Baruun
Urt

I N N E R   M O N G O L I A

•Changchun
•Jilin

Vladivostok•

Sapporo•

HOKKAIDŌ

J A

•Baotou
•Hohhot
Tangshan•

Shenyang• •Fushun
Anshan•

Yalu

•Ch'ŏngjin

NORTH
KOREA

Kanggye•

Aomori•

O B I

GOBI

BEIJING ⊕
Shijiazhuang• •Tianjin

Sinŭiju•
Dalian•
(Darien)

Bo
Hai

Hamhŭng•

•P'yŏngyang

SEA OF
JAPAN
(EAST SEA)

Sendai•

P A N

HONSHŪ

Miller Cylindrical Projection

SCALE 1:33,000,000
1 CENTIMETER = 330 KILOMETERS; 1 INCH = 520 MILES

0 200 400 600 800 1000 1200
KILOMETERS

40°

•Taiyuan

Huang
(Yellow)

Incheon• ⊕**SEOUL**
SOUTH
Daejeon• KOREA

Nagoya•
Kyōto•

N
•Luoyang
Xi'an•

•Jinan
•Zhengzhou

Qingdao•

YELLOW
SEA

Daegu•
Busan•
(Pusan)

Kōbe•
Hiroshima•
Ōsaka

TŌKYŌ
Kawasaki

Yokohama•

0 200 400 600 800 1000 1200
STATUTE MILES

•Xinyang
Hefei•

•Nanjing
Jeju-do

Nagasaki•

Shikoku

Fukuoka•

Izu Shotō

NAMPŌ   SHOTŌ

•Wuhan

Chang Jiang
(Yangtze)

SHANGHAI•
Hangzhou•

EAST

Kyūshū

30°

Chongqing•
Changsha•
Nanchang•

CHINA

SEA

NANSEI SHOTŌ
(RYUKYU ISLANDS)

Okinawa•

Bonin Islands
(Ogasawara Guntō)
Japan

Guiyang•
Fuzhou•

Daitō
Islands
Japan

PACIFIC

Nanning•
•Macau
(Aomen)

Guangzhou•
(Canton)

•Hong Kong
(Xianggang)

Taiwan Strait

Taipei•

•Kaohsiung

Taiwan

Volcano Is.
(Kazan Rettō)

Iwo To (Iwo Jima)
Japan

TROPIC OF CANCER

Haiphong•
noi

Luzon Strait

TAIWAN
The People's Republic of China
claims Taiwan as its 23rd
province. Taiwan's government
(Republic of China) maintains
that there are two political entities.

Batan Is.

PHILIPPINE

SEA

20°

OCEAN

Hainan

Babuyan Is.

Xisha Qundao
(Paracel Is.)
Administered
by China
Claimed by
Vietnam

LUZON

**NORTHERN
MARIANA
ISLANDS**
U.S.

•Da Nang

VIETNAM

•Manila ⊕ Quezon City

•Saipan
•Rota

thani

Mindoro

PHILIPPINES

•Guam
U.S.

10°

Penh• •Nha Trang

Ho Chi Minh City•
(Saigon)

Panay

Samar

Leyte

M I C R O N E S I A

Spratly Is.

Negros

Palawan

SULU

Yap Is.

FEDERATED STATES OF MICRONESIA

Davao•

MINDANAO

•Melekeok

PALAU

C A R O L I N E   I S L A N D S

•Palikir

Bandar Seri
Begawan

⊕

SEA

SPRATLY ISLANDS
The scattered islands and reefs called the Spratly
Islands are claimed by Brunei, China, Malaysia,
the Philippines , and Vietnam. The Spratlys
possess rich fishing grounds and potential oil.

S O U T H

BRUNEI

CELEBES
SEA

A Y S I A

ORE

B O R N E O
(KALIMANTAN)

Manado•

Halmahera

Biak•

BISMARCK

Admiralty
Islands
Manus

MELAN

0°

GREATER

Balikpapan•

SULAWESI
(CELEBES)

Makassar Strait

Buru

Kendari•

Ceram

M O L U C C A S

Jayapura•

N E W

G U I N E A

ARCHIPELAGO

New
Ireland

New Britian

Bougainville•

Santa Isabel•

N
UNDA ISLANDS

JAKARTA
ung •Semarang
ava •Surabaya

Makassar•

I N D O N E S I A

Bali
Lombok
Sumbawa

BANDA SEA

Yamdena

Dolak

IRIAN
JAYA

PAPUA
NEW GUINEA

New Georgia•

•Honiara
Guadalcanal•

Malaita•

SOLOMON
ISLANDS

S I A

JAVA
LESSER S

Flores

Dili

Timor

TIMOR-LESTE
(EAST TIMOR)

Sumba

ARAFURA

SEA

Port Moresby ⊕

0°

CHINA FROM SPACE

This composite panorama presents a striking image of China, from sweeping mountain systems with the frozen Himalaya, to the sere Gobi desert, and a lush southeast. It was created by merging hundreds of images captured by two Landsat satellites, along with data collected by a topographic radar system carried by the space shuttle *Endeavour*. Images gathered by Landsat 7 and supplemented by Landsat 5 were selected and combined into a mosaic to eliminate cloud cover and show the land as it typically appears during the growing season. The 14.5-ton, shuttle-mounted topographic radar employed two antennas, one carried in the payload bay, the other on a 200-foot-long boom. Each antenna captured slightly different images of the terrain. Those inputs were processed to produce a detailed digital topographic model, here exaggerated eight times for visual effect.

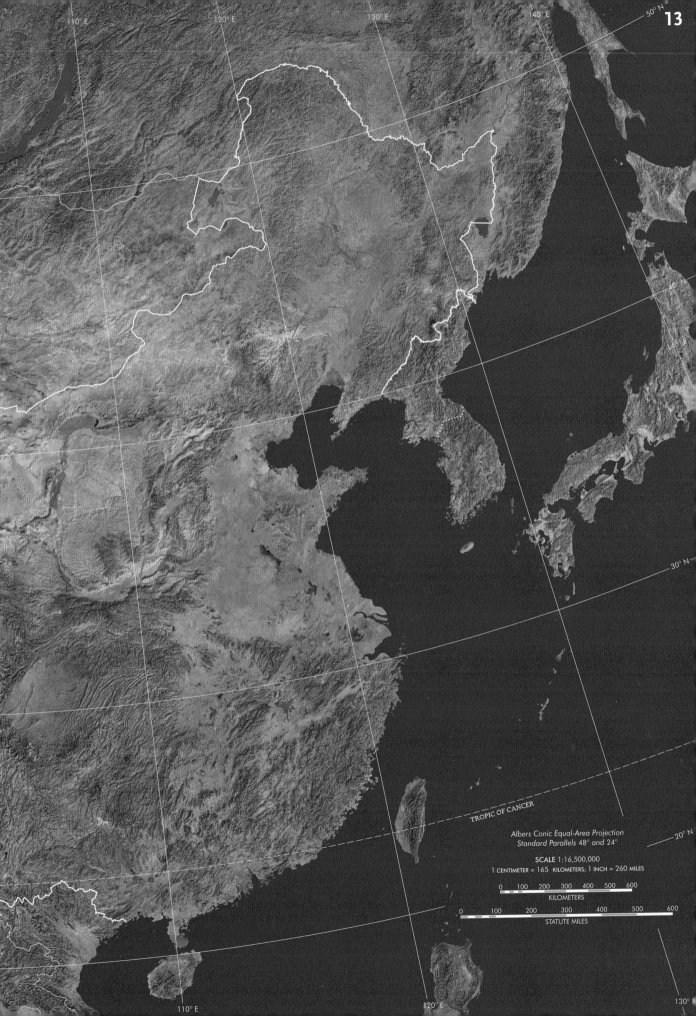

50° N

110° E

120° E

130° E

140° E

40° N

50° N

30° N

20° N

TROPIC OF CANCER

Albers Conic Equal-Area Projection
Standard Parallels 48° and 24°

SCALE 1:16,500,000
1 CENTIMETER = 165 KILOMETERS; 1 INCH = 260 MILES

| 0 | 100 | 200 | 300 | 400 | 500 | 600 |

KILOMETERS

| 0 | 100 | 200 | 300 | 400 | 500 | 600 |

STATUTE MILES

110° E

120° E

130°

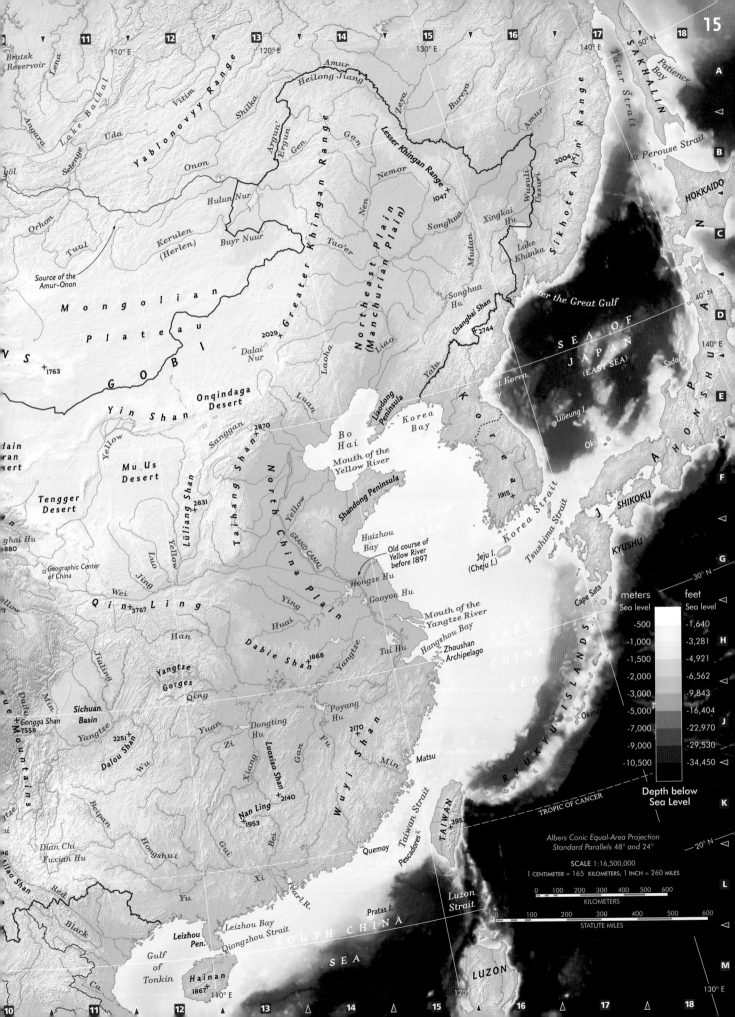

11 110° E 12 120° E 13 14 15 130° E 16 17 140° E 18

Bratsk
Reservoir
Lena

Angara

Selenge
Orhon
Gol

Tuul

Source of the
Amur-Onon

M o n g o l i a n

P l a t e a u

1763

G O B I

Yin Shan

Onqindaga
Desert

Mu Us
Desert

Tengger
Desert

880

Geographic Center
of China

Qin Ling 3767

Han

Jialing

Sichuan
Basin

Gongga Shan
7558

Dalou Shan

2251

Yangtze

Min

Wu

Dian Chi
Fuxian Hu

Red

Black

Ca

Yablonovyy Range

Lake Baikal

Vitim

Uda

Shilka

Onon

Hulun Nur

Kerulen
(Herlen)

Buyr Nuur

Argun'
Ergun

Gen.

Dalai
Nur

2029

Laoha

Sanggan

Yellow

Lüliang Shan

2831

Luo

Jing

Wei

Yuan

Dalou Shan

Beipan

Hongshui

Amur

Heilong Jiang

Gan

Nemor

Nen

Tao'er

Songhua

Taihang Shan

2870

North China Plain

GRAND CANAL

Yellow

Ying

Huai

Dabie Shan 1868

Yangtze

Yangtze
Gorges

Qing

Dongting
Hu

Zi

Xiang

Luoxiao Shan

2140

Nan Ling
1953

Gui

Bei

Xi

Yu

Lesser Khingan Range

1047

Greater Khingan Range

Northeast Plain
(Manchurian Plain)

Liao

Songhua
Hu

Changbai Shan

2744

Yalu

Liaodong
Peninsula

Bo
Hai

Mouth of the
Yellow River

Shandong Peninsula

Haizhou
Bay

Old course of
Yellow River
before 1897

Hongze Hu

Gaoyou Hu

Tai Hu

Mouth of the
Yangtze River

Hangzhou Bay

Zhoushan
Archipelago

Yellow

Poyang
Hu

Gan

Fu

2170

Wuyi Shan

Min

Matsu

Quemoy

Pearl R.

Pratas I.

Leizhou Bay

Leizhou
Pen.

Gulf
of
Tonkin

Hainan
1867

110° E

Qiongzhou Strait

SOUTH CHINA

SEA

Mudan

Xingkai
Hu

Lake
Khanka

Wusuli
Ussuri

Amur

2004

Sikhote Alin' Range

East Korea
Bay

K
o
r
e
a

1915

YELLOW
SEA

Jeju I.
(Cheju I.)

Korea Strait

Tsushima Strait

EAST
CHINA
SEA

RYUKYU ISLANDS

Okinawa

TAIWAN 3952

Taiwan Strait

Pescadores

Luzon
Strait

LUZON

120° E

Peter the Great Gulf

SEA OF
JAPAN
(EAST SEA)

Ulleung I.

Oki

Sado

SHIKOKU

KYUSHU

H O N S H U

Tatar
Strait

SAKHALIN

Patience
Bay

La Perouse Strait

HOKKAIDO

TROPIC OF CANCER

50° N

40° N

140° E

30° N

20° N

130° E

A

B

C

D

E

F

G

H

J

K

L

M

A

B

C

D

E

F

G

H

J

K

L

M

50°N 60°E

6   7   8

80°E   90°E

KAZAKHSTAN

⊛ Astana
(Aqmola)

R
U
S

ALTAY MOUNTAIN

M

Habahe • Altay
Jeminay • Burqin
Tacheng • Hoboksar • Fuhai • Fuyun
Emin • Qinghe
Toli • Junggar Pendi • Ertai
Karamay (Dzungarian Basin)
Bole • Jinghe • Bajiantan
Huocheng • Yining Ebinur Usu • Shihezi • Jiangjunmiao
(Gulja) Hu Dushanzi • Manas
Zhaosu Gongliu Nilka • Changji Qitai
Ürümqi ⊙ Bogda • Mori
Tekes • Xinyuan Shan
Baicheng • Lunta Hejing • Toksun Turpan Hami
Wushi Xinhe • Kuqa • Yanqi Turpan Pendi (Kumul)
Akqi • Aksu Yuli Kuruktag Sitian
Kalpin • Awat Bosten Hu
Kashi • Artux XINJIANG UYGUR Xingxingxia
(Kashgar) Shule (SINKIANG) Bei Shan Hongliuyuan
Yopurga • Bachu Tarim Lop Nur Dunhuang Anxi Jiayuguan
Yengisar • Markit TARIM PENDI Ikanbujmal Subei Yumen
Shache Taklimakan Shamo Ruoqiang Miran Aksay Qilia
Taxkorgan • Yecheng ALTUN SHAN Da Qaidam
Mingteke Pishan Hotan Qiemo Qarqan Baxkorgan Mangnai Iqe Delingha
Moyu Lop Ruoqiang Xorkol Gas Hure Qaidam Pendi Qing
Hotan • Qira Yutian Ayakkum Hu Hu Urt Boluntay Golmud Dulan
Yutian Minfeng Aqqikkol Hu Qimantag Moron QINGHA
Boundary KUNLUN SHAN Hoh Xil Budongquan Gyaring
claimed by India AKSAI Tielongtan Ulan Ul Shan Wudaoliang Hu Ngoring Hu
Changmar Hoh Xil Shan Yugê Hars
Boundary Boundary claimed by India QING ZANG GAOYUAN Tanggula Shan Zadoi Yushu
claimed by Pakistan Rutog Lumajangdong (PLATEAU OF TIBET) Nangqên
Co Amdo Riwoqê
Nganglong Kangri Nyima Sog Dengqên Qamdo
Ga'gyal Gêrzê XIZANG Nagqu Baxoi Bamba
Boundary Zanda (TIBET) Markam
claimed by China Barga Lunggar Coqên Nyainqêntanglha Shan Bomi
Burang Gangdisê Shan Zhari Nam Lhari Rawu Mêdog
Zhabdün Namco Danxung Maizhokunggar Nyingchi Zayü
Gyirong Saga Xigazê Lhasa ⊙ Yarlung Boundary
Quxü Gonggar Zangbo claimed by China
Lhazê Gyangzê
Mount Everest Kangmar Cona
(Qomolangma, Sagarmatha) Yadong BHUTAN A
+ 8850 (29,035 ft) Kathmandu ⊛ Thimphu

UZBEKISTAN

TURKMENISTAN
60°E
Dushanbe ⊛

AFGHANISTAN

Kabol
(Kabul) ⊛

Islamabad ⊛

PAKISTAN
30°N

Bishkek ⊛

KYRGYZSTAN

TAJIKISTAN

Hindu Kush

Karakoram

KASHMIR

New Delhi ⊛

NEPAL

INDIA

TROPIC OF CANCER

20°N

ARABIAN
SEA

40°N

Ganga
(Ganges)

BANGLADESH

⊛ DHAKA

Baosha
Tengchong
Luxi
Wanding

MYANMAR
(BURMA)

70°E

Naw Pyi Taw ⊛

BAY OF BENGAL

70°E   80°E   90°E

1   2   3   4   5   6   7   8

CHINA map labels

ASIA

MONGOLIA

Ulaanbaatar (Ulan Bator)

GOBI

INNER MONGOLIA

NEI MONGOL

HEILONGJIANG

Mohe · Tahe · Huma

Genhe · Oroqen · Jagdaqi · Heihe
Xunke
Sunwu · Jiayin
Ergun Youqi · Nenjiang · Morin Wuyiling · Xinqing
Manzhouli · Jala Nur · Yakeshi · Dawa · Nehe · Bei'an · Yichun · Fujin
Hailar · Qiqhar · Hailun · Tieli · Jiamusi · Baoshan
Xin Barag Youqi · Longjiang · Suihua · Hulan · Yilan · Qitaihe · Hulin
Xin Barag Zuoqi · Arxan · Jalaid Qi · Daqing · Anda · Harbin · Didao · Jixi
Ulanhot · Baicheng · Zhaodong · Shuangcheng · Hengshan · Mudanjiang · Dongning
Hulingol · Taonan · Da'an · Songyuan · Fuyu · Yushu · Dongjingcheng
Bairin · Dehui · Jiutai · Jilin · Dunhua · Yanji
Zuoqi · Tongliao · Changchun · **JILIN**
Erenhot · Gongzhuling · Huadian
Xilinhot · Linxi · Ongniud Qi · Siping · Liaoyuan · Meihekou · Longjing
Duolun · Chifeng · Kaiyuan · Tieling · Hunjiang · Tonghua
LIAONING · Fushun · Changbai Shan
Taibus Qi · Lingyuan · Jinzhou · **Shenyang** · Huanren
Shangdu · Jining · **HEBEI** · Chengde · Huludao · Yingkou · Dandong · **NORTH KOREA**
Bayan Obo · Hohhot · Zhangjiakou · Qinhuangdao · Fengcheng · P'yŏngyang
Wuyuan · Zhanghua · Xuanhua · **BEIJING SHI** · Wafangdian
Linhe · Baotou · Togtoh · **Datong** · Great Wall · **Tangshan** · Jinzhou · Pulandian
Dengkou · Xar Burd · Dongsheng · Shuozhou · **BEIJING (Peking)** · **Tianjin** · Tanggu · Dalian (Dairen) · Korea Bay
Wuhai · Hainan · Shenmu · Xinzhou · **Baoding** · Renqiu · **TIANJIN SHI** · Bo Hai
Wuda · Yulin · **HEBEI** · Hekou · Yantai · Weihai
Shizuishan (Dawukou) · Pingluo · Suide · **Shijiazhuang** · Dezhou · Binzhou · Kenli · Wendeng
Jinchang · Xincheng · **Yinchuan** · Wuzhong · Yuci · **Taiyuan** · Linqing · Zibo · Weifang · Laiyang
Qingtongxia (Xiaoba) · Dingbain · Xingtai · **Jinan** · Boshan · **Qingdao**
Zhongwei · **NINGXIA HUIZU** · Yan'an · Handan · Anyang · **SHANDONG**
Wuwei · Yongdeng · Huanxian · Huachi · Linfen · Changzhi · Zoucheng · Xintai · **YELLOW SEA**
Baiyin · Jingyuan · Houma · Puyang · Heze · Jining · Tengzhou · Linyi · Rizhao
Minhe · **Lanzhou** · Guyuan · Xifeng · Yuncheng · Jiaozuo · **Zhengzhou** · Shangqiu · Weishan · Lianyungang (Xinpu)
Linxia · Lintao · Longxi · Qin'an · **Luoyang** · Bozhou · Xuzhou · Yancheng
Hezuo · Longxi · Pingliang · Tongchuan · **HENAN** · Zhoukou · Huaibei · Huaiyin · **JIANGSU**
Luqu · **Tianshui** · Xianyang · **Xi'an** · Pingdingshan · Luohe · Jieshou · Bengbu · Xinghua · Dongtai
Dangchang · Fengxian · Weinan · Zhumadian · Fuyang · Zhenjiang · Taizhou
Zoigê · Wudu · Lüeyang · Liuba · **Qin Ling** · Nanyang · Huainan · **Nanjing** · Jiangyin
Aba · Songpan · Wenxian · Ningqiang · Zaoyang · Xinyang · Lu'an · **Hefei** · **Wuxi** · **SHANGHAI**
Pingwu · Jiangyou · Bazhong · Chengkou · Xiangfan · Guangshui · **ANHUI** · Suzhou · **SHANGHAI SHI**
Mianyang · Langzhong · Daxian · Hanzhong · Shiyan · Laohekou · Anqing · Huzhou · Jiaxing · Yuyao
Deyang · Nanchong · Suizhou · Xiaogan · Macheng · **Hangzhou** · Ningbo
Chengdu · Suining · Enshi · Yichang · **Wuhan** · Ezhou · Huangshi · Huangshan · Shaoxing · Zhuji · **EAST CHINA SEA**
SICHUAN · Zhongxian · **HUBEI** · Zhicheng · Shashi · Xiantao · Xianning · Jiujiang · Jingdezhen · Jiandi
Ya'an · Fengdu · Three Gorges Dam · Yingcheng · Jianli · Jiande · **ZHEJIANG** · Linhai · Taizhou (Jiaojiang, Haimen)
Leshan · **Chongqing** · Fuling · Shishou · Yueyang · Changde · Changsha · Shangrao · Huangyan · Luqiao
Zigong · Luzhou · Nanchuan · **Nanchang** · Yingtan · Rui'an · Wenzhou
Yibin · Junlian · Tongzi · Meitan · Yiyang · **Changsha** · Fu'an · Xiapu · Aojing
Yuexi · Zhenxiong · Gulin · Zunyi · Huaihua · Jishou · Xiangtan · Zhuzhou · Xinyu · Linchuan · Pucheng · Luoyuan · Matsu
Zhaotong · Weining · **GUIZHOU** · Shaoyang · Pingxiang · Hengyang · Shaowu · Fuzhou
Lupanshui · **Guiyang** · Kaili · Jingzhou · Songbai · Leiyang · Sanming · **FUJIAN** · Chilung (Keelung)
Xuanwei · Anshun · Dushan · Rong'an · Yongzhou · Zixing · Ganzhou · Longyan · Xianyou · Putian · Taipei (Taibei)
Zhanyi · Qujing · Dachang · Luorong · Liannan · Lipu · Lechang · Shaoguan · Zhangzhou · Quanzhou · Hsinchu
Qingyuan · Meizhou · Xiamen · Raoping · **Taichung**
Kunming · Shiping · Bose · **GUANGXI ZHUANGZU** · Wuzhou · Shilong · Huizhou · Jieshi · **Shantou (Swatow)** · Tainan · Taitung
Anning · Kaiyuan · Binyang · Rongxian · Yulin · **GUANGDONG** · Jieyang · Haimen · **Kaohsiung** · Pingtung
Gejiu · Wenshan · Jingxi · **Nanning** · **Guangzhou (Canton)** · **Shenzhen** · **TAIWAN**
Hekou · Qinzhou · Dongzhen · Gaozhou · Jiangmen · **Macau** · **Hong Kong**
Pingxiang · Maoming · Yangjiang · **MACAU (AOMEN) S.A.R.** · **HONG KONG (XIANGGANG), S.A.R.**
VIETNAM · Beihai · Zhanjiang · Dongsha
Leizhou · Xuwen · Xuwen
Hanoi · Gulf of Tonkin · Lingao · Haikou · **HAINAN** · **SOUTH CHINA SEA**
Chengmai · Qionghai
Danzhou · Dongfang · Tongshi · Wanning
Sanya

SEA OF JAPAN (EAST SEA)

JAPAN

TŌKYŌ

SOUTH KOREA

SEOUL

Korea Strait · Tsushima Strait

PHILIPPINE SEA

TROPIC OF CANCER

PHILIPPINES

TAIWAN
The People's Republic of China claims Taiwan as its 23rd province. Taiwan's government (Republic of China) maintains that there are two political entities.

Albers Conic Equal-Area Projection
Standard Parallels 48° and 24°

SCALE 1:16,500,000
1 CENTIMETER = 165 KILOMETERS; 1 INCH = 260 MILES

| 0 | 100 | 200 | 300 | 400 | 500 | 600 |
KILOMETERS

| 0 | 100 | 200 | 300 | 400 | 500 | 600 |
STATUTE MILES

S.A.R. .... Special Administrative Region

Regional Map Coverage Key

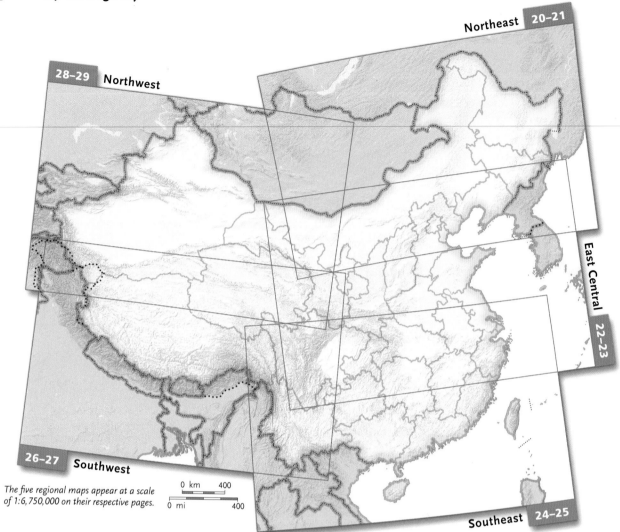

28–29 Northwest

Northeast 20–21

East Central 22–23

26–27 Southwest

Southeast 24–25

The five regional maps appear at a scale of 1:6,750,000 on their respective pages.

0 km 400
0 mi 400

Pronunciation Guide

a	vowel, as in far	**j**	consonant, as in jeep	**u**	vowel, as in too, also as the French "u" in "tu" or the German umlauted "u" in München
b	consonant, as in be	**k**	consonant, as in kind, strongly aspirated		
c	consonant, as "ts" in its			**v**	is only used to produce foreign and national minority words and local dialects
ch	consonant, as "ch" in church, strongly aspirated	**l**	consonant, as in land		
		m	consonant, as in me		
d	consonant, as in do	**n**	consonant, as in no	**w**	used as a semi-vowel in syllables beginning with "u" when not preceded by consonants, pronounced as in want
e	vowel, as "uh" in but	**o**	vowel, as "aw" in law		
ei	diphthong, as in way	**p**	consonant, as in par, strongly aspirated		
f	consonant, as in foot			**x**	consonant, as "sh" in she
g	consonant, as in go	**q**	consonant, as "ch" in cheek	**y**	used as a semi-vowel in syllables beginning with "i" or "u" when not preceded by consonants, pronounced as in yet
h	consonant, as in her, strongly aspirated	**r**	consonant, pronounced as "r" but not rolled, or like "z" in azure		
		s	consonant, as in sister		
i	vowel, two pronunciations, 1) as in eat 2) as in sir in syllables beginning with the consonants c, ch, r, s, sh, z, zh	**sh**	consonant, as "sh" in shore	**z**	consonant, as in zero
		t	consonant, as in top, strongly aspirated	**zh**	consonant, as "j" in jump
ie	diphthong, as in yes				

See page 106 for a more detailed pronunciation explanation.

Regional Map Key

POPULATED PLACES

BEIJING ● Over 5,000,000

Guangzhou ● 3,000,000 – 5,000,000

Xinyang ● 1,000,000 – 2,999,999

Huzhou ● 100,000 – 999,999

Turpan ● 10,000 – 99,999

Jingtai ● Under 10,000

⊛ Capital

◉ Administrative regional capital

MAP SYMBOLS

▫ Point of interest

Three Gorges Dam ⌐ Dam

Bogda Feng + Peak with elevation
5445 in meters

-154. Depression with elevation in meters

3003 ⤳ Pass with elevation in meters

SAMPLE SCALE

Albers Conic Equal-Area Projection
Standard Parallels 50° and 40°

SCALE 1:6,750,000
1 CENTIMETER = 68 KILOMETERS; 1 INCH = 106 MILES

0   50   100   150   200   250
KILOMETERS

0   50   100   150   200   250
STATUTE MILES

TRANSPORTATION

═══ Super highway

┄┄┄ Super highway under construction

─── Highway

─── Other road

▭▭▭ Railroad

- - - Ferry

· · · Canal

HUMAN FEATURES

· · · · · International boundary

· — · · Disputed international boundary

· · · · · · Claimed boundary

· · · · · International boundary water demarcation

· · · · · Administrative regional boundary

▪━▪━▪ Great Wall

KASHMIR Historic or cultural region

NATURAL FEATURES

─── Perennial drainage

←─── Intermittent drainage

─── Intermittent coastline

▱ Area below sea level

▒ Area subject to inundation

░ Swamp and/or wetland

▚ Sand and/or gravel

Glacier and/or icefield

Geographic Equivalents

Bandao	peninsula	Jie	road, street	Ringco	lake
Bei	north	Kangri	mountain, peak, range	Shadi	desert
Bögeni	reservoir	Khrebet	mountain range	Shamo	desert
Caka	lake	Köl-i	lake	Shan	mountain-s, range
Chi	lake	Kou	estuary, river mouth	Shankou	mountain pass
Co	lake	La	pass	Shi	municipality
Da	great, greater	Lam	avenue, road	Shotō	archipelago
Dao	island	Liedao	archipelago, islands	Shuiku	reservoir
Ding	mountain	Ling	mountain-s, range	Tag	mountains
Do	island-s, rock-s	Lu	road, street	Tao	island-s
Dong	east	Nan	south	Wan	bay, gulf
Feng	mount, peak	Nanshan	south mountain	Xi	west
Gang	harbor	Nur	lake, salt lake	Xia	gorge
Gaoyuan	plateau	Nuur	lake	Xiao	lesser, little
Guan	pass	Ozero	lake	Xiang	lane
Guba	bay, gulf	Pao	lake	Yanchi	salt lake
Gum	desert	Pendi	basin	Yang	ocean
Hai	lake, sea	Proliv	strait	Yumco	lake
Haixia	channel, strait	Pubu	waterfall	Yunhe	canal
He	river	Qu	canal	Zaliv	bay, gulf
Hu	lake, reservoir	Qum	desert	Zangbo	river
Jiang	river	Qundao	archipelago, islands	Zhotasy	mountains
Jiao	cape	Ri	mountain, peak		

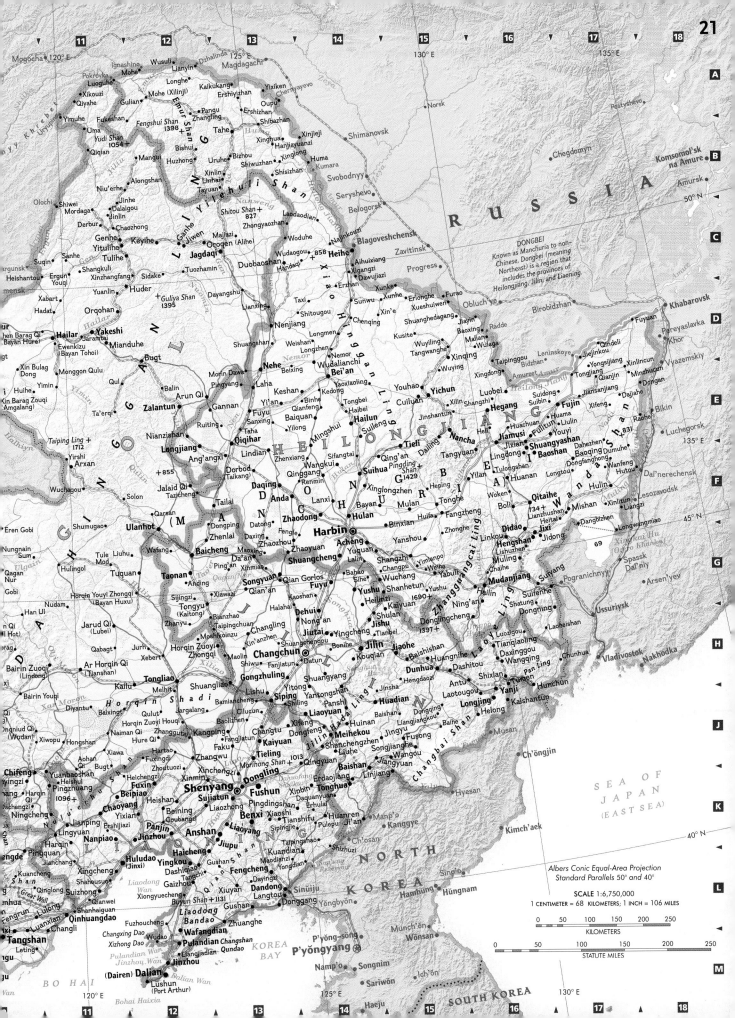

MONGOLIA

NEI MONGOL GAOYUAN

ALXA GAOYUAN
Badain Jaran Shamo

Tengger Shamo

Hobq Shamo

Ulan Buh Shamo

Mu Us Shamo (Ordos)

NINGXIA HUIZU

QINGHAI

GANSU

SICHUAN

SHAANXI

Qin Ling

CHONGQING

YUNNAN

GUIZHOU

HUNAN

HUBEI

HENAN

SHANXI

ANYEMAQEN SHAN

A'nyemaqen Shan

Qinghai Hu

Selected place names:

Bor Ul Shan, Saihan Toroi, Ejin Qi, Yagan, Sogo Nur, Adun Gol, Ulan Sum, Mandal, Tohom, Sonid Youqi (Saihan Tal), Ondor Sum

Shuangcheng, Lüyuan, Jiuquan Satellite Launch Center, Bayan Mod, Xar Burd, Wuyuan, Hanggin Houqi, Urad Qianqi, Linhe, Baotou, Hohhot, Jining, Xinghe

Zhangye, Shandan, Jinchang, Minqin, Wuhai, Wuda, Shizuishan (Dawukou), Hainan, Huangquqiao, Dongsheng, Datong, Huairen, Shuozhou

Wuwei, Yinchuan, Qingtongxia, Wuzhong, Yulin, Xinzhou, Taiyuan, Yuci, Shijiazhuan

Xining, Baiyin, Lanzhou, Guyuan, Yan'an, Linfen, Changzhi

Linxia, Dingxi, Pingliang, Qingyang, Hancheng, Houma, Jincheng, Anyang, Hebi

Tianshui, Baoji, Xianyang, Xi'an, Weinan, Sanmenxia, Luoyang, Zhengzhou, Kaifeng

Hanzhong, Ankang, Shiyan, Nanyang, Xinyang, Zhumadian

Guangyuan, Mianyang, Deyang, Chengdu, Nanchong, Wanxian, Zhongxiang, Jingmen, Yingcheng

Suining, Neijiang, Zigong, Chongqing, Fuling, Fengdu, Yichang, Jingzhou, Shashi

Leshan, Yibin, Luzhou, Changde, Yiyang, Changsha

Xichang, Zhaotong, Zunyi, Huaihua, Loudi, Xiangtan, Zhuzhou

THREE GORGES DAM — China's Three Gorges Dam is due to become the largest hydroelectric dam on Earth by 2009

Northwest 28–29
Southwest 26–27
Southeast 24–25

Southwest 26-27

MYANMAR (BURMA)

THAILAND

LAOS

VIETNAM

SICHUAN

YUNNAN

GUIZHOU

GUANGXI ZHUANGZU

SHAANXI

CHONGQING

HAINAN

HAINAN
The province of Hainan
administers the Chinese islands in
the South China Sea.

GULF OF TONKIN

TROPIC OF CANCER

Grid references: A B C D E F G H J K L M / 1 2 3 4 5 6 7 8

100° E, 105° E, 110° E, 30° N, 25° N, 20° N

Cho La, Dêgê, Chola Shan 6168, Garzê, 5992+, Barkam, Guangyuan, Hexi, Ziyang, Ankang, Shiy, Jomda, Toba, Baiyü, Zhag'yab, Luhuo (Zhaggo), Jinchuan (Quqên), Lixian, Maoxian (Fengyi), Jiuding Shan +4984, Beichuan, Jiangyou, Bazhong, Cangxi, Nanjiang, Wangcang, Tongjiang (Nuojiang), Langao, Zhushan, Zhuxi, Fangxian

Gonjo, Zogang (Wangda), Batang (Hekou), Litang, Dawu (Xianshui), Danba (Zhanggu), Qianning, +5734, Xiaojin, 5300+, Wenchuan, Mianzhu, Mianyang, Santai, Zitong, Zhongjiang, Shehong, Nanbu, Shiqiao, Xuanhan, Daxian, Kaixia, Kaijiang, Yunyang, Fengjie, Wushan, Badong

Markam (Gartog), 6204+, Kangding, 6070+, Ya'an, Hanyuan (Fulin), Leshan, Zigong, Neijiang, Suining, Huaying, Liangping, Dianjiang, Zhongxian, Fengdu, Shizhu, Xuan'en, Hefeng, 2359

Zayü (Gyigang), Namni Pass, Dégén (Songmai), Moirigkawagarbo 6740, 6032+, Zhongdian, Jiulong, Shimian, Ebian (Shaping), Muchuan, Yibin, Nanxi, Luzhou, Hejiang, Qijiang, +2251 Jinfo Shan, Nanchuan, Wulong, Daozhen, Zheng'an, Xishui, Pengshui, Zhangjiajie, Yongshun

Gongshan, 5396+, Ninglang, Yulongxue Shan 5596, Lijiang, Xichang Satellite Launch Center, Zhaojue, Butuo, Daguan, Zhaotong, Ludian +4050, Bijie, Dafang, Qianxi, Xifeng, Zunyi, Meitan, Fenggang, Yinjiang, Sinan, Jiangkou, Tongren, Huaihua, Zhijiang, Hongjiang, +1934

Panzhihua, Lixi, Huidong, Huize, Xuanwei, Weining, Lupanshui, Anshun, Guiyang, Kaili, Leigong Shan 2179, Liping, Rongjiang, Congjiang, Miao'er Shan 2142+, Guilin

Baoshan, Tengchong, Dali, Fengyi, Dayao, Yuanmou, Zhanyi, Qujing, Fuyuan, Panxian, Pu'an, Xingren, Anlong, Xingyi, Hechi, Liuzhou, Luzhai, Lipu

Kunming, Anning, Haikou, Yuxi, Eshan, Tonghai, Jiangchuan, Huaning, Mile, Luxi, Luoping, Longlin, Xilin, Guangnan, Bose, Tianyang, Tiandong, Nandan, Huanjiang, Yishan, Liuzhou, Yongfu, Yangshuo

Chuxiong, Shiping, Jianshui, Gejiu, Mengzi, Wenshan, Funing, Napo, Debao, Jingxi, Tiandeng, Long'an, Daxin, Wuming, Binyang, Guigang, Yulin

Simao, Jiangcheng, Jinping, Hekou, Lao Cai, Ha Giang, Cao Bang, Chongzuo, Longzhou, Pingxiang, Munan Pass, Lang Son, Nanning, Yongning, Hengxian, Rongxian

Menghai, Jinghong, Phôngsali, Yen Bai, Tuyen Quang, Ningming, Shangsi, Fangchenggang, Dongxing, Mong Cai, Qinzhou, Beihai, Lianjiang, Zhanjiang, Leizhou

Mengla, Dien Bien, Son La, Hoa Binh, Hanoi, Haiphong, Hong Gai, Cam Pha, Weizhou Dao, Leizhou Bandao (Luichow Peninsula), Xuwen, Hai

Chiang Rai, Chiang Mai, Lampang, Phayao, Nan, Louangphrabang, Xiangkhoang, Xaignabouri, Nam Dinh, Thanh Hoa, Vinh, Ha Tinh, Sanya, HAINAN

Uttaradit, Phrae, Viangchan (Vientiane), Loei, Udon Thani, Khammouan, Dong Hoi, Phitsanulok, Tak

HENAN

Xinye
Xinyang
Zaoyang
Suizhou
Yicheng
Zhangxhang
Guangshui
Guangshan
Shangcheng
Dawu
Xiaochang
Hong'an
Macheng
Luotian
Tiantangzhai 1868
Dabie Shan
Lu'an
Huoshan
Shucheng
Sanhezhen
Jinzhai
Lujiang
Hefei
Chaohu

East Central
22-23

Huainan
Yangzhou
Yizheng
Zhenjiang
Danyang
120° E
Rudong (Juegang)
Tongzhou
Nantong
Qidong

Nanjing
Ma'anshan
Changzhou
Jiangyin
Changshu
Chongming Dao
Chongming Dao
Mouth of the Yangtze

JIANGSU
Dangtu
Liyang
Yixing
Wuxi
Kunshan
SHANGHAI
SHANGHAI SHI

Anlu
Yingcheng
Hanchuan
Xiaogan
Wuhan
Hanyang
Ezhou
Huanggang
Huangshi
Wuxue

Tianmen
Qianjiang
Xiantao

HUBEI

Chaohu
Wuwei
Wuhu
Tongling
Anqing
Huaining
Taihu

ANHUI
Xuanzhou
Ningguo
Jiuhua Shan
1342
Guichi
Shitai
Jingde
Jixi
Huang Shan
Lianhua Feng 1873

Deqing
Haiyan
Xiaoyang Shan
Huzhou
Jiaxing
Songjiang
Jinshan

DA YUNHE
GRAND CANAL

Hangzhou Wan
Shengsi Liedao
ZHOUSHAN
QUNDAO

30° N

Hangzhou
Yuyao
Zhoushan
Putuo (Shenjiamen)
Zhoushan Dao
Beilun

EAST CHINA SEA

Hong Hu
Honghu
Jiayu
Puqi
Xianning
Wuning
Yangxin
Guling

Xiushui
Tongcheng
Chongyang
Huangshan

Jiujiang
De'an
Fuliang
Jingdezhen
Dexing

Shaoxing
Zhuji
Shengzhou
Pujiang
Dongyang
Yiwu
Xianju
Ninghai
Xiangshan
Shipu
Niutou Shan

Yueyang
Linxiang

Anxiang
Nanxian

Dongting
Hu

Pingjiang
1596
Xiangyin
Wangchang

Changsha
Zhuzhou
Xiangtan
Loudi
Zhuzhou
Liling
Xiangdong
Pingxiang

Ningxiang

JIANGXI
Yifeng
Gao'an
Jin
Zhangshu
(Qingjiang)

Anyi
Xinjian
Nanchang
Fengcheng
Linchuan
Nanchang

Leping
Boyang
Yugan
Poyang Hu
Xin Jiang Shuiku

Jingdezhen
Dexing

Yanshan
Guangfeng
Songyang
Qingtian
Yueqing

ZHEJIANG
Quzhou
Xianju
Linhai
Huangyan
Luqiao
Taizhou (Jiaojiang, Haimen)
Wenling
Kanmen
Yuhuan Dao

Shangrao
Yingtan
Changshan
Yushan
Jiangshan
Yongkang
Lishui

Shaoxing

Tonggu

Yichun
Xinyu
Fenyi
Jiuling Shan
1790

Xintian
Pucheng
Wuyishan
Qingyuan
Shouning
Zhenghe
Zherong
Fu'an
Sansha

Huangmao Jian
1921
Wencheng
Wenzhou
Rui'an
Pingyang
Aojing
Xiaojiang
Jinxiang
Fanshan

25° N

D

E

F

Loudi
Hengshan
Youxian
Chaling
Anren
Xinshi
Leiyang

Ji'an
Jishui
Ji'an
Yongxin
Taihe

Lianhua
1918
Anfu
Lichuan
Nanfeng
Jianning

Nancheng
Guangze
Shaowu
Jian'ou
Shunchang
Zhouning
Gutian

Nanping
Jiangle
Shunchang
Pingnan
Luoyuan
Lianjiang

Matsu

Kōbi Shō
Senkaku Shotō
Uotsuri Shima
(Diaoyu Qundao)
Administered by Japan
Claimed by China

Pengjia Yü

JAPAN

Hengyang
Songbai
Yangming Shan 1704
Matianxu
Xintian
Guiyang
Jiahe
xian

Nanfengmian
2120
Yongxing
Guidong

Wan'an
Ningdu
Shicheng
Xingguo
Mingxi
Yuxi
Sanming
Yong'an
Gutian
Minqing
Fuzhou
Changle
Fuqing
Pingtan
Haitan Dao

Nansei Shotō
(Ryukyu Islands)
Yaeyama Rettō
Ishigaki Shima
Yonaguni
Jima
Iriomote
Jima

Hateruma Shima

25° N

G

Chenzhou
Guidong
Shikengkong
1902
Lianzhou
Yangshan

Ganzhou
Shangyou
Chongyi
Dayu

Tangjiang
Changting
Yudu
Ruijin

Liancheng
Zhangping
Datian
Yongchun
Dehua

Daiyun Shan
1856
Putian
Xianyou
Quangang

Nan'an
Quanzhou
Jinjiang
Anhai

Tanshui
Sanchung
Taoyuan
Yangmingshan
Chilung (Keelung)

Yangmei
Hsinchu
Chungli
Panchiao
Taipei (Taibei)

Houlung
Yüanli
Shalu
Toufen
Miaoli
Fengyüan

Suao

Matianxu
Xintian

Lechang
Honggong
Nanxiong
Xunwu
Wuping
Yongding

Shaoguan
Qujiang

Anyuan
Dingnan
Pingyuan
Jiaoling
Tong'an
Xiamen (Amoy)
Kinmen (Quemoy)
Kinmen
Xiamen Gang

Zhangzhou
Nanjing
Longhai
Zhangpu

Taichung
Changhua
Yüanlin
Nantou
Touliu
Puli
Fenglin
Hualien (Hualian)

TAIWAN

Chungyang Shanmo

Yingde
Guandu
Lianping
Longchuan

Meizhou
Xingning
Wuhua
Fengshun
Raoping
Zhao'an (Xibu)
Dongshan (Xibu)

Makung
Penghu
(Pescadores)

Yü Shan
3952
Yüli

Chengkung

TAIWAN

TROPIC OF CANCER

H

Qingyuan
Fogang

Heyuan
Boluo

Jieyang
Jiexi
Hongyang
Chaoyang
Chenghai
Shantou (Swatow)
Haimen
Haimen Wan

Chaozhou

Chiai
Hsinying
Matou
Hsinhua
Tainan
Chishan

Pingtung
Chaochou
Taitung

Kaohsiung
Fengshan
Pingtung
Tungkang
Tawu

Lü Tao

Kuanshan

Guangzhou
Canton
Foshan
Panyu
Huangpu
Zengcheng
Shilong
Dongguan
Huizhou
Huidong
Lufeng
Haifeng
Shanwei
Jieshi
Jiazi
Jinghai

GUANGDONG

Zhaoqing

Xinhui
Jiangmen
Zhongshan
Zhuhai
Xiaolan
Humen
Shenzhen
Huiyang

Jiulong (Kowloon)
HONG KONG (XIANGGANG), S.A.R.
Hong Kong

Dayushan (Lantau Island)

Liuchiu Yü
Hengchun
Oluan Pi
Chihsing Yen

TAIWAN
The People's Republic of China
claims Taiwan as its 23rd
province. Taiwan's government
(Republic of China) maintains
that there are two political entities.
Dongsha, Kinmen, Matsu, and
Penghu islands are administered by Taiwan.

Lan Yü
Hsiaohungtou Yü

Bashi Channel

Y'Ami

Itbayat

J

Taishan
Pingsha
Guanghai
Zhuhai

MACAU
MACAU (AOMEN), S.A.R.

Gaolan Dao

Hailing Dao
Zhapo
Dongping
Beijin Gang
Xiachuan Dao
Shangchuan Dao
Zhu Jiang (Pearl R.)

SOUTH CHINA SEA

Dongsha
Dongsha
(Pratas I.)

LUZON
STRAIT

BATAN ISLANDS

Batan
Sabtang

20° N

K

Albers Conic Equal-Area Projection
Standard Parallels 30° and 20°

SCALE 1:6,750,000
1 CENTIMETER = 68 KILOMETERS; 1 INCH = 106 MILES

0   50   100   150   200   250
KILOMETERS

0   50   100   150   200   250
STATUTE MILES

S.A.R. .... Special Administrative Region

115° E

22-23

26-27

Balintang Channel

Babuyan

Calayan
Dalupiri
Camiguin
Fuga
BABUYAN
ISLANDS
Babuyan Channel

Aparri

Laoag
Vigan

PHILIPPINES

Tuguegarao

LUZON

120° E

Santiago

L

M

KAZAKHSTAN

KYRGYZSTAN

UZB.

TAJIKISTAN

AFGHAN.

PAKISTAN

KASHMIR

INDIA

XINJIANG

(SINKIANG)

TARIM PENDI

Taklimakan Shamo

TIAN SHAN

JUNGGAR
(DZUNGARIA)

XIZANG

(TIBET)

KUNLUN

KARAKORAM RANGE

RAKSAI CHIN

LADAKH

SILK ROAD
An ancient trade route, linking China
with Europe, the Silk Road follows the
southern edge of the Tian Shan mountains
to Kashgar, before leaving China. The Silk
Road concept is being used today to develop
trade between China and Central Asia.

UYGURS
The western Xinjiang region is known as
East Turkestan, or Chinese Turkestan,
because of the Uygurs—a Muslim people
who speak a Turkic language.

KASHMIR
India and Pakistan both claim Kashmir—a
disputed region of some 10 million people.
India administers only the area south of the line
of control. Pakistan controls northwestern Kashmir.
China took eastern Kashmir from India in a 1962 war.

Southwest
26-27

Country Themes

To summarize the many facets of modern China and map their extent, the following section examines 21 themes divided into two groups: the Natural and the Human. Each theme is, perhaps, comparable to a voice in a complex piece of music: each is distinct but influences all the others, and the combination of effects enriches the whole.

When the world's most populous nation, ranking fourth in largest area, transforms itself in only a few decades, the music is played in many keys, loudly, and not to everyone's taste. But attention should be paid.

Landforms

LANDFORM DISTRIBUTION

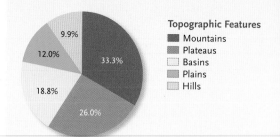

Topographic Features
- Mountains
- Plateaus
- Basins
- Plains
- Hills

9.9%
12.0%
33.3%
18.8%
26.0%

WHEN THE INDIAN TECTONIC PLATE pushed into Eurasia 50 million years ago, it provided the constant force needed to raise the world's highest mountains, the Himalaya, and the imposing Plateau of Tibet, which towers over the rest of China. The "roof of the world" has an average elevation of more than 14,000 feet (4,267 meters) and an area four times the size of Texas. All of western China is dominated by a complex pattern of deep basins (the Turpan Depression bottoms out at 505 feet, or 154 meters, below sea level) and steep ranges that owe their origins to the massive pileup of the Indian and Eurasian plates.

Included within China's immense territory (it is almost the same size as the U.S.) are diverse and singular landscapes. Stepping down 10,000 feet (3,048 meters) from the high mountains of the west into central China is the world's largest loess plateau, a heavily eroded landscape of wind-deposited silt piled hundreds of feet deep. Eastern China is dominated by low, undulating plains but is not without diversity. The world's largest karst landscape covers much of southeastern China and includes dramatic limestone towers hundreds of feet high, along with countless sinkholes and caverns.

The contrast in China's landforms is reflected in its human land use pattern. The high, barren areas of western China are scarcely used, while the gentler, eastern parts contain some of the most intensely cultivated areas in the world, along with more than a billion people.

Tian Shan: *Chinese for "Heavenly Mountains," this range stretches across central Asia and forms China's border with Kyrgyzstan.*

Dzungarian B
T I A N S
TARIM BASIN
Taklimakan Desert
K U N L U N M O U
P L A T E A U
T I B E
Gangdise Range
H I M A L

CHINA'S LANDFORMS

Plains
- Littoral low plain
- Delta plain
- Undulating or flat plain
- Fan-like plain
- Sloping plain
- Intermountain wide valley or basin

High Plains
- High plain composed of gradual relief monadnock or wide valley
- High plain composed of terrace or valley
- High plain with rugged and broken surface

Platforms
- Low platform
- High platform

Hills and Mountains
- Hill
- Low mountain
- Middle mountain
- High mountain
- Very high mountain

Plateaus
- Relatively complete plateau
- Relatively broken plateau
- Hilly plateau
- Mountainous plateau

Other Structures
- Depression
- Desert, sandy area, and Gobi
- Micro high land
- Alluvial fan
- Volcanic cone
- Glacier
- River

Qomolangma (Mount Everest): *The world's highest mountain (29,035 ft; 8,850 m) straddles the China-Nepal border.*

Huangtu Gaoyuan: *This loess plateau is the largest in the world; its windblown silt is fertile but prone to erosion.*

Three Gorges: Rising water levels from the Three Gorges Dam will alter the spectacular scenery of Qutang, Wu Xia, and Xiling Gorges.

Poyang Lake: One of China's largest freshwater lakes, Poyang Lake varies greatly by season, creating wetlands ideal for migratory birds.

Karst: Distinctive limestone peaks and caves have been formed by extensive erosion throughout southern China.

Pearl River Delta: Economic development since the 1980s has transformed this former agricultural area into a vast urban tract.

White lines represent administrative boundaries

For more detail of China's physical features, see pages 14–15.

Lesser Khingan Range

Greater Khingan Range

Northeast Plain (Manchurian Plain)

N

pan Depression

un Shan

Qilian Shan

Qaidam Basin

MAINS

F

A

Hengduan Shan

Daxue Mountains

Sichuan Basin

G O B I

Mu Us Desert

Taihang Shan

North China Plain

Qin Ling

Wuyi Shan

TAIWAN

Hainan

Land Cover

LAND COVER DISTRIBUTION

LAND COVER DISTRIBUTION

FOREST — **15.8%**

Evergreen needleleaf forest 3.8%
Evergreen broadleaf forest 0.4%
Deciduous needleleaf forest 0.2%
Deciduous broadleaf forest 0.9%
Woodland 8.3%
Mixed forest 2.2%

OTHER — **32.4%**

Water 1.2%
Urban and built-up areas 0.1%
Barren and desert 14.7%
Cropland: 16.4%

GRASSLAND & SHRUBLAND — **51.8%**

Wooded grassland 11.4%
Grassland 18.0%
Open shrubland 21.3%
Closed shrubland 1.1%

Pie chart labels: Forest 15.8%; Grassland & Shrubland 51.8%; Other 32.4%

CHINA IS A LARGE COUNTRY with a great variety of land cover. The southeast has a warm, humid climate, capable of supporting lush, semitropical vegetation such as forest cover and rice croplands. The north-central and northeast areas have a dry climate and grassland or woodland land cover, often converted to grass grains croplands. The northwest is arid with a semidesert vegetation, while the southwest is also arid but at a very high altitude. Most human influence on land cover in the western regions occurs near reliable water, with herding spread throughout wide expanses. The large population in eastern China has resulted in one of the most human-altered landscapes in the world, mostly in the form of agriculture. Cities are another major type of land cover, with steady growth of built-up areas along the eastern coast over the past 20 years. China's new economy will most likely affect additional land cover alterations through features such as the Three Gorges Dam.

LAND COVER TYPES

EVERGREEN NEEDLELEAF FOREST Forest dominates, with a canopy coverage of more than 60%; tree height exceeds 16 ft (5 m). This land cover is typical of the boreal (northern) region.

EVERGREEN BROADLEAF FOREST Forest dominates, with a canopy coverage of more than 60%; tree height exceeds 16 ft (5 m). Such forests, which include tropical rain forests, dominate in the tropics.

DECIDUOUS NEEDLELEAF FOREST Forest dominates, with a canopy coverage of more than 60%; tree height exceeds 16 ft (5 m). Trees respond to cold seasons by shedding their leaves simultaneously.

DECIDUOUS BROADLEAF FOREST Forest dominates, with a canopy coverage of more than 60%; tree height exceeds 16 ft (5 m). In dry or cold seasons, trees shed their leaves simultaneously.

WOODLAND Land has herbaceous or woody under-stories and tree canopy cover of 40% to 60%; tree height exceeds 16 ft (5 m) and may be evergreen or deciduous.

MIXED FOREST Forest dominates, with a canopy coverage of more than 60%; tree height exceeds 16 ft (5 m). Both needleleaf and deciduous types appear, with neither having coverage of less than 25% or more than 75%.

WATER

URBAN AND BUILT

BARREN AND DESERT Exposed soil, sand, or rocks are typical; the land never has more than 10% vegetated cover during any time of year.

CROPLAND Crop-producing fields make up more than 80% of the landscape.

WOODED GRASSLAND Land has herbaceous or woody understories and tree canopy cover of 10% to 40%; tree height exceeds 16 ft (5 m) and may be evergreen or deciduous.

GRASSLAND Land has continuous herbaceous cover and less than 10% tree or shrub canopy cover.

OPEN SHRUBLAND Shrubs are dominant, with a canopy cover between 10% and 40%; they do not exceed 7 ft (2 m) in height and can be evergreen or deciduous. The remaining land is either barren or characterized by annual herbaceous cover.

CLOSED SHRUBLAND Bushes or shrubs dominate, with a canopy coverage of more than 40%. Bushes do not exceed 16 ft (5 m) in height; shrubs or bushes can be evergreen or deciduous. Tree canopy is less than 10%.

Barren and Desert: *The Taklimakan Desert in western China is among the world's largest shifting sand deserts.*

Open Shrubland: *Shrubland, such as this in a Gobi Desert valley, is China's most wide-spread type of land cover.*

Grassland: *Flocks of sheep graze in an expansive meadow in Gansu Province, a major center for animal husbandry.*

Evergreen Broadleaf Forest: *Bamboo groves in the biologically rich Qin Mountains of Shaanxi Province*

White lines represent administrative boundaries

Cropland: *A network of rice paddies in Hunan Province — one of many modes of cultivation in China*

Today's land cover researchers interpret satellite imagery, which includes a measure of radiation reflected off the Earth's surface. Specific vegetation types have different values in the imagery, so ranges of values are grouped together in the classifications shown here.

Fresh Water

FOUR LARGEST RIVERS	ANNUAL FLOW MILLIONS OF CUBIC FEET (MILLIONS OF METERS³)	DRAINAGE AREA SQUARE MILES (KM²)	LENGTH MILES (KM)
CHANG JIANG (YANGTZE)	33,594,842 (951,300)	1,808,500 (4,683,994)	3,915 (6,379)
ZHU (PEARL)	11,788,036 (333,800)	453,690 (1,175,052)	1,376 (2,214)
SONGHUA	2,690,978 (76,200)	557,180 (1,443,090)	1,434 (2,308)
HUANG (YELLOW)	2,334,300 (66,100)	752,443 (1,948,818)	3,395 (5,464)

CHINA'S WATER USE

- Agricultural
- Industrial
- Domestic

6.6%
25.7%
67.7%

LACK OF WATER RESOURCES and environmental degradation, particularly in the north, are the key constraints limiting sustainable development in China. China's annual per capita water availability is around 2,300 cubic meters—a quarter of the world's average. This amount, however, is distributed unevenly, with most of the precipitation falling in the south. The northern arid plateau is the country's industrial and agriculture center but receives only 2 to 31 inches (5 to 80 centimeters) of rainfall a year. This puts the 47 percent of China's population that lives in the north at a high level of water stress, with annual per capita water availability of less than 750 cubic meters. Exploitation of water resources is exacerbated by pollution. Less than 15 percent of the population is connected to operational treatment plants, and because most cities and industries are located along rivers, pollution levels are very high, with some waters in the north categorized as unfit even for industrial use.

Groundwater resources are not immune from problems. Two-thirds of the water demand is met by groundwater, but exploitation is rampant, causing land subsidence and saltwater intrusion, and rendering many groundwater sources undrinkable.

ACCESS TO SAFE DRINKING WATER

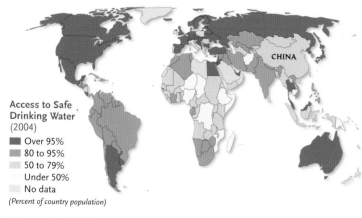

Access to Safe Drinking Water (2004)

- Over 95%
- 80 to 95%
- 50 to 79%
- Under 50%
- No data

(Percent of country population)

RURAL AND URBAN ACCESS TO SAFE DRINKING WATER

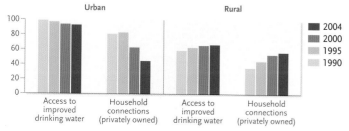

Urban

Rural

- 2004
- 2000
- 1995
- 1990

Access to improved drinking water

Household connections (privately owned)

Access to improved drinking water

Household connections (privately owned)

KAZAKHSTAN

KYRGYZSTAN

TAJ.

PAK.

INDIA

NEPAL

BHUT

Ili

Tarim

Kaxgar

Yarkant

Hotan

Indus

Shiquan

Maquan

Ya

FRESH WATER

More than 300 million rural inhabitants do not have access to safe drinking water. Even in major cities, people experience periodic water shortages. To alleviate this, in 2002 the Chinese government initiated construction of the South-North Water Transfer, a huge diversion project that will bring water from the Yangtze River in the south to the Hai, Huai, and Yellow Rivers in the north. Three channels (eastern, central, and western routes), two of which are over 621 mi (1,000 km) long, are necessary. Water withdrawal from the Yangtze will, however, reduce needed sediments to the coast and raise the concentration of pollutants. Social effects such as resettlement and displacement will also occur.

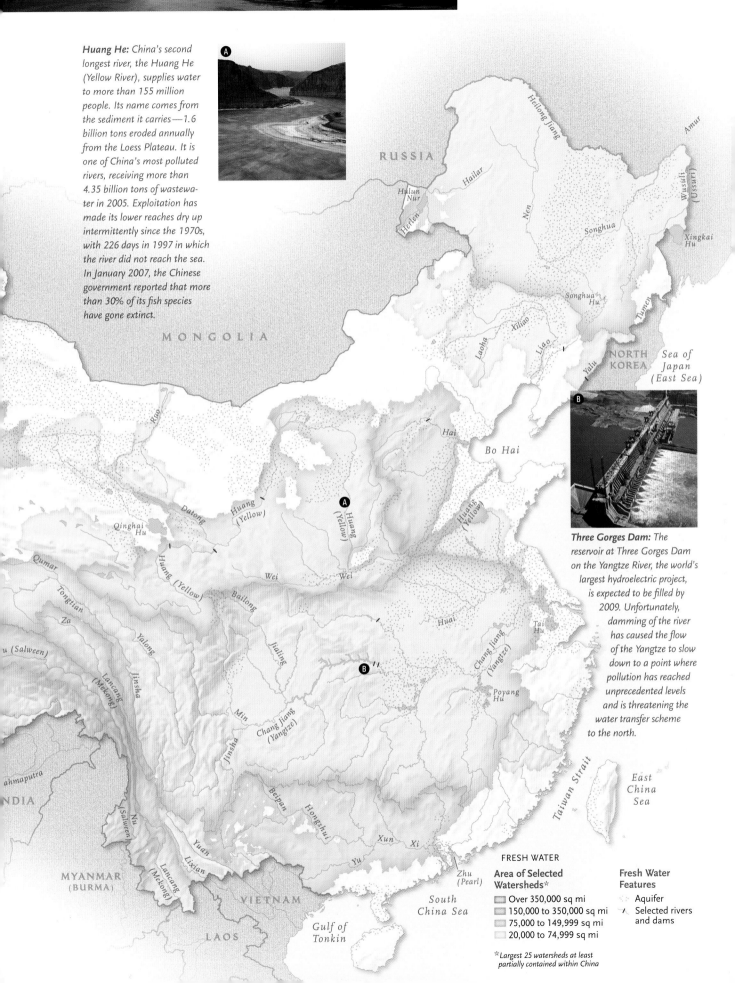

Huang He: China's second longest river, the Huang He (Yellow River), supplies water to more than 155 million people. Its name comes from the sediment it carries—1.6 billion tons eroded annually from the Loess Plateau. It is one of China's most polluted rivers, receiving more than 4.35 billion tons of wastewater in 2005. Exploitation has made its lower reaches dry up intermittently since the 1970s, with 226 days in 1997 in which the river did not reach the sea. In January 2007, the Chinese government reported that more than 30% of its fish species have gone extinct.

Three Gorges Dam: The reservoir at Three Gorges Dam on the Yangtze River, the world's largest hydroelectric project, is expected to be filled by 2009. Unfortunately, damming of the river has caused the flow of the Yangtze to slow down to a point where pollution has reached unprecedented levels and is threatening the water transfer scheme to the north.

FRESH WATER

Area of Selected Watersheds*

- Over 350,000 sq mi
- 150,000 to 350,000 sq mi
- 75,000 to 149,999 sq mi
- 20,000 to 74,999 sq mi

Fresh Water Features

- Aquifer
- Selected rivers and dams

*Largest 25 watersheds at least partially contained within China

Climate

CHINA IS A LAND OF DIVERSE CLIMATES, support-ing a wide range of vegetation, landscapes, cultures, and lifestyles. The southeastern part of the country is subtropical, characterized by mild winters and hot and humid summers. It is also wet, lying directly in the path of moisture-bearing winds from the South China Sea. Northeastern China experiences cold, dry winters and mild, moist summers. Close proximity to the Siberian High produces the country's lowest winter temperatures. Extensive areas of northern and north-western China, shielded from the ocean by mountain ranges, are extremely arid. Summer temperatures vary widely with elevation, ranging from China's hottest in low-lying valleys, to pleasantly cool in the mountains.

The Plateau of Tibet dominates southwestern China's climate. Winters are cold and dry, but tem-peratures are moderated by the relatively low latitude and distance from the Siberian High. Summers are generally cool to cold, depending on elevation. The plateau acts as a formidable barrier to moisture-bearing winds flowing north and northwestward from the Bay of Bengal and the South China Sea. As a result, the southeastern flank of the plateau is relatively wet, while the northern and western regions are very dry, even in summer.

Monsoons: *People with colorful rain ponchos ride bicycles and mopeds in the rain on a June day in Shanghai. Heavy rains from the summer monsoon (see description below) can cause severe flooding in China's densely populated southeast—in some years resulting in the loss of many lives as well as billions of dollars in damage. In contrast, China's cooler, drier northern areas are often affected by fierce sand and dust storms caused by northerly winds carrying cold, dry air from Siberia (see The Siberian High, below). This phenomenon is known as the "winter monsoon."*

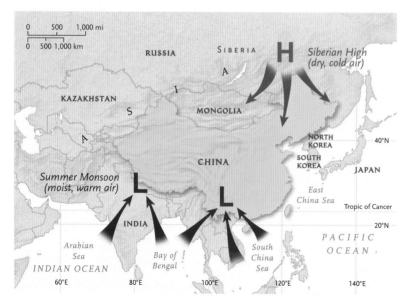

THE SUMMER MONSOON

The summer monsoon, responsible for the bulk of China's precipitation, is an inland flow of moist air off the ocean that occurs when the land becomes warmer than the ocean. The main routes of monsoonal moisture are into Tibet from the Bay of Bengal, and through southeastern China from the South China Sea. Unlike the Plateau of Tibet, which is an effective barrier to moisture, the relatively flat terrain of south-eastern China allows heavy rains to penetrate well inland.

THE SIBERIAN HIGH

The Siberian High is a center of dry, cold air that develops each winter over eastern Siberia. This air mass flows outward from its center into northern China, as well as Mongolia and Korea, producing generally clear, dry winter weather. Winter minimum temperatures in extreme northern China average -22°F (-30°C) and below, which can be colder than those found at high eleva-tions on the Plateau of Tibet. Winter temperatures rise steadily as one moves southward, away from the Siberian High.

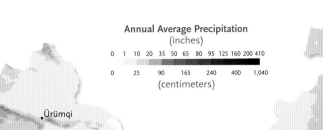

PRECIPITATION

Patterns of precipitation in China are related primarily to elevation and exposure to monsoonal winds. Southeastern China and windward mountain slopes are typically wettest, while areas sheltered by mountains in the northwest are driest. Summers are generally wet and winters dry.

Annual Average Precipitation
(inches)

0 1 10 20 35 50 65 80 95 125 160 200 410

0   25   90   165   240   400   1,040
(centimeters)

- Harbin
- Ürümqi
- Beijing
- Wuhan
- Lhasa
- Guangzhou

TEMPERATURE

Temperature patterns across China are primarily related to elevation, latitude, and proximity to the coast. Summer temperatures are highest at low elevations away from the coast. Winter temperatures are lowest in northern China, near the Siberian High, and on the Plateau of Tibet.

JANUARY
AVERAGE LOW
TEMPERATURES

PLATEAU OF TIBET

Average Temperature (°F)

-35 -30 -25 -15 -10 0 10 20 32 40 50 60 70 80 90 100 110

-37 -34 -32 -26 -23 -18 -12 -7 0 4 10 16 21 27 32 38 43
Average Temperature (°C)

CLIMOGRAPHS

Climographs for several cities across the country show patterns of temperature and precipitation throughout the year. China has a wide variety of climate types, including extremes in both temperature and precipitation.

—— Temperature (°F)   ▉ Precipitation (inches)

JULY
AVERAGE HIGH
TEMPERATURES

- Nanjing
- Wuhan
- Chongqing

THE "THREE OVENS"

The Yangtze River cities of Chongqing, Wuhan, and Nanjing, famous for their intense summer heat and humidity, are called the "Three Ovens" of China. However, China's hottest summer temperatures are found in western low-lying basins, where a typical July day reaches 104°F (40°C).

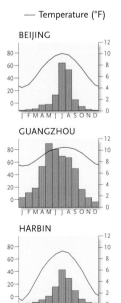

BEIJING

LHASA

GUANGZHOU

ÜRÜMQI

HARBIN

WUHAN

Biodiversity

AT A GLANCE

	CHINA	BRAZIL	UNITED STATES	WORLD
TOTAL DOCUMENTED SPECIES* (2004)	38,023	63,603	24,990	257,874
TOTAL ENDEMIC SPECIES* (2004)	18,585	2,444	4,871	ALL SPECIES
TOTAL THREATENED SPECIES (2006)	804	721	1,178	27,816
RECENTLY EXTINCT SPECIES	8	17	254	888

*Includes amphibians, birds, fish, mammals, reptiles, and vascular plants.

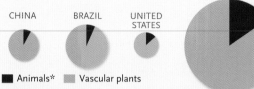

CHINA   BRAZIL   UNITED STATES   WORLD

■ Animals* ■ Vascular plants

*Includes amphibians, birds, fish, mammals, and reptiles.

WITHIN CHINA IS A VAST ARRAY OF ECOSYSTEMS comprising a total of 133 ecoregions that ranges from icy peaks to tropical rain forests and from arid plateaus to wetlands fed by a multitude of rivers.

This heterogeneity of habitats has generated extremely diverse fauna and flora. Within the boundaries of China are portions of three biodiversity hotspots: the mountains of Central Asia, Himalaya, and Indo-Burma. In addition, the Mountains of Southwest China biodiversity hotspot falls entirely within China. With over 12,000 vascular plant species, about 30 percent of which are endemic, this hotspot is arguably the most botanically rich temperate region in the world. Vertebrate species richness is also high, including 92 species of freshwater fish, 92 reptiles, 611 birds, 90 amphibians, and 237 mammals.

Alarmingly, much of China's spectacular biodiversity is threatened with extinction. According to the 2006 IUCN Red List of Threatened Species, 804 species found in China are listed as globally threatened. The best way to ensure that these species do not disappear altogether is to conserve the places where they live; these places are termed key biodiversity areas (KBAs) and are global conservation priorities. Although KBA identification has yet to be undertaken comprehensively for China, the Alliance for Zero Extinction has identified 23 sites that form the highest-priority subset of KBAs; each contains the entire global population of one or more highly threatened species. Additionally, a total of 445 Important Bird Areas (IBAs) have been identified, representing KBAs for bird species, and KBAs for all threatened vertebrates have been identified in southwest China.

Five Flower Lake in Jiuzhai Gou, a designated UNESCO World Heritage site, is home to a vast array of species, many of which are threatened. Among its inhabitants is the giant panda.

THREATENED SPECIES*

Giant panda

Red panda

Indochinese tiger   *Snow leopard*

The giant panda and red panda are just 2 of over 400 threatened Chinese species. Habitat loss and degradation are widespread risks and some species, such as the tiger and snow leopard, also face the harvesting of their pelts and bones for use in traditional ceremonies and medicines.

CHINA'S ENDEMIC SPECIES

Many species threatened with extinction in China are endemic, meaning that they are found nowhere else on Earth. One such species, the Yangtze River dolphin (Baiji), has just become extinct.

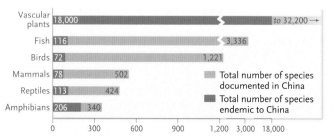

Vascular plants 18,000 — to 32,200 →
Fish 116 / 3,336
Birds 72 / 1,221
Mammals 78 / 502
Reptiles 113 / 424
Amphibians 206 / 340

■ Total number of species documented in China
■ Total number of species endemic to China

0   300   600   900   1,200   3,000   18,000

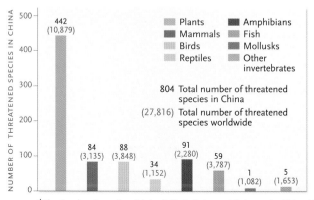

NUMBER OF THREATENED SPECIES IN CHINA

Plants 442 (10,879)
Mammals 84 (3,135)
Birds 88 (3,848)
Reptiles 34 (1,152)
Amphibians 91 (2,280)
Fish 59 (3,787)
Mollusks 1 (1,082)
Other invertebrates 5 (1,653)

■ Plants ■ Amphibians
■ Mammals ■ Fish
■ Birds ■ Mollusks
■ Reptiles ■ Other invertebrates

804 Total number of threatened species in China
(27,816) Total number of threatened species worldwide

*Threatened species are those listed as Critically Endangered, Endangered, or Vulnerable.

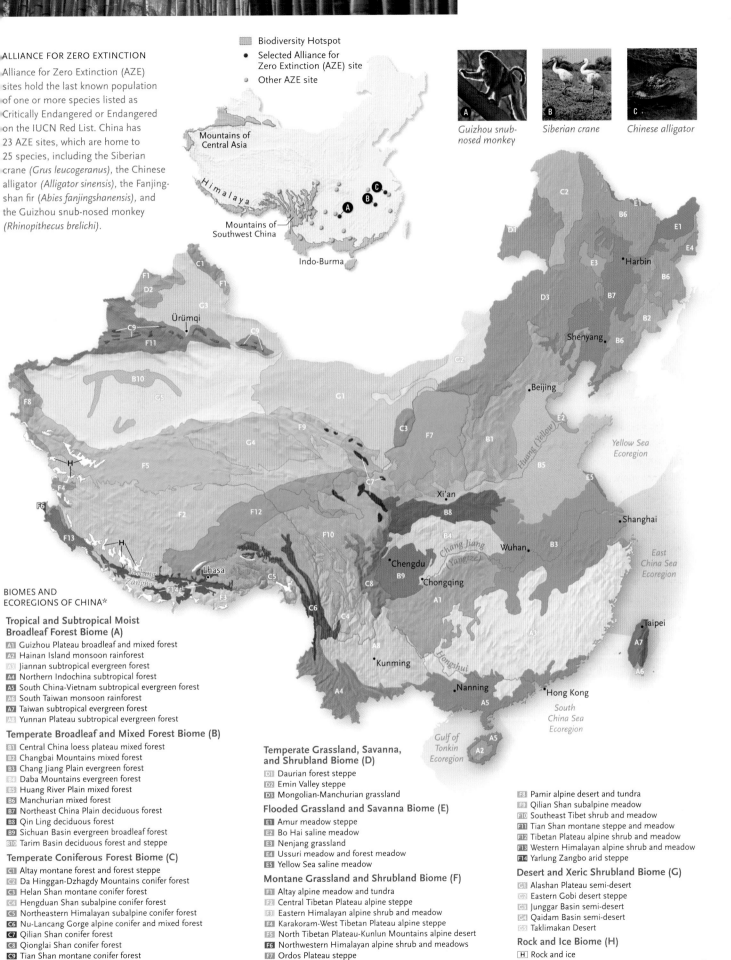

Biodiversity Hotspot

● Selected Alliance for Zero Extinction (AZE) site

● Other AZE site

ALLIANCE FOR ZERO EXTINCTION

Alliance for Zero Extinction (AZE) sites hold the last known population of one or more species listed as Critically Endangered or Endangered on the IUCN Red List. China has 23 AZE sites, which are home to 25 species, including the Siberian crane (*Grus leucogeranus*), the Chinese alligator (*Alligator sinensis*), the Fanjing-shan fir (*Abies fanjingshanensis*), and the Guizhou snub-nosed monkey (*Rhinopithecus brelichi*).

Guizhou snub-nosed monkey

Siberian crane

Chinese alligator

Mountains of Central Asia

Himalaya

Mountains of Southwest China

Indo-Burma

BIOMES AND ECOREGIONS OF CHINA*

Tropical and Subtropical Moist Broadleaf Forest Biome (A)
- A1 Guizhou Plateau broadleaf and mixed forest
- A2 Hainan Island monsoon rainforest
- A3 Jiannan subtropical evergreen forest
- A4 Northern Indochina subtropical forest
- A5 South China-Vietnam subtropical evergreen forest
- A6 South Taiwan monsoon rainforest
- A7 Taiwan subtropical evergreen forest
- A8 Yunnan Plateau subtropical evergreen forest

Temperate Broadleaf and Mixed Forest Biome (B)
- B1 Central China loess plateau mixed forest
- B2 Changbai Mountains mixed forest
- B3 Chang Jiang Plain evergreen forest
- B4 Daba Mountains evergreen forest
- B5 Huang River Plain mixed forest
- B6 Manchurian mixed forest
- B7 Northeast China Plain deciduous forest
- B8 Qin Ling deciduous forest
- B9 Sichuan Basin evergreen broadleaf forest
- B10 Tarim Basin deciduous forest and steppe

Temperate Coniferous Forest Biome (C)
- C1 Altay montane forest and forest steppe
- C2 Da Hinggan-Dzhagdy Mountains conifer forest
- C3 Helan Shan montane conifer forest
- C4 Hengduan Shan subalpine conifer forest
- C5 Northeastern Himalayan subalpine conifer forest
- C6 Nu-Lancang Gorge alpine conifer and mixed forest
- C7 Qilian Shan conifer forest
- C8 Qionglai Shan conifer forest
- C9 Tian Shan montane conifer forest

Temperate Grassland, Savanna, and Shrubland Biome (D)
- D1 Daurian forest steppe
- D2 Emin Valley steppe
- D3 Mongolian-Manchurian grassland

Flooded Grassland and Savanna Biome (E)
- E1 Amur meadow steppe
- E2 Bo Hai saline meadow
- E3 Nenjang grassland
- E4 Ussuri meadow and forest meadow
- E5 Yellow Sea saline meadow

Montane Grassland and Shrubland Biome (F)
- F1 Altay alpine meadow and tundra
- F2 Central Tibetan Plateau alpine steppe
- F3 Eastern Himalayan alpine shrub and meadow
- F4 Karakoram-West Tibetan Plateau alpine steppe
- F5 North Tibetan Plateau-Kunlun Mountains alpine desert
- F6 Northwestern Himalayan alpine shrub and meadows
- F7 Ordos Plateau steppe
- F8 Pamir alpine desert and tundra
- F9 Qilian Shan subalpine meadow
- F10 Southeast Tibet shrub and meadow
- F11 Tian Shan montane steppe and meadow
- F12 Tibetan Plateau alpine shrub and meadow
- F13 Western Himalayan alpine shrub and meadow
- F14 Yarlung Zangbo arid steppe

Desert and Xeric Shrubland Biome (G)
- G1 Alashan Plateau semi-desert
- G2 Eastern Gobi desert steppe
- G3 Junggar Basin semi-desert
- G4 Qaidam Basin semi-desert
- G5 Taklimakan Desert

Rock and Ice Biome (H)
- H Rock and ice

*Terrestrial Ecoregions are lettered and numbered according to biome. Marine Ecoregions are labeled on the map in blue. Visit the Terrestrial Ecoregions online map at www.nationalgeographic.com/wildworld.

Protected Areas

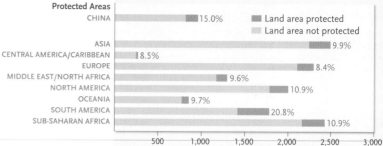

AT A GLANCE

Protected Areas

CHINA	15.0%

■ Land area protected
■ Land area not protected

ASIA	9.9%
CENTRAL AMERICA/CARIBBEAN	8.5%
EUROPE	8.4%
MIDDLE EAST/NORTH AFRICA	9.6%
NORTH AMERICA	10.9%
OCEANIA	9.7%
SOUTH AMERICA	20.8%
SUB-SAHARAN AFRICA	10.9%

500   1,000   1,500   2,000   2,500   3,000
TOTAL LAND AREA (millions of hectares)

RANGING FROM THE TUNDRA TO THE TROPICS, China's 3.7 million square miles (9.6 million square kilometers) incorporate a wealth of ecosystems, including deserts, grasslands, temperate and tropical forests, and wetlands. Its extensive marine areas range from the frigid northern seas to the vibrant coral reefs of the South China Sea. These varied habitats harbor one of the world's richest concentrations of biodiversity, including over 32,000 species of higher plants and more than 6,000 vertebrate species.

The protected areas of China are a network of nature reserves, forest parks, heritage preserves, scenic areas, and non-hunting areas. A variety of agencies administer these areas to preserve and protect native ecosystems, their inhabitants, the processes on which they rely, and important cultural sites. Since the first one was established in 1956 on Dinghu Mountain, Guangdong Province, protected areas have expanded to cover around 15 percent of the country, somewhat higher than the global average of 11 percent. While preserving natural and cultural sites, these areas also provide opportunities for public education, ecotourism, and sustainable use of natural resources.

Wuyi Shan, One of China's 33 World Heritage Sites: *Selected for protection and preservation, World Heritage sites are areas identified by UNESCO as having outstanding natural or cultural importance to humanity. One of 33 such sites in China, Wuyi Shan embodies both categories. The high-quality habitat in Fujian Province, which is home to one of the most remarkable subtropical forests on Earth, harbors many ancient, relict plant species, some endemic to China, and a significant diversity of reptile, amphibian, and insect species. The clear waters of the Nine-bend River wind through idyllic gorges and along archaeological ruins. In the 11th century C.E., the many temples and monasteries of Wuyi Shan were the birthplace of Neo-Confucianism, the influence of which eventually spread across East and Southeast Asia and dominated the region's intellectual landscape for centuries. Nearby at Chengcun, massive city walls enclose a Han dynasty administrative capital built in the first century B.C.E.*

CHINA'S PROTECTED AREAS OVER TIME

NUMBER OF PROTECTED AREAS

2,000 / 1,800 / 1,600 / 1,400 / 1,200 / 1,000 / 800 / 600 / 400 / 200 / 0

1,977 protected sites in 2007

China's first nature reserve established in 1956

Data Not Available

145,382,413 ha

1950   1960   1970   1980   1990   2000   2010

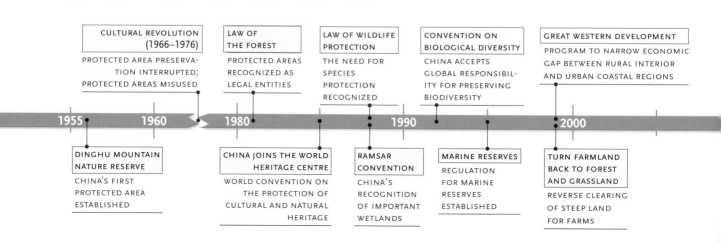

CULTURAL REVOLUTION (1966–1976)	LAW OF THE FOREST	LAW OF WILDLIFE PROTECTION	CONVENTION ON BIOLOGICAL DIVERSITY	GREAT WESTERN DEVELOPMENT
PROTECTED AREA PRESERVATION INTERRUPTED; PROTECTED AREAS MISUSED	PROTECTED AREAS RECOGNIZED AS LEGAL ENTITIES	THE NEED FOR SPECIES PROTECTION RECOGNIZED	CHINA ACCEPTS GLOBAL RESPONSIBILITY FOR PRESERVING BIODIVERSITY	PROGRAM TO NARROW ECONOMIC GAP BETWEEN RURAL INTERIOR AND URBAN COASTAL REGIONS

1955   1960   1980   1990   2000

DINGHU MOUNTAIN NATURE RESERVE	CHINA JOINS THE WORLD HERITAGE CENTRE	RAMSAR CONVENTION	MARINE RESERVES	TURN FARMLAND BACK TO FOREST AND GRASSLAND
CHINA'S FIRST PROTECTED AREA ESTABLISHED	WORLD CONVENTION ON THE PROTECTION OF CULTURAL AND NATURAL HERITAGE	CHINA'S RECOGNITION OF IMPORTANT WETLANDS	REGULATION FOR MARINE RESERVES ESTABLISHED	REVERSE CLEARING OF STEEP LAND FOR FARMS

TERRESTRIAL AND MARINE PROTECTED AREAS

Terrestrial Protected Areas

Protected lands in China provide critical habitat for rare and imperiled species like the giant panda and South China tiger, protect globally important cultural sites, and preserve areas of relative wilderness in a rapidly urbanizing landscape.

Marine Protected Areas

Of natural, scientific, and educational value, China's marine preserves protect coral reefs, estuaries, islands, shorelines, and marine wetlands, securing habitat for endangered species like the white-flag dolphin and ensuring the viability of these delicate ecosystems.

CHINA'S PROTECTED AREAS: STATISTICS

Protected Area Type	Number	Total Area
National protected areas	1,977	145,382,413 hectares
World Heritage Sites	33	2,947,075 hectares
UNESCO-MAB Biosphere Reserves	26	6,377,611 hectares
Wetlands of International Importance (Ramsar)	30	2,937,454 hectares

PROTECTED AREAS*

- National protected area
- UNESCO-MAB Biosphere Reserve
- Wetlands of International Importance (Ramsar)

World Heritage Sites
- Cultural
- Natural
- Mixed (site with both cultural and natural value)

*Not all areas have equal levels of protection and conservation management. For a list of official management categories, see http://www.unep-wcmc.org/protected_areas/categories

Data for map, above, and graph, bottom left, from UNEP-World Conservation Monitoring Centre (UNEP-WCMC), May 2007

Map labels: Huang (Yellow); Chang Jiang (Yangtze); Hongshui; Yellow Sea; East China Sea; South China Sea; Gulf of Tonkin

WORLD HERITAGE SITE CATEGORIES

Cultural Heritage Site: Lijiang

Remarkable for its preservation of an authentic townscape, Lijiang, in Yunnan Province, displays a unique architectural blend of several cultures and centuries. Perched on uneven land at an important commercial and strategic junction, the city boasts a still-functioning ancient water supply system of sophisticated design.

Natural Heritage Site: Wulingyuan

Home to many endangered plants and animals, the landscape of Hunan Province's Wulingyuan is a singular one. Some 3,000 sandstone columns and peaks tower as high as 984 ft (300 m) over gorges full of streams cascading down waterfalls into pools. Numerous caves pierce the land, and two natural land bridges bind it.

Mixed Heritage Site: Emei Shan Scenic Area

Of natural and cultural importance, Sichuan Province's Emei Shan Scenic Area is home to diverse habitats, from subtropical to subalpine pine forests with trees over 1,000 years old. The Great Buddha of Leshan, the largest Buddha in the world, towers 233 ft (71 m) over the meeting of three rivers.

Environmental Issues

AT A GLANCE			
	CHINA	UNITED STATES	JAPAN
LAND PROTECTED FOR BIODIVERSITY, 2005	14.9%	23.2%	8.6%
FOREST AREA CHANGE, SINCE 1990	0.8%	1.0%	-1.0%
AGRICULTURAL LAND AREA CHANGE, SINCE 1990	4.2%	-3.5%	-8.8%
ANNUAL CARBON DIOXIDE EMISSIONS PER CAPITA, 2003	3.2 TONS	20 TONS	9.9 TONS
ANNUAL OZONE-DEPLETING (CFC*) EMISSIONS, 2004	17,903 ODP** TONS	1,154 ODP** TONS	0 ODP** TONS
ANNUAL MUNICIPAL WASTE COLLECTED, 2003	148,565,000 TONS	222,863,000 TONS (2005)	54,367,000 TONS

*Chlorofluorocarbons   **Ozone depleting potential

CHINA'S PHENOMENAL ECONOMIC GROWTH and development of the past 20 years has come at an unsustainable environmental price. Many of its cities are among the world's most polluted. The land is increasingly degraded, water resources are scarce and deteriorating in quality, and air pollution affects the entire region.

China has over 20 percent of the world's population but only 7 percent of global farmland; thus, land is precious. Overgrazing and deforestation contribute to some of the world's worst erosion. Already at least 20 percent desert, China loses more than 1,158 square miles (3,000 square kilometers) of land to desertification each year.

Water supplies are equally problematic: With the same approximate water resources as Canada supporting 100 times the population, China has one-quarter of the global per capita average. Seventy percent of all cities experience shortages. In addition, sewage and industrial pollutants contaminate many of the rivers, lakes, and underground supplies.

China's economic explosion has been fueled by an energy system that relies on coal for more than 60 percent of its needs, making the country the world's second largest emitter of greenhouse gases and the largest producer of sulfur dioxide, causing acid rain throughout East Asia. Nearly a quarter of all deaths in the countryside are associated with respiratory diseases. In the cities, almost 600,000 people are expected to die prematurely from air pollution each year until 2020.

In Linfen, a young boy rides behind his mother, his face shielded against air pollution. One of China's most polluted cities, Linfen is located in Shanxi Province, the heart of the country's rapidly expanding coal industry. Residents of the city claim to literally choke on coal dust in the evenings, and clinics report rising cases of bronchitis, pneumonia, and lung cancer. Lead poisoning occurs in high rates in children, and arsenic in the water supply has caused a province-wide epidemic of arsenicosis. China's energy-hungry economic expansion has resulted in hundreds of often unregulated coal mines, steel factories, and tar refineries that have parched the land, fouled the air, and poisoned the water. The national dependence on coal results in strong opposition to environmental improvement by business interests and corrupt officials.

GLOBAL IMPACT OF POLLUTION

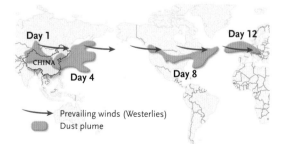

In early 1990, a huge dust plume from China's Taklimakan Desert traveled 12,000 miles (19,000 km) in about two weeks, crossing the Pacific Ocean, North America, and the Atlantic Ocean to settle atop the French Alps. These dust events can transport heavy metal, fungal, bacterial, and viral pollution.

CARBON DIOXIDE (CO₂) EMISSIONS

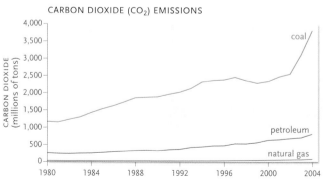

In the early 21st century, China's CO2 emissions began to increase dramatically, in tandem with the country's tremendous economic growth. By 2005, China was the world's second highest overall greenhouse gas emitter (after the U.S.), with coal combustion for industrial uses being by far the largest source.

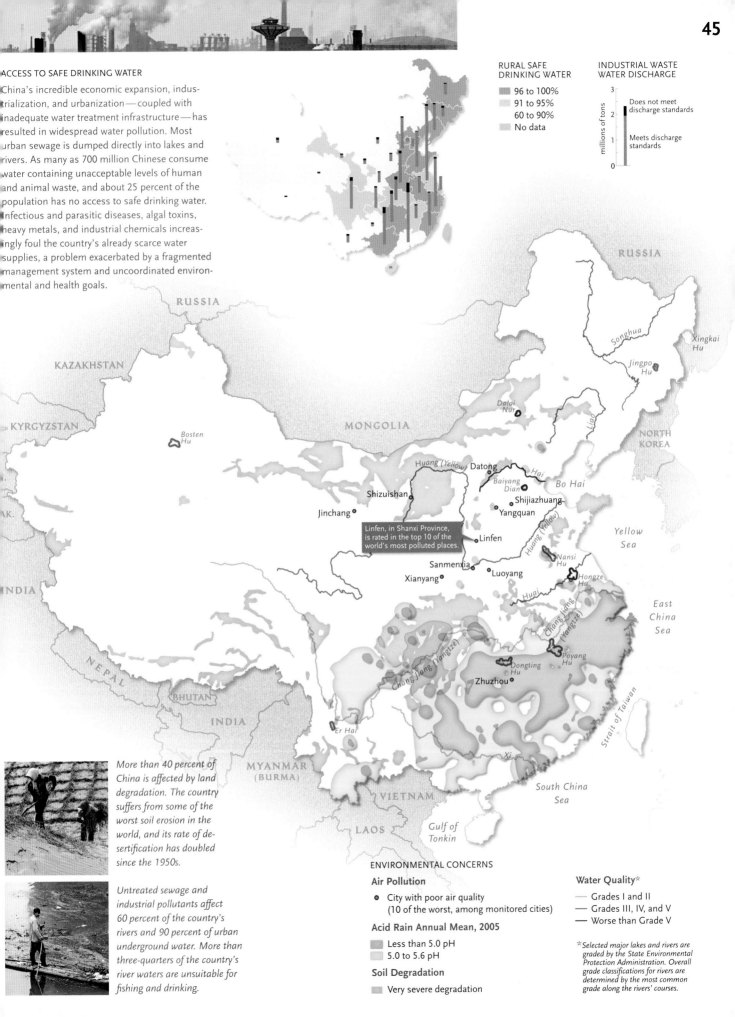

ACCESS TO SAFE DRINKING WATER

China's incredible economic expansion, industrialization, and urbanization—coupled with inadequate water treatment infrastructure—has resulted in widespread water pollution. Most urban sewage is dumped directly into lakes and rivers. As many as 700 million Chinese consume water containing unacceptable levels of human and animal waste, and about 25 percent of the population has no access to safe drinking water. Infectious and parasitic diseases, algal toxins, heavy metals, and industrial chemicals increasingly foul the country's already scarce water supplies, a problem exacerbated by a fragmented management system and uncoordinated environmental and health goals.

RURAL SAFE DRINKING WATER
- 96 to 100%
- 91 to 95%
- 60 to 90%
- No data

INDUSTRIAL WASTE WATER DISCHARGE

millions of tons
3
2
1
0

Does not meet discharge standards

Meets discharge standards

Linfen, in Shanxi Province, is rated in the top 10 of the world's most polluted places.

More than 40 percent of China is affected by land degradation. The country suffers from some of the worst soil erosion in the world, and its rate of desertification has doubled since the 1950s.

Untreated sewage and industrial pollutants affect 60 percent of the country's rivers and 90 percent of urban underground water. More than three-quarters of the country's river waters are unsuitable for fishing and drinking.

ENVIRONMENTAL CONCERNS

Air Pollution
- City with poor air quality (10 of the worst, among monitored cities)

Acid Rain Annual Mean, 2005
- Less than 5.0 pH
- 5.0 to 5.6 pH

Soil Degradation
- Very severe degradation

Water Quality*
- Grades I and II
- Grades III, IV, and V
- Worse than Grade V

**Selected major lakes and rivers are graded by the State Environmental Protection Administration. Overall grade classifications for rivers are determined by the most common grade along the rivers' courses.*

Population

AT A GLANCE

TOTAL POPULATION	1,313,424,000 PEOPLE
MALE LIFE EXPECTANCY	70 YEARS
FEMALE LIFE EXPECTANCY	73 YEARS
GROWTH RATE	0.6% ANNUAL INCREASE
FERTILITY RATE	1.6 BIRTHS PER WOMAN
GENDER RATIO AT BIRTH	119 MALES PER 100 FEMALES*
MINORITY POPULATION	104,490,000 PEOPLE

*The natural gender ratio at birth is 105 males per 100 females.

WORLD POPULATION

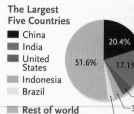

The Largest Five Countries
- China
- India
- United States
- Indonesia
- Brazil

Rest of world

20.4%
51.6%
17.1%
2.9%

WITH SLIGHTLY LESS TERRITORY and three-quarters as much arable land as the United States, China has a population that is is well over four times greater and is the largest of any country in the world. The gentle terrain and temperate climate of the plains, coastline, and especially megacities of the east are home to about 90 percent of China's people, mainly ethnic Hans. In contrast, the mountains, high plateaus, and deserts of China's west and north have been only lightly settled, mainly by ethnic minorities.

After civil war ended in 1949, improved health and living conditions accelerated population growth. Then the Great Leap Forward and associated famine of 1959–61 not only hastened the death of 30 million people but also drastically reduced childbearing. Following this population check, fertility increased rapidly with the restoration of more normal times and Mao Zedong's pro-natalist outlook. By 1970 Chinese women were giving birth at a rate of about six children each.

Realizing that economic growth could not keep pace with such rapid population expansion, the state soon adopted mandatory family-planning policies, and fertility dropped to significantly less than the replacement rate of about two children per woman by the end of the 20th century. In fact, projected trends suggest that China's population will stabilize and even decline well before mid-century. This change will introduce demographic issues typically associated with more developed countries, such as an expansive aging population and a shrinking workforce.

Newborns in a Chinese maternity ward

FAMILY PLANNING AND THE DEMOGRAPHIC TRANSITION

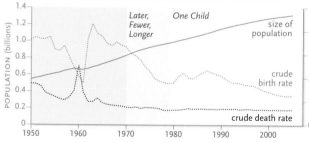

China's state-mandated family-planning policies have helped reduce the birthrate, slowing population growth that would otherwise boom due to a decreased death rate. The "Later, Fewer, Longer" policy, instituted during the 1970s, encouraged women to have children later in life, to have fewer children, and to wait longer between pregnancies. Under the "One Child" policy, introduced in 1979, penalties are assessed to most urban couples—mainly the Han—who have more than one offspring.

POPULATION STRUCTURE

Graphic pyramids show at a glance the structure of a given population according to age and gender. When the sides slope to a broad base, the population is growing quickly due to increased births and lower infant mortality. A bulge in a pyramid, such as 25 to 39-year-olds in 2020, marks a particularly large cohort, often with strong economic and social influence. A narrow base such as in the 2050 pyramid suggests a future population decline.

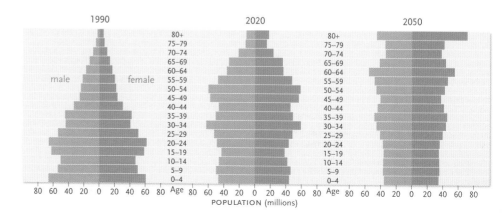

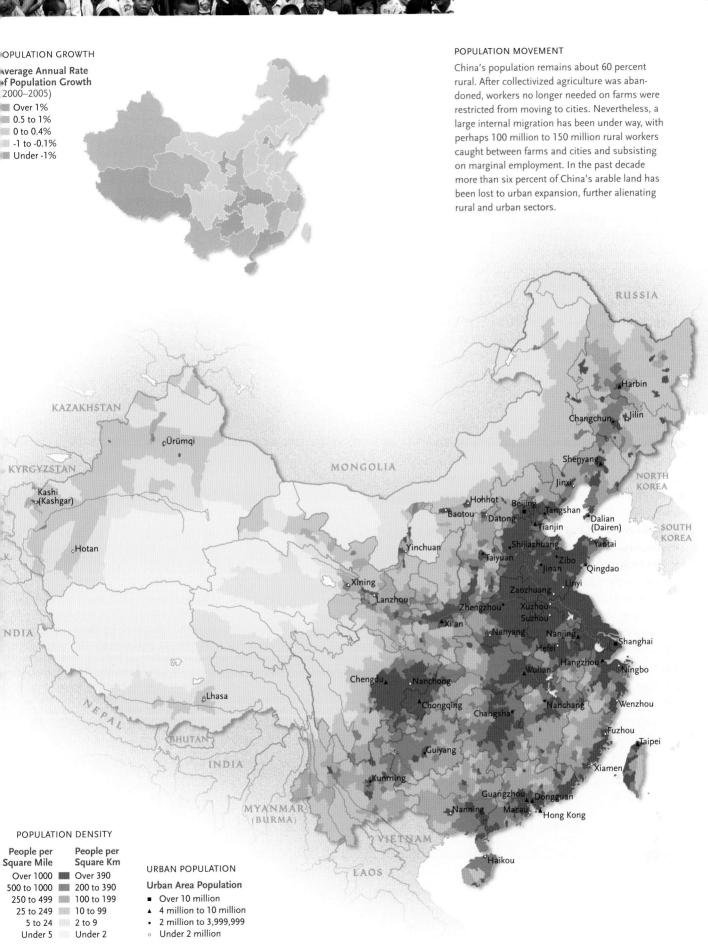

POPULATION GROWTH

Average Annual Rate of Population Growth
(2000–2005)

- Over 1%
- 0.5 to 1%
- 0 to 0.4%
- -1 to -0.1%
- Under -1%

POPULATION MOVEMENT

China's population remains about 60 percent rural. After collectivized agriculture was abandoned, workers no longer needed on farms were restricted from moving to cities. Nevertheless, a large internal migration has been under way, with perhaps 100 million to 150 million rural workers caught between farms and cities and subsisting on marginal employment. In the past decade more than six percent of China's arable land has been lost to urban expansion, further alienating rural and urban sectors.

POPULATION DENSITY

People per Square Mile	People per Square Km
Over 1000	Over 390
500 to 1000	200 to 390
250 to 499	100 to 199
25 to 249	10 to 99
5 to 24	2 to 9
Under 5	Under 2

URBAN POPULATION

Urban Area Population

- ■ Over 10 million
- ▲ 4 million to 10 million
- • 2 million to 3,999,999
- ○ Under 2 million

Urbanization

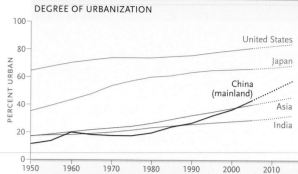

DEGREE OF URBANIZATION

CHINA IS CURRENTLY UNDERGOING a rapid rural-urban transition and transformation. Though it is not easy to measure the momentum precisely (owing to the country's complex and changing system of urban definitions), the latest official statistics show that by 2005 mainland China's urban population had reached 562 million, or 43 percent of the national total. In absolute numbers, China has the largest urban population in the world.

Rural-urban migration and urban reclassifications (newly designated towns and city districts) have been the major contributors to urbanization since the late 1970s. China's urbanization path has deviated from the standard model somewhat, in part because of the country's command economy legacy. The government uses strong measures to regulate rural-urban migration, and the system of local urban governments also forms a rigid political hierarchy. In 2005, China had 661 cities and 19,522 towns, and their distribution was very uneven. Because of the complexity in definition, the city population sizes shown on the map to the right are estimates.

Most expect China to continue on the path of fast urbanization for the coming two decades. It is very likely that China will pass the mark of being 50 percent urban by 2010 and that its urban population will increase by at least another 300 million people in the next 15 years. The huge increased demand for employment, urban infrastructure, and social services will pose a challenge to the government.

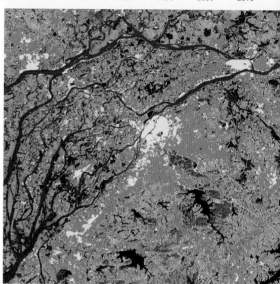

■ Urban area in 1988
▓ Urban area in 1999

This Landsat 7 ETM satellite image has been overlaid with data showing the extent of urban growth in the Dongguan area.

Dongguan's Urban Growth: *If China is the "world's factory," Dongguan is one of the cores. Thirty years ago, no one imagined that this slow agricultural county in the proximity of Hong Kong would today be one of the favorite outsourcing destinations of Hong Kong's and Taiwan's investments. This city is one of China's largest export-processing centers, employing millions of low-cost migrant laborers from many parts of China. In 2005, the city had a population of about 6.6 million, three-quarters of whom were migrant workers, typically young women and men. Dongguan also has one of the most skewed social and demographic structures of any Chinese city.*

THE URBAN-RURAL DIVIDE

China has huge rural-urban disparities, among the worst in the world. The urban to rural ratio of per capita income (including all sources) is likely in the range of 3:1 or 4:1. These disparities are created partly by the faster pace of growth in the urban industrial sector than in agriculture and, more importantly, by institutions and policies. For the three decades of Mao's era, China's development strategy favored industry. Government policies gave urban residents state-guaranteed food, jobs, housing, and access to an array of subsidized welfare and social services, while rural residents had few of these. Furthermore, migration from rural to urban areas was strictly controlled. Since the late 1970s, this rigid segmentation has been loosened somewhat, but discrimination against peasants and peasant migrants remains. Promoting agricultural development and improving the standard of living of China's peasantry mass remain serious challenges.

URBAN-RURAL ECONOMIC DIFFERENCES

Consumer Items
(per 100 households, 2005)

	URBAN	RURAL
MOBILE PHONES	137	50
COLOR TELEVISIONS	135	84
WASHING MACHINES	96	40
REFRIGERATORS	91	20
AIR CONDITIONERS	81	6
CAMERAS	47	4
COMPUTERS	42	2
STEREO SYSTEMS	29	13
VIDEO RECORDERS	15	3

URBAN
$1,382

68.9%
23.4%
1.7%
6.0%

RURAL
$565

68.3%
25.4%
4.4%
1.9%

Per Capita Income
(2005)

■ Wages and salaries
■ Business and self-employment
▨ Properties
▓ Subsidies and remittances

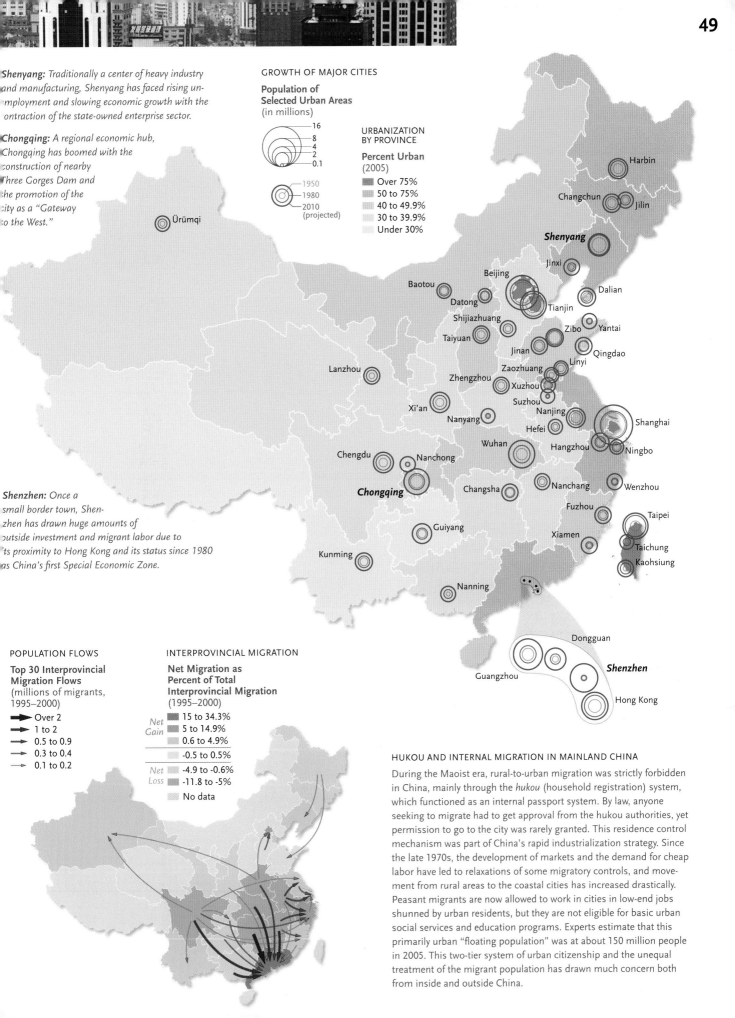

Shenyang: Traditionally a center of heavy industry and manufacturing, Shenyang has faced rising unemployment and slowing economic growth with the contraction of the state-owned enterprise sector.

Chongqing: A regional economic hub, Chongqing has boomed with the construction of nearby Three Gorges Dam and the promotion of the city as a "Gateway to the West."

Shenzhen: Once a small border town, Shenzhen has drawn huge amounts of outside investment and migrant labor due to its proximity to Hong Kong and its status since 1980 as China's first Special Economic Zone.

GROWTH OF MAJOR CITIES

Population of Selected Urban Areas
(in millions)

16
8
4
2
0.1

1950
1980
2010
(projected)

URBANIZATION BY PROVINCE

Percent Urban
(2005)

- Over 75%
- 50 to 75%
- 40 to 49.9%
- 30 to 39.9%
- Under 30%

Cities labeled on map

Harbin, Changchun, Jilin, Shenyang, Jinxi, Dalian, Ürümqi, Baotou, Datong, Beijing, Tianjin, Shijiazhuang, Zibo, Yantai, Taiyuan, Jinan, Qingdao, Lanzhou, Zhengzhou, Zaozhuang, Linyi, Xuzhou, Xi'an, Nanyang, Suzhou, Nanjing, Shanghai, Hefei, Hangzhou, Ningbo, Wuhan, Chengdu, Nanchong, Changsha, Nanchang, Wenzhou, Chongqing, Fuzhou, Guiyang, Xiamen, Taipei, Taichung, Kaohsiung, Kunming, Nanning, Dongguan, Guangzhou, Shenzhen, Hong Kong

POPULATION FLOWS

Top 30 Interprovincial Migration Flows
(millions of migrants, 1995–2000)

- Over 2
- 1 to 2
- 0.5 to 0.9
- 0.3 to 0.4
- 0.1 to 0.2

INTERPROVINCIAL MIGRATION

Net Migration as Percent of Total Interprovincial Migration
(1995–2000)

Net Gain
- 15 to 34.3%
- 5 to 14.9%
- 0.6 to 4.9%

- -0.5 to 0.5%

Net Loss
- -4.9 to -0.6%
- -11.8 to -5%

- No data

HUKOU AND INTERNAL MIGRATION IN MAINLAND CHINA

During the Maoist era, rural-to-urban migration was strictly forbidden in China, mainly through the *hukou* (household registration) system, which functioned as an internal passport system. By law, anyone seeking to migrate had to get approval from the hukou authorities, yet permission to go to the city was rarely granted. This residence control mechanism was part of China's rapid industrialization strategy. Since the late 1970s, the development of markets and the demand for cheap labor have led to relaxations of some migratory controls, and movement from rural areas to the coastal cities has increased drastically. Peasant migrants are now allowed to work in cities in low-end jobs shunned by urban residents, but they are not eligible for basic urban social services and education programs. Experts estimate that this primarily urban "floating population" was at about 150 million people in 2005. This two-tier system of urban citizenship and the unequal treatment of the migrant population has drawn much concern both from inside and outside China.

Human Development Indicators

AT A GLANCE

	1990	2004	DEFINITION
MALNUTRITION	16%	12% (2003)	Population that is undernourished
UNDER-5 MORTALITY	49	31	Mortality rate of children under age 5 (per 100,000)
MATERNAL MORTALITY	89	50 (2000)	Mortality rate of women in childbirth (per 100,000 live births)
GENDER EQUALITY IN SCHOOL ENROLLMENT	86:100	90:100 (2000)	Female-to-male ratio in elementary school
DRINKING WATER ACCESS	70%	77%	Population with sustainable access to an improved water source
SANITATION ACCESS	23%	44%	Population with sustainable access to improved sanitation

CHINA'S FUTURE PROSPECTS depend on a healthy, well educated population and geographically balanced social development. These goals represent major challenges for the Chinese government and society. After decades in which the strong hand of government was used to bring about rapid improvements in access to health and education in the rural areas and steep declines in childbearing, new policy measures are needed to respond to the opportunities and hardships associated with market-oriented economic growth.

China's Human Development Index (HDI), a composite of health, education, and other social indicators, has risen steadily since the late 1970s, and the life expectancy, primary school enrollment, and literacy of the country's 1.3 billion citizens are comparable to those in other middle-income countries. Overall, the country faces huge regional disparities in the population's welfare, with the HDI in the economically advanced region of Shanghai being almost 55 percent higher than it is in the disadvantaged area of Tibet. Throughout the country, and particularly in low-income provinces, girls have poorer health and education outcomes than boys. Ethnic minorities also have significantly worse health status and higher rates of illiteracy.

The most striking test of public policy will be in the health sector, where China is experiencing an explosive increase in noninfectious disease, particularly ailments resulting from changes in diet, physical activity, and tobacco use. Health care financing and structure will have to adjust drastically to respond adequately.

EDUCATIONAL ATTAINMENT

The majority of Chinese adults are literate, and most have completed the compulsory nine years of schooling. Rural provinces lag, however, and throughout China girls are less likely than boys to be able to read and write.

Maximum Educational Attainment
(2005)

- No schooling
- Primary school
- Junior secondary school
- Senior secondary school
- College or higher

6.3%   5.6%
14.1%
32.4%
41.6%
MALE

4.8%
10.8%   15.1%
35.1%   34.2%
FEMALE

HUMAN DEVELOPMENT

Human Development Index (HDI) Value
(2005)

- Over 0.80
- 0.75 to 0.80
- 0.70 to 0.74
- 0.58 to 0.69

ILLITERACY

Percent Illiterate
(2005)

- Over 40%
- 15 to 40%
- 10 to 14.9%
- 7 to 9.9%
- Under 7%

Illiteracy by Gender
(2005)

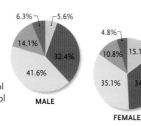

—20%
—10%
MALES   FEMALES

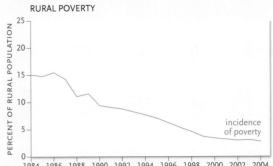

POVERTY

China's growth and social development has been dramatic but shared unequally across the vast country, with rural citizens, western provinces and women benefiting least. According to government statistics, the number of poor people in rural areas decreased dramatically, from 250 million in 1978 (about one-third of the rural population) to 42 million in 1998 (less than one-twentieth of the rural population). However, poverty has become increasingly concentrated, with about two-thirds of the rural poor living in the western provinces. Recent research suggests that inequality between genders and between rural and urban areas is increasing as more market-based economic growth has emerged, and as the government has played a more limited role in providing a social safety net for the poor. The government has identified balancing growth and equity as one of its top concerns as the country strives for a *xiaokang*, or "all-around well-off" society, on its way to overall modernization.

RURAL POVERTY

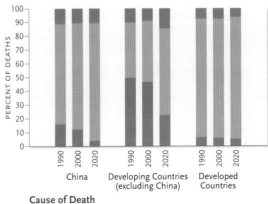

Tobacco Use: *Nearly two-thirds of all Chinese men over the age of 15 smoke, and an increasing number of women are taking it up. Despite the severity of the health consequences, dealing with the problem is complex, both because of a lack of awareness of the dangers (more than half of all male doctors smoke) and the economic power of the government-run tobacco industry.*

THE EPIDEMIOLOGIC TRANSITION

In the past 50 years, China's demographic transition (see Urbanization, p. 48) has been matched by an epidemiologic transition. The rates of child deaths from preventable causes, such as diarrheal disease and respiratory disease, are still quite high in poor, rural areas, but the current leading causes of death and disability in China are noncommunicable diseases in adults — particularly cardiovascular and lung diseases and cancer.

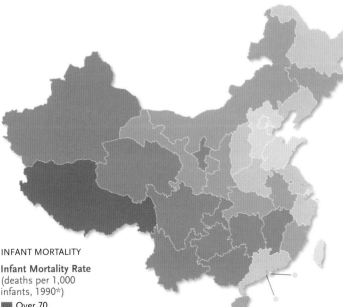

BIRTH RATE

Crude Birth Rate
(births per 1,000 persons, 2005)

- Over 14
- 12 to 14
- 9 to 11.9
- Under 9

INFANT MORTALITY

Infant Mortality Rate
(deaths per 1,000 infants, 1990*)

- Over 70
- 35 to 70
- 20 to 34
- 15 to 19
- Under 15

*Most recent data available. Current mortality patterns should be similar, though actual values may have changed since 1990.

Cause of Death

- Injury
- Noncommunicable disease
- Communicable disease

Global Burden of Disease data consider countries with established market economies and European countries that formerly had Socialist economies to be developed; all other countries are considered developing. Baseline predictions for 2020 are shown, though they reflect uncertainty.

Religion, Philosophy, and Language

THERE ARE A NUMBER OF RELIGIONS in China. Some are indigenous, such as Confucianism and Daoism. Others are imported from abroad, such as Buddhism, Islam, and Christianity. Among the latter, Buddhism is the only foreign religion that has been widely adopted in Chinese culture.

Since the 1949 revolution, Marxism and atheism have been the official dogmas. During the Cultural Revolution (1966–76), all religions suffered persecution. In recent years, however, Buddhist and Daoist temples have been restored, and traditional religious observations, such as temple worship and pilgrimage, have returned.

Unlike the Chinese Mandarin language—which the government has used to assert its influence throughout the country—no single religion dominates in China. It is difficult to provide a breakdown of the numbers of adherents, because aside from religious professionals (such as Buddhist monks and Daoist priests), the majority of the people cannot be said to be followers of any one religion exclusively. They are familiar with the basic teachings of Confucianism of filial piety and courtesy, as well as the Daoist and Buddhist emphases on meditation and compassion.

Legend:
- Buddhist
- Daoist
- Confucianist
- ◉ Daoist and Buddhist
- ○ Daoist, Buddhist and Confucianist

Map labels: Temple of Heaven (Beijing); Heng Shan Bei; Wutai Shan; Tai Shan; Lao Shan; Qufu (birthplace of Confucius); Hua Shan; Song Shan; Tholing Monastery; Kangrinboqê Feng (Mt. Kailash); Jokhang Temple & Potala Palace (Lhasa); Tashilhunpo Monastery; Wudang Shan; Qingcheng Shan; Jiuhua Shan; Putuo Shan; Emei Shan; Heng Shan Nan

SACRED SITES

Sacred sites in China include mountaintop monasteries built by Daoist and Buddhist monks, many of which preserve traditional Chinese architecture. Myths and legends are often associated with these sites, some of which have become pilgrimage destinations.

CHINESE CHARACTERS

Chinese characters appeared 3,500 years ago during the Shang dynasty. To know 3,000 characters out of the 50,000 total number is sufficient to read newspapers. Pictographs, created by drawing the objects, are believed to be earlier written characters (see "horse" pictograph, below). Ninety percent of the current characters are meaning-sound characters—i.e., each character is formed by a meaning element and a sound element (see examples below).

Evolution of a Chinese Pictograph: "Horse"

| 1400 B.C.E. | 1100 B.C.E. | 221 B.C.E. | 220 C.E. | after 1956 C.E. |

Meaning-Sound Characters

MEANING ELEMENT	SOUND ELEMENT	CHARACTER
氵 "water"	青 qíng, "green"	清 qíng, "clean"
日 "sun"	青 qíng, "green"	晴 qíng, "sunny"

The Yin-Yang symbol represents the dualistic nature of the universe—an idea common to China's main belief systems.

THREE PRIMARY SCHOOLS OF THOUGHT

The keystone of philosophy in China has always been humanism, with the circumstances of the times shaping the details of each of the most popular ideologies. Confucianism focuses on relationships between people, while Daoism centers on the relationship between humans and nature. Buddhism, introduced to China from India about 2,000 years ago, fit nicely with these preexisting philosophies and has persisted as a popular religious practice today. Each of these three schools of thought has played a defining role in Chinese belief systems, and the Chinese culture owes much of its richness to the wisdom and inspiration contained within them.

CONFUCIANISM: Popularized by the sage Confucius in the sixth century B.C.E., the values of Confucianism have been arguably the most influential in shaping Chinese thought and values. Famous for his many insightful quotes such as *"What you do not want done to yourself, do not do to others,"* Confucius centered his wide-ranging teachings on establishing harmonious interpersonal relationships, focusing on humaneness and respect—especially for elders and parents.

DAOISM: Inspired by the sage Laozi's writing of the Daodejing (Tao Te Ching), Daoism has pervaded Chinese thought for more than 2,000 years. Associated with nature due to its origin in China's agrarian history, Dao is the force behind the natural order and keeps the universe balanced. Daoism's teachings include complementary dualism (represented by yin and yang), and are commonly expressed and symbolized through the practice of martial arts such as *tai ji quan* (tai chi chuan).

BUDDHISM: The Buddha, or "awakened one," reached enlightenment in India in about the fifth century B.C.E. Buddhism grew based on his vision and teachings, which promote liberation from suffering through the threefold cultivation of morality, meditation, and wisdom. Chinese Buddhism has evolved its own distinct forms, often incorporating Confucianist and Daoist principles which account for its distinctive characteristics not found in Buddhist traditions elsewhere. The form most commonly practiced in China today combines elements of the Pure Land and Chan (Zen) sects.

Turkic
- Ⓐ Kazak
- Ⓑ Kirgiz
- Ⓒ Salar
- Ⓓ Tatar
- Ⓔ Tuva
- Ⓕ Uygur
- Ⓖ Uzbek
- Ⓗ Western Yugur

Manchu-Tungus
- Ⓔ Ewenki
- Ⓗ Hezhe
- Ⓜ Manchu
- Ⓞ Oroqen
- Ⓧ Xibo

Mongolian
- Ⓐ Bao'an
- Ⓑ Dagur
- Ⓒ Dongxiang
- Ⓓ Eastern Yugur
- Ⓔ Mongolian
- Ⓕ Monguor

Indo-European
- Ⓡ Russian
- Ⓣ Tajik

Miao-Yao
- Ⓐ Bunu
- Ⓑ Miao (Hmong)
- Ⓒ She
- Ⓓ Yao (Mian)

Korean
- Korean

Minority Languages
(percentage of speakers)
- Kam-Tai
- Tibeto-Burman
- Turkic
- Miao-Yao
- Mongolian
- Korean
- Other

1.6%
3.4%
7%
15%
35%
11%
27%

Austronesian
- Ⓗ Huihui (Cham)
- Taiwan-Austronesian

Austroasiatic
- Ⓑ Blang
- Ⓓ De'ang
- Ⓙ Jing (Vietnamese)
- Ⓥ Va

Kam-Tai
- Ⓐ Bouyei
- Ⓑ Cun
- Ⓒ Dai
- Ⓓ Gelao Isolate
- Ⓔ Kam
- Ⓕ Lakkia
- Ⓖ Li
- Ⓗ Lingao
- Ⓘ Mak
- Ⓙ Maonan
- Ⓚ Mulam
- Ⓛ Sui
- Ⓜ Yanghuang
- Ⓝ Zhuang

Tibeto-Burman
- Ⓐ Achang
- Ⓑ Bai
- Ⓒ Bogar-Lhoba
- Ⓓ Canglo-Monba
- Ⓔ Cuona-Monba
- Ⓕ Darang-Deng
- Ⓖ Derung (Drung)
- Ⓗ Geman-Deng
- Ⓙ Gyarong
- Ⓙ Hani
- Ⓚ Jingpo
- Ⓛ Jino
- Ⓜ Lahu
- Ⓝ Lisu
- Ⓞ Naxi
- Ⓟ Nu
- Ⓠ Pumi
- Ⓡ Qiang
- Ⓢ Tibetan
- Ⓣ Tujia
- Ⓤ Yi
- Ⓥ Yidu-Lhoba
- Ⓦ Zaiwa

MINORITY LANGUAGES

There are 55 minority groups in China, with half of the minority languages belonging to the Sino-Tibetan family, including the Kam-Tai, Miao-Yao, and Tibeto-Burman groups. About 19 belong to the Altaic family, consisting of Manchu-Tungus, Mongolian, and Turkic languages. Austronesian languages can also be heard in Taiwan.

Dialects
(percentage of speakers)
- Mandarin
- Wu
- Min
- Jin
- Yue
- Hakka
- Xiang
- Gan
- Other

3%
3%
4%
5%
6%
7%
1%
68%

Mandarin Supergroup
- Ⓐ Beifang
- Ⓑ Beijing
- Ⓒ Jiaoliao
- Ⓓ Jianghuai
- Ⓔ Lanyin
- Ⓕ Northeastern
- Ⓖ Southwestern
- Ⓗ Zhongyuan
- Ⓘ Bilingual (Southwestern Mandarin & Tuhua)

Min Supergroup
- Ⓐ Minbei
- Ⓑ Mindong
- Ⓒ Minnan
- Ⓓ Minzhong
- Ⓔ Puxian
- Ⓕ Qiongwen
- Ⓖ Shaojiang

Other Groups
- Danzhou (unclassified)
- Gan
- Hui
- Hakka
- Ⓗ Hakka (scattered)
- Jin
- Pinghua
- Ⓢ Shaozhou Tuhua
- Wu
- Xiang
- Ⓧ Xianghua
- Yue (Cantonese)
- Other languages & dialects
- No data

CHINESE DIALECTS

The Chinese language spoken by the majority Han people (90%) is classified in the Sino-Tibetan language family. The Chinese language is monosyllabic and tonal, with little inflection. There are seven major dialects, with mutually unintelligible regional variants. However, Chinese characters are not phonetically based, and are used as a script for speakers of various dialects.

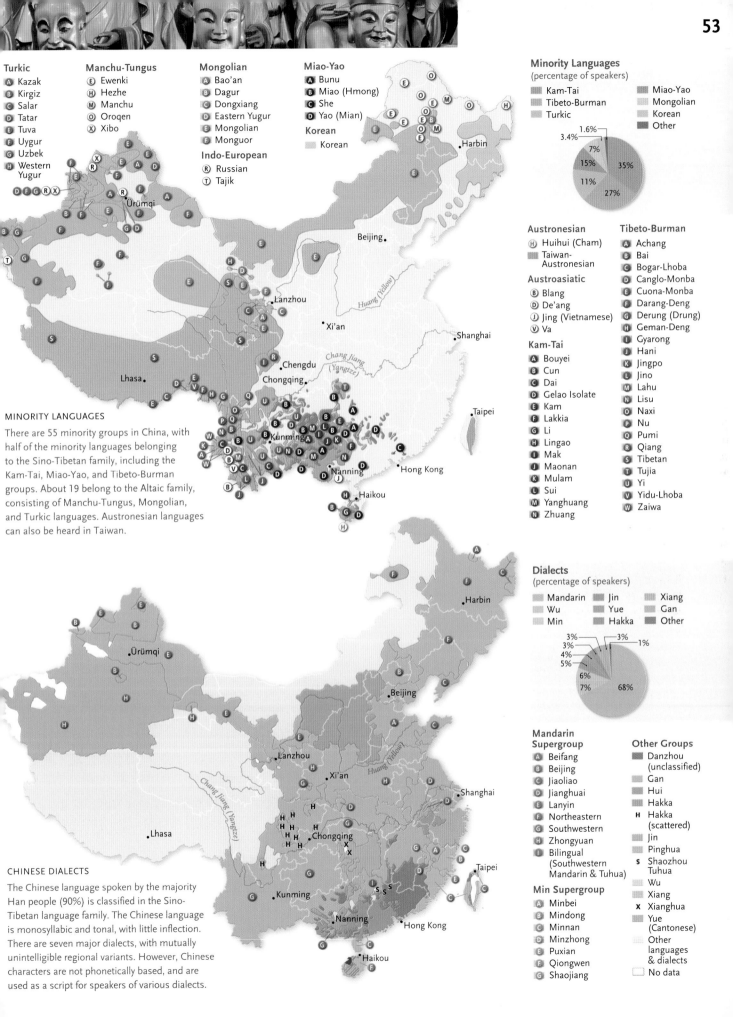

Way of Life

	2005	AT A GLANCE	
		SHANGHAI	NEW YORK
TOTAL POPULATION		17.78 MILLION	18.35 MILLION
PERCENT FEMALE		49.8%	51.8%
PERCENT MALE		50.2%	48.2%
AREA		2,400 SQUARE MILES	6,720 SQUARE MILES
POPULATION DENSITY		7,408 PERSONS/SQUARE MILE	2,731 PERSONS/SQUARE MILE
AVERAGE PER CAPITA INCOME (U.S. dollars)		$2,500	$31,200
UNEMPLOYMENT RATE		4.4%	6.8%
PERSONS PER HOUSHOLD		3.0	2.7
COLLEGE EDUCATED		18%	34.8%
METRO/SUBWAY TICKET (2007)		$0.39	$2.00

THE CHINESE CREATED one of the world's great cultural traditions based on the needs of an agrarian society. Its main themes include a reverence for nature and an obligation to family, since these were values that were essential to maintaining prosperity in early China. Much of the traditional and modern Chinese way of life has a basis in one or both of these themes, although the modern way of life is rapidly adapting to include elements of modern Western society.

Often guided by Confucianism, the Chinese way of life has utilized the collective wisdom, ingenuity, and creativity of the most populous society in the history of the world. This unprecedented collection of ideas and practices has formed a culture that has given the world some of its richest traditions in language, philosophy, religion, architecture, literature, and art.

SOCIAL RELATIONS AND GENDER

Traditionally, a Chinese family formed an invaluable, self-sufficient social network. Rather than being considered inside or outside a family, people were viewed as being "nearer to" or "further from" a person, with individual relationships based on that perceived distance. In this patrilineal and patriarchal society, the network was usually centered on the eldest male, who held the wealth and power of the family. Since a family's legacy depended on male heirs, females were considered less desirable and held very few rights. Recently, however, the family in China has undergone a dynamic shift in values, with the roles of men and women becoming more equal.

TRADITIONAL CHINESE MEDICINE

Drawing on the experience and wisdom of the ancient Chinese civilization, traditional medicine in China can be mysterious to anyone not familiar with its doctrine. Its basic belief is that the human body and the environment are interrelated and in harmony with one another, and that any illness or misfortune is due to an imbalance in the dualistic system of forces called the yin and the yang. The overall aim of traditional Chinese medicine is to keep the yin and the yang in proper balance. A complicated and ancient process of pulse taking determines any imbalance, and common treatments to restore the proper bodily balance include herbs, moxibustion (burning of moxa, or mugwort herb, near the skin), and acupuncture.

EDUCATION

At the time of the establishment of the People's Republic of China in 1949, 80 percent of China's 500 million people were illiterate. At that time, the Communist Party established successful policies that expanded education beyond the elite class to the proletariat. However, the 1966–1976 Cultural Revolution led to a major collapse in China's education system, which shut down schools across the country. The ensuing shortage of educated workers stalled China's economic growth for decades. China now has a nine-year compulsory-schooling system, and enrollment in universities continues to rise, producing the skilled workers needed for China's rapid modernization. The government follows one of Deng Xiaoping's principles that "Education should be geared to the needs of modernization, of the world, and of the future."

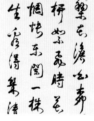

CALLIGRAPHY

According to legend, a man named Cangjie created Chinese characters, having been inspired by the characteristics and beauty of animal footprints and other natural objects. And although modern calligraphy utilizes several different standard scripts, the fundamental inspiration, as in all arts in China, is nature. The deep respect for calligraphy in China is earned by the ability of the advanced form to combine a multitude of life-simulating brushstrokes into a delicately balanced whole. A master of the art of Chinese calligraphy is thought to possess good *qi*, or life force, evidenced in the artist's ability to capture the form of natural objects.

LANDSCAPE GEOMANCY

With a deep affinity for the natural world and its cycles, the Chinese have long been adept at utilizing the subtlest differences in surroundings. Over time, they developed landscape geomancy, a system of divination that throughout history has sought the best location and orientation for man-made structures such as cities and dwellings. The most well-known system of geomancy is called feng shui. The goal of its practice is to harmonize the artificial and natural environment by situating human elements to maximize the positive energy in a space. Often dismissed and labeled a pseudo-science, feng shui is misunderstood by many Westerners but is gaining in popularity around the world.

CHINESE CUISINE

Growing conditions have long favored rice in the south of China and wheat in the north, and the use of these staples today largely defines the difference between northern and southern Chinese cuisines. As the population of China grew and cooking fuel became scarce, early Chinese developed techniques to cook and eat food more efficiently. The stir-fry has its origins in the practice of cooking food in smaller pieces, which takes less time and fuel, while early chopsticks were used to pluck bits of food from the fire. As cooking techniques evolved and more ingredients became available, Chinese ingenuity eventually led to the creation of the geographically separate "four schools" of cuisine (map, at right). Each school has its definitive characteristics: Sichuan is famous for its spicy tradition, for example, and Cantonese for its use of a wide variety of ingredients. Modern times have produced a multitude of local variations on these original ideas, leading to popular dishes like Peking Roast Duck. Chinese cuisine has since become popular worldwide, and many other cultures have incorporated elements of it to form their own flavors of Chinese food.

CHINESE FESTIVALS

Chinese Lantern Festival

Chinese New Year

Rich in culture and history, traditional festivals—each with its own unique character—form a critical aspect of Chinese culture. Moon worship was common in China thousands of years ago, based on the belief that the phases of the moon and the growth and decline of life are connected. Most traditional festivals are determined by the Chinese calendar, which is based on the cycles of the moon and sun. Most festivals fall on a specific day of a certain lunar month, although some—such as Chinese New Year (end of the 12th month) and Winter Solstice—coincide with significant events in the Chinese calendar.

　　Double numbers hold a special significance in Chinese culture—there is a Chinese saying meaning "good things come in pairs," and major festivals are held on the 1st day of the 1st lunar month, the 5th day of the 5th lunar month, the 7th day of the 7th lunar month, and the 9th day of the 9th lunar month. During the prosperous Tang dynasty (618–906 C.E.), traditional festivals became less involved with mysticism and instead focused on entertainment. Today, popular festivals such as Chinese New Year and the Dragon Boat Festival are world famous for the colorful and inspiring images they create.

ENGLISH	CHINESE	DATE	DESCRIPTION
Spring Festival (New Year's Day)	新年，农历新年	1st day of 1st lunar month	*Fireworks after midnight, visiting in-laws*
Lantern Festival	元宵节	15th day of 1st lunar month	*Celebration of first full moon, lantern parade, and lion dance*
Tomb Sweeping Day	清明节	Solar longitude 15° (~April 5)	*Cleaning and offering at family tombs*
Dragon Boat Festival	端午节	5th day of 5th lunar month	*Commemorating ancient poet Qu Yuan, dragon boat racing*
The Night of Sevens	七夕	7th day of 7th lunar month	*Romantic holiday, sometimes called Chinese Valentine's Day*
Spirit Festival	中元节	15th day of 7th lunar month	*Make offerings to ancestors and the dead, burn paper money*
Moon Festival	中秋节	15th day of 8th lunar month	*Celebrate the legend of the moon goddess Chang'e*
Double Ninth Festival	重阳节，重阳	9th day of 9th lunar month	*Autumn outing and mountain climbing*
Winter Solstice	冬至	Solar longitude 270° (~Dec. 22)	*Ancestor worship, feast day, "Chinese Thanksgiving"*
Laba Festival	腊八节	8th day of 12th lunar month	*The day Buddha self-enlightened*
Chinese New Year's Eve	除夕，大年夜	Last day of 12th lunar month	*Fireworks, followed by at least a 10-course meal with a whole fish entrée symbolizing the abundance of the coming year.*

Chinese Mid-Autumn (Moon) Festival *One of the most popular holidays in China, the Mid-Autumn Festival, or Moon Festival, traditionally celebrated the summer's harvest by bringing families together to worship the moon. Today the immensely popular mooncake dominates the festival, which features parades and lantern fairs (above).*

URBAN LIFE: Urban life in China is fast-paced, crushingly crowded, and a bustle of activity. Hordes of pedestrians and bicyclists, along with rapidly increasing numbers of motorists, clog the streets and squares of most large cities. Urban Chinese typically work 8 to 12 hours a day, spending their growing incomes on things once considered luxuries, like mobile phones and air conditioners. Urbanites also enjoy a widening variety of services, arts, and entertainment options that are supported by the metropolitan makeup of their populations. Development is rampant in China's cities, with new offices, roads, and apartment buildings unable to keep up with the growing number of businesses and citizens. As a result of the increased opportunities being offered to China's urban residents, more rural Chinese are joining their ranks. It is becoming a nearly impossible task, however, for the cities to provide housing and services for the millions of hopeful villagers lured each year by the city lifestyle.

RURAL LIFE: Life in rural China is every bit as hardworking as the cities but lacks the crowded hustle and many of the modern luxuries. Communist rule improved the lifestyle of rural Chinese by introducing a system of communes and,

later, collectives that provided steady work for most citizens. More recent policies have allowed rural citizens to offer services on the free market rather than fulfill government contracts for agricultural products. Many rural Chinese are now buying motorcycles and household appliances, and except in remote areas, most villagers have access to electricity. However, as China modernizes, more villagers are being forced to abandon the traditional way of Chinese life in order to provide for their families.

Tourism

	2006	AT A GLANCE
TOURISM REVENUE		34 BILLION U.S. DOLLARS (4.5% OF GDP)
IMPACT ON EMPLOYMENT		17.4 MILLION JOBS (2.3% OF TOTAL EMPLOYMENT)
PROJECTED GROWTH		8.7% ANNUALLY FROM 2007 TO 2016
SHARE OF WORLD TOURISM		5.5%
TOTAL TOURIST ARRIVALS		124,940,000
FOREIGN TOURIST ARRIVALS		22,210,000
COMPATRIOT* TOURIST ARRIVALS		102,730,000
OUTBOUND TOURIST DEPARTURES		34,520,000
DOMESTIC TOURIST VISITS		1,394,000,000

*Residents of Taiwan, Hong Kong, and Macau

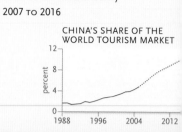

CHINA'S SHARE OF THE WORLD TOURISM MARKET

EVER SINCE THE ECONOMIC REFORMS and renewed openness that occurred in China in the late 1970s, tourism has gained increasing importance as a growth industry at both national and local levels. With its enormous variety of features—bustling cities, wild and spectacular landscapes, ethnic diversity, numerous World Heritage sites and other cultural and historical marvels—the country offers something for travelers of nearly all tastes and interests.

Indeed, following a sustained effort in this sector over the past 20 years (both in terms of government policy changes and investment), China has now become a major destination for foreign travelers. In 2005, international visits numbered some 20 million, with revenue totaling around $30 billion U.S. By 2015, the UN World Tourism Organization predicts that China will be the top tourist destination worldwide. Its domestic market has already become the largest in terms of tourist numbers (around 1.2 billion in 2005).

Also remarkable is the potential for huge numbers of Chinese to themselves become foreign tourists in the coming years. Officials, commercial representatives, and students have historically been most likely to travel abroad, but this is changing as incomes grow and travel restrictions ease. With big growth increases likely to persist in the coming years, China's tourism industry stands as another symbol of its economic vigor.

Crosswaters Ecolodge, set in a nature reserve, was built using local materials and craftspeople, regionally inspired design, and with a strong eye toward environmental protection. With proper management, ecotourism can help in the sustainable development of China's natural areas and socially and ecologically diverse inland regions.

VISITOR ARRIVALS AND TOURISM RECEIPTS

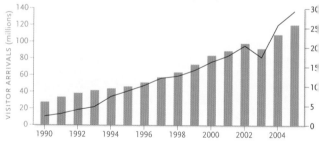

OUTBOUND TOURISM

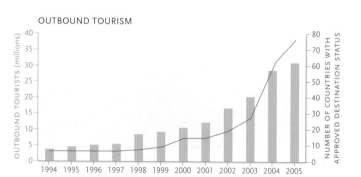

Most outbound Chinese travelers head to destinations in Asia, with about 70% going to Hong Kong or Macau and another 20% to other Asian countries. However, countries on every continent maintain Approved Destination Status for Chinese tour groups, and enjoy the $1,000 per day that an average Chinese tourist spends abroad.

DOMESTIC TOURISM

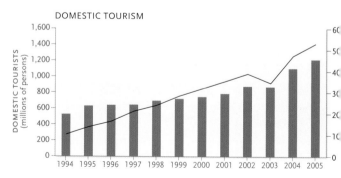

Shaking off the severe acute respiratory syndrome scare of 2003, domestic tourism has continued on its huge upward trend as the Chinese enjoy greater disposable incomes and more leisure time. The three "Golden Week" holidays—Chinese New Year, International Labor Day, and National Day—are by far the busiest times to travel, and stimulate tourism earnings significantly.

TOP SOURCES OF FOREIGN TOURISTS

Of the 22 million foreign tourist arrivals in China in 2006, well over half of visitors were from other Asian countries. Not included in this number are approximately 100 million visits from Chinese compatriots in Hong Kong, Macau, and Taiwan and other Chinese nationals living overseas. The bulk of inbound tourists are destined for the eastern provinces, which offer a combination of business destinations and attractions for sightseeing.

1.	South Korea	3,924,000	6.	Singapore	828,000	(number of visits, 2006)
2.	Japan	3,746,000	7.	Philippines	704,000	
3.	Russia	2,405,000	8.	Mongolia	631,000	
4.	United States	1,710,000	9.	Thailand	592,000	
5.	Malaysia	910,000	10.	United Kingdom	553,000	

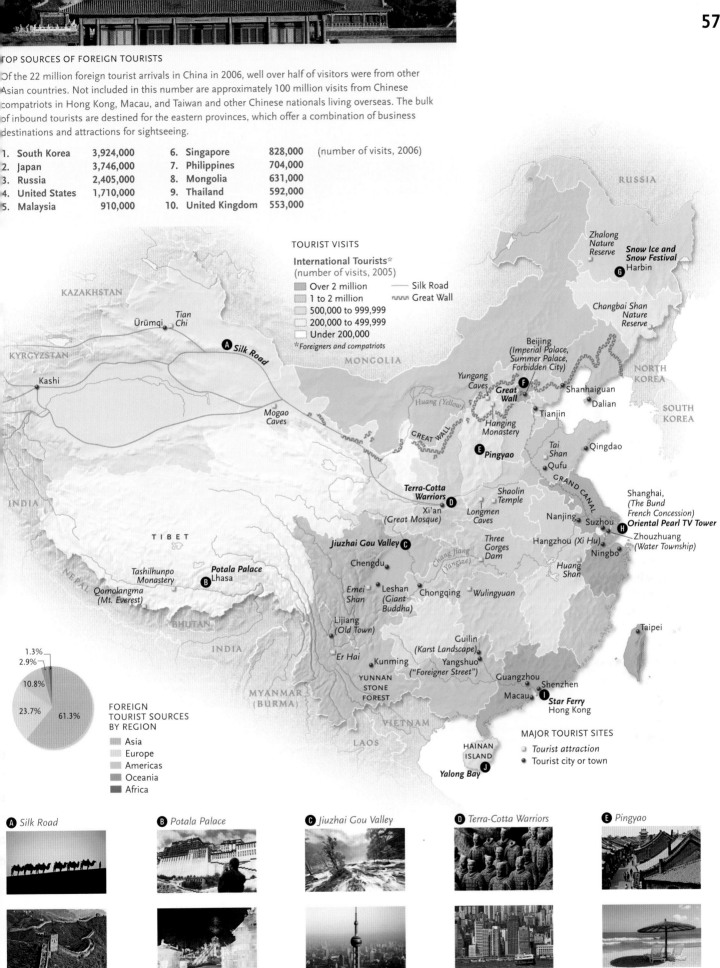

TOURIST VISITS

International Tourists*
(number of visits, 2005)
- Over 2 million
- 1 to 2 million
- 500,000 to 999,999
- 200,000 to 499,999
- Under 200,000

— Silk Road
ᙆᙆᙆ Great Wall

*Foreigners and compatriots

FOREIGN TOURIST SOURCES BY REGION

1.3%
2.9%
10.8%
23.7%
61.3%

- Asia
- Europe
- Americas
- Oceania
- Africa

MAJOR TOURIST SITES
- ◻ Tourist attraction
- ● Tourist city or town

Ⓐ *Silk Road*

Ⓑ *Potala Palace*

Ⓒ *Jiuzhai Gou Valley*

Ⓓ *Terra-Cotta Warriors*

Ⓔ *Pingyao*

Ⓕ *Great Wall*

Ⓖ *Ice and Snow Festival*

Ⓗ *Oriental Pearl TV Tower*

Ⓘ *Star Ferry, Hong Kong*

Ⓙ *Yalong Bay*

Economy

AT A GLANCE					Compound Annual Growth Rate
GDP-PPP* per Capita	1980	1990	2000	2006	1980 to 2006
CHINA	$420	$1,310	$3,853	$6,761	11.3%
TAIWAN	$3,726	$10,554	$22,067	$28,790	8.2%
HONG KONG	$6,256	$15,711	$25,694	$33,940	6.7%
JAPAN	$8,929	$18,789	$25,894	$32,617	5.1%
UNITED STATES	$12,104	$22,921	$34,344	$43,538	5.0%

*GDP is calculated using the Purchasing Power Parity (PPP) method.

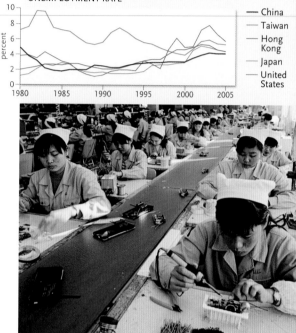

UNEMPLOYMENT RATE

— China
— Taiwan
— Hong Kong
— Japan
— United States

CHINA TODAY HAS one of the world's largest econo-mies. During the past 30 years its average annual GDP growth rate has increased more than 8%, probably the highest of any country. In 2006 China's GDP was esti-mated at $2.5 trillion, nearly one-fifth that of the United States. During the early years of communist control, 1949–1977, the country had a centrally directed and planned economic system with erratic performance and economic stagnation after 1957. Following the death of Chairman Mao Zedong in 1976 came a series of economic reforms based on free market principles, in both agriculture and the urban economy. Among the changes were decentralization, encouragement of foreign investment, comparative advantage, and regional specialization of production.

China emphasized its greatest comparative advan-tages in an almost endless supply of low-cost, hard-working labor from the rural areas and a large supply of relatively low-cost land and related resources. Rapid eco-nomic growth followed, along with an increased structural change or shift in the economy. Production of manufac-tured goods accelerated, and workers began to move off the farms and into towns and cities to factory jobs and a variety of service jobs or to jobs in construction and transportation. Thus the economic output of the country shifted to a greater emphasis on manufactured goods and their export.

Unfortunately, the new wealth has not been distributed evenly, and income is increasingly in the hands of the powerful and connected, largely in the coastal provinces.

Special Economic Zones (SEZs): A strategy to link China's growth with the global economy emerged in the 1980s with the establish-ment of SEZs along the southeast coast near Hong Kong and farther north. Overseas investment flowed in, and factories were set up to take advantage of the low-cost labor and land in adjacent lo-cations such as Shenzhen (site of China's first SEZ, in which the fac-tory women above are soldering) and Dongguan. Twenty years later coastal China—especially its southeastern provinces—has become a leading center of manufacturing. This export-oriented strategy has allowed China to accumulate more than $1 trillion in foreign exchange reserves, mostly in U.S. dollar-denominated debt instru-ments. It has also powered China's economic growth and pulled tens of millions of citizens out of poverty even as the country re-structures its fiscal and monetary systems to reach full compliance with its recent membership in the World Trade Organization.

WHERE THE WORK IS DONE

The pie charts below depict variations in employ-ment between urban and rural locations and among different administrative regions. The diameter of each circle is proportional to the size of the labor force in enterprises in the various sectors. On the rural side, the blue at upper left shows the share of the labor force in township and village enterprises.

In many cases these are privately owned and invested yet disguised as publicly owned. On the urban side, orange indicates the influence of the state-owned sector on the economy even as the transition from socialism proceeds. The yellow (private sector), when paired with the red (foreign-funded), shows the power of global connections.

TYPES OF ENTERPRISES

Number of Persons Employed (2005)

Rural	**Urban**
Township village enterprise	State-owned
Private	Hong Kong, Macau, and Taiwan funded
Self-employed	Foreign funded
Other	Private
	Self-employed
	Other

Administrative Divisions

Highest: 56.6 million employed

Anhui · Beijing · Chongqing · Fujian · Gansu · Guangdong · Guangxi Zhuangzu · Guizhou · Hainan · Hebei · Heilongjiang · Henan · Hubei · Hunan

CHINA'S THREE SECTORS

The sectors of China's economy (graphs at right) tell the story of economic growth over time: the share of production in farming declines while the share in manufacturing and producer services grows. Shifts in employment follow suit.

DOMINANT SECTOR

Percentage of Regional GDP (2005)

Agriculture
- Green dot indicates a province in which agriculture accounts for more than 20% of its regional output

Industry / Services
- 50 to 70%
- Less than 50%
- No data

Agriculture includes farming, forestry, animal husbandry, and fisheries. **Industry** includes mining, quarrying, manufacturing, production and supply of electricity, water, and gas. **Services** includes circulation (transportation, storage, telecommunications, wholesale/retail, etc.), and other (banking, insurance, etc.)

PERSONS EMPLOYED BY SECTOR

COMPOSITION OF GDP BY SECTOR

CHINA'S PRODUCTIVITY

Productivity in China's economy is the key to growth and progress and improvement in the well-being of its people. It can be measured as an increase in the value of output in relation to the cost of labor or capital inputs; the goal is for the value of output to rise faster than the cost of labor or capital inputs. China's continuing success is in part the result of continuing increases in productivity.

ECONOMIC OUTPUT

U.S. Dollars per Square Kilometer (2003)
- $5,000 to $15,000
- $1,000 to $4,999
- $100 to $999
- $25 to $99
- $0 to $24
- No data

Special Economic Zones labeled in brown

NUMBER OF WORKERS

Persons Employed by Sector (2005)

- Services
- Industry
- Agriculture

AVERAGE YEARLY WAGE PER WORKER (U.S. dollars, 2005)

	Agriculture	Industry	Services
1.	Shanghai........ $3,093	Shanghai...$5,324	Beijing.......$4,938
2.	Zhejiang..........$2,980	Tianjin......$3,845	Shanghai...$4,627
3.	Xizang (Tibet)..$2,488	Beijing......$3,718	Zhejiang....$4,125
1.	Hebei................ $731	Jiangxi.......$1,647	Gansu.....$1,713
2.	Liaoning............ $753	Hunan......$1,787	Shanxi....$1,731
3.	Heilongjiang...... $754	Hainan.....$1,803	Jiangxi....$1,777

(see "China's Three Sectors" above for category descriptions)

SHANGHAI SHI
Pudong District of Shanghai

Xiamen
Shantou
Shenzhen
HONG KONG
Zhuhai
MACAU
Hainan

Lowest: 1.4 million employed

Jiangsu · Jiangxi · Jilin · Liaoning · Nei Mongol · Ningxia Huizu · Qinghai · Shaanxi · Shandong · Shanghai · Shanxi · Sichuan · Tianjin · Xinjiang Uygur · Xizang (Tibet) · Yunnan · Zhejiang

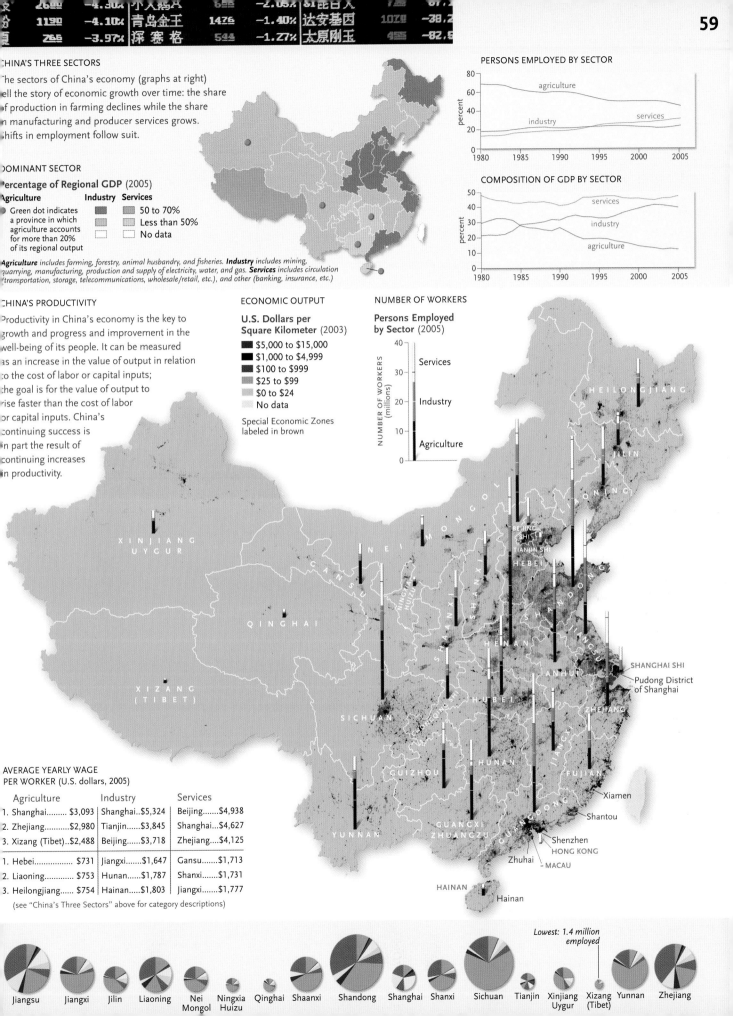

Trade

AT A GLANCE

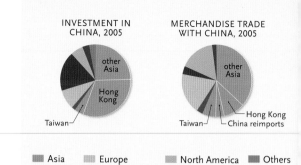

INVESTMENT IN
CHINA, 2005

MERCHANDISE TRADE
WITH CHINA, 2005

Asia   Europe   North America   Others
Africa   Latin America   Oceania

Thousands of containers wait for their ships to come in at the port of Shenzhen, in southern China. A fishing village only 20 years ago, it has become one of the world's busiest ports. Nearby Hong Kong, a Special Administrative Region of China, remains the world's busiest port, re-exporting goods made on the mainland.

SIX CENTURIES AGO, Chinese "treasure ships" carrying diplomats, silk, porcelain, and tea sailed the Indian Ocean as far as East Africa. Bustling commercial ties with its neighbors helped establish China at the time as the wealthiest and most technologically advanced country in the world. But by 1500, China had turned inward, and centuries of relative economic decline and political turmoil followed. Thus China's reemergence in the past 30 years as a major trading nation is one of the great stories of our time. One-fifth of humankind has rejoined the global economy.

The rural land reforms that began under the communist reformer Deng Xiaoping in 1978 were followed by the opening of China's economy to foreign trade and investment. Abandoning Chairman Mao Zedong's vision of national "self-sufficiency," China embarked on an aggressive program of lowering import tariffs, privatizing state-owned industries, and welcoming foreign multinationals to open plants within China.

China's economic opening reached a milestone in 2001 with its entry into the World Trade Organization, which resulted in further tariff reductions and the opening of service sectors such as banking and insurance to more foreign competition. Since 1982, average tariffs on imports to China have dropped from 50 percent to less than 10 percent. From one of the most closed economies, China has become one of the world's most open.

The result of trade and broader economic reforms has been spectacular. China's economy has grown by an average of almost 10 percent per year since 1977, moving China up the rankings of the world's largest economies from tenth in 1980 to fourth in 2006. China's share of global trade has risen tenfold since reforms began, and it now routinely attracts more direct foreign investment than any other developing country.

China's rapid rise as a global trading giant has benefited its trading partners with investment and export opportunities and a wider array of affordable goods, but it has also raised worries. China's growing trade surplus and its move into more high-end products has aroused political opposition in the United States and other developed countries. A major challenge confronting Western policymakers will be to understand and accommodate China's reemergence as a major player in the global economy.

RE-EXPORTS, AND CHINA'S ROLE AS A REASSEMBLY PLATFORM

Goods stamped "Made in China" have become ubiquitous in global markets, but the label obscures a more complex reality. Many products exported from China contain parts and materials imported form other countries. For example, laptop computers, DVD players, and iPods assembled in China for export contain sophisticated parts made elsewhere in East Asia, with research, development, and design from the United States and shipping and other logistical support from Hong Kong. China has become the last link in a deep and intricate supply chain running from Europe, North America, and throughout East Asia.

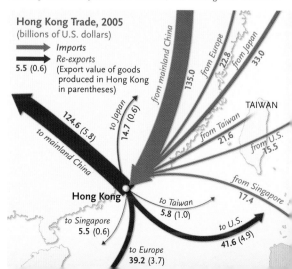

Hong Kong Trade, 2005
(billions of U.S. dollars)

→ Imports
→ Re-exports
5.5 (0.6) (Export value of goods produced in Hong Kong in parentheses)

from mainland China 135.0
from Europe 22.8
from Japan 33.0
to Japan 14.7 (0.6)
to mainland China 124.6 (5.8)

TAIWAN

from Taiwan 21.6
from U.S. 15.5
from Singapore 17.4

Hong Kong

to Taiwan 5.8 (1.0)
to Singapore 5.5 (0.6)
to U.S. 41.6 (4.9)
to Europe 39.2 (3.7)

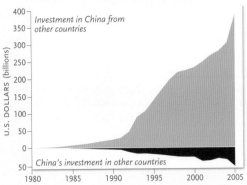

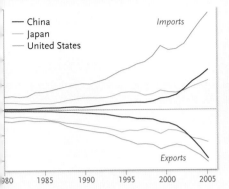

FOREIGN COMMODITIES TRADE

China
Japan
United States

Imports

Exports

1980 1985 1990 1995 2000 2005

TRADE AND FOREIGN DIRECT INVESTMENT

Foreign-owned firms in China have played the leading role in its rise as the world's number three exporting nation. Foreign firms have flocked to China because of its low labor costs, booming domestic market, and generally open economy. More than half of China's exports are produced by foreign-owned companies and their affiliates in China. Global producers have brought technology, innovation, higher wages, and better working conditions to millions of Chinese workers. The total stock of foreign investment in China now exceeds $600 billion, two-thirds of that in the manufacturing sector.

FOREIGN DIRECT INVESTMENT (FDI)

Investment in China from other countries

U.S. DOLLARS (billions)

400
350
300
250
200
150
100
50
0
50

China's investment in other countries

1980 1985 1990 1995 2000 2005

United Kingdom
$13 billion

Austria
Switzerland
Croatia, Slovenia
Belgium, Czech Republic, Denmark, France, Germany, Ireland, Luxembourg
Netherlands, U.K.

Iraq
$0.4 billion

CHINA

South Korea
$32.2 billion

Japan **$52.3 billion**
(highest amount invested in China)

South Korea, Taiwan
Japan
North Korea

Taiwan
FDI: **$42.7 billion**
(and largest merchandise trade surplus, $58 billion)

United States
$114 billion
merchandise trade deficit with China)

United States
FDI: **$52 billion**

British Virgin Islands
$1.5 billion

Sudan
$0.3 billion

Cayman Islands
$7.9 billion
(highest amount of Chinese investment)

The Cayman Islands, British Virgin Islands, and Bermuda attract large amounts of investment in the form of banks and financial holding companies or services.

Nigeria
$0.1 billion

Singapore
$27.5 billion

Samoa
$4.5 billion

Most of China's outward investment is portfolio investment, which means non-controlling investments in securities, government bonds, and bank accounts. Exceptions are places such as Nigeria and Sudan, in which China invests directly in energy production—with controlling ownership.

Japan, South Korea, Hong Kong, Taiwan, and the United States invest heavily in mainland China's manufacturing sector through direct investments where the investor has a controlling share in the assets.

Mauritius
$0.6 billion

MERCHANDISE* TRADE BALANCE WITH CHINA (2005)
(millions of U.S. dollars)

Positive | 20,000 to 40,000
Trade | 1,000 to 19,999
Balance | 10 to 999

Negative | 0 to -99
Trade | -100 to -999
Balance | -1,000 to -9,999
| -10,000 to -24,999
| -25,000 to -120,000

*Includes fuels, minerals, metals, chemicals, machinery, office and telecom equipment, agricultural products, textiles, clothing, and other manufactures.

FOREIGN DIRECT INVESTMENT (2004)
(millions of U.S. dollars)

Investment from China to Other Countries

500 to 9,999
200 to 499
100 to 199
50 to 99
1 to 49

Investment in China from Other Countries

10,000 to 60,000
500 to 9,999
200 to 499
100 to 199
50 to 99
1 to 49

Foreign Direct Investment *refers to an investment made to acquire lasting interest in enterprises operating outside of the economy of the investor.*

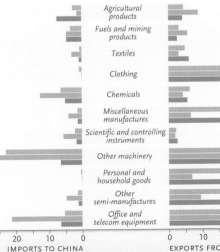

Agricultural products
Fuels and mining products
Textiles
Clothing
Chemicals
Miscellaneous manufactures
Scientific and controlling instruments
Other machinery
Personal and household goods
Other semi-manufactures
Office and telecom equipment

30 20 10 0   0 10 20 30 40 50 60 70 80

IMPORTS TO CHINA
(billions of U.S. dollars)

EXPORTS FROM CHINA
(billions of U.S. dollars)

TRADE WITH THE TRIAD

China's trade with the most advanced economies—the U.S., Japan, and the European Union—has been booming. China runs a trade surplus with them, exporting an array of consumer goods eagerly purchased by wealthy Westerners and importing more sophisticated components and capital machinery.

European Union*
Japan
United States
*Excludes Bulgaria and Romania

CHINA'S TOP FIVE IMPORT AND EXPORT COMMODITIES, 2005

	(billions of U.S. dollars)
Imports	
1. Mechanical and electrical products	350.4
2. High and new-tech products	197.7
3. Crude oil	47.7
4. Rolled steel	24.6
5. Iron ore	18.4
Exports	
1. Mechanical and electrical products	426.7
2. High and new-tech products	218.2
3. Automatic data processing machines	76.3
4. Garments	60.3
5. Parts for automatic data processing equipment	28.4

Food and Agriculture

2003	CHINA	WORLD
ARABLE LAND	137,124,000 HECTARES	1,402,317,000 HECTARES
IRRIGATED LAND	37%	20%
PERMANENT CROPS	11,533,000 HECTARES	138,255,000 HECTARES
TRACTORS	7 PER 1,000 HECTARES	20 PER 1,000 HECTARES
FERTILIZER USE	39,605,000 TONS	147,917,000 TONS
UNDERNOURISHED POPULATION	12%	14%
AGRICULTURAL EXPORTS (U.S. DOLLARS)	$20.8 BILLION	$604.3 BILLION
PER CAPITA DAILY CONSUMPTION	2,940 CALORIES	2,800 CALORIES

Note: 100 hectares equal one square kilometer

FEEDING A FIFTH OF THE WORLD'S POPULATION on less than a tenth of the world's arable land in a nation whose territory encompasses extremes of climate and topography has been a formidable challenge for China.

After the 1949 revolution, property of rural land-owners was confiscated and many were beaten to death or executed. Peasants were given small plots, but farming was soon collectivized into "People's Communes." That wrenching change—combined with cycles of bad weather and diversion of rural funds to industrial production—contributed to millions of deaths in one of the worst famines in history.

After the reforms of 1978, farmers were allocated land to cultivate independently, but they were not given rights of ownership. Over the ensuing decades, the government gradually decontrolled farm prices, gave farmers more discretion about what they could plant, and allowed them to keep profits from farm sales.

Over 200 million individual families account for most of China's farm production. While labor-intensive small plot farming is effective for raising crops such as fruits and vegetables, it is less so for land-intensive crops such as grains and oilseeds. Farm productivity has grown due to stronger incentives and improved technology, but it is difficult to achieve high earnings with small land holdings averaging just a few acres per family.

Beginning in the 1990s, 100 million to 200 million laborers left farms to seek employment opportunities in cities. Industrialization and mining activity cascaded over the countryside, sparking thousands of protests over land confiscation and pollution.

Guangxi Zhuangzu Autonomous Region presents a landscape of water-filled terraces. Terracing, used for centuries in China, is a labor-intensive but effective way to maximize the amount of arable land.

LIVESTOCK PRODUCTION

China is the world's largest producer and consumer of pork. Most pig raising is done by families with only a few animals, but larger commercial-style operations—often with foreign investment—are increasing, as are exports. Chickens, geese, and ducks also are raised, mainly in small-scale operations, sometimes under conditions that could allow for the spread of diseases such as avian influenza. Most poultry, including 4.7 billion chickens, is consumed locally. Herding of sheep, goats, cattle, and yaks is done mostly in grasslands of remote areas in the north and west. As demand for meat increases, especially in cities, this area of husbandry should prosper.

LIVESTOCK DENSITY
(per square kilometer)

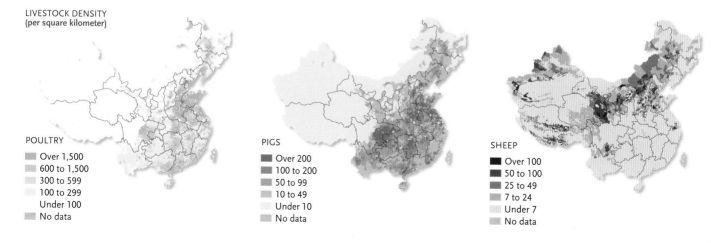

POULTRY
- Over 1,500
- 600 to 1,500
- 300 to 599
- 100 to 299
- Under 100
- No data

PIGS
- Over 200
- 100 to 200
- 50 to 99
- 10 to 49
- Under 10
- No data

SHEEP
- Over 100
- 50 to 100
- 25 to 49
- 7 to 24
- Under 7
- No data

CALORIC SUPPLY

With its emphasis on cereals and vegetables, the typical Chinese diet is relatively healthful. Recently, however, there has been a rise in the consumption of meat and dairy products—especially in urban areas—bringing with it an increase in obesity, heart disease, and diabetes.

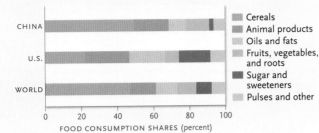

CHINA

U.S.

WORLD

- Cereals
- Animal products
- Oils and fats
- Fruits, vegetables, and roots
- Sugar and sweeteners
- Pulses and other

0   20   40   60   80   100
FOOD CONSUMPTION SHARES (percent)

CROP PRODUCTION

Grains dominate the diet throughout China, with rice being the primary food crop in the south and wheat (often used for noodles and dumplings) most popular in the north. Corn and root crop production are also significant, especially in the northern regions, and China has long been one of the world's leading potato producers. Rapid economic development and urbanization—and associated environmental impacts—have meant increased pressures on the amount of available cropland, a trend that is expected to continue.

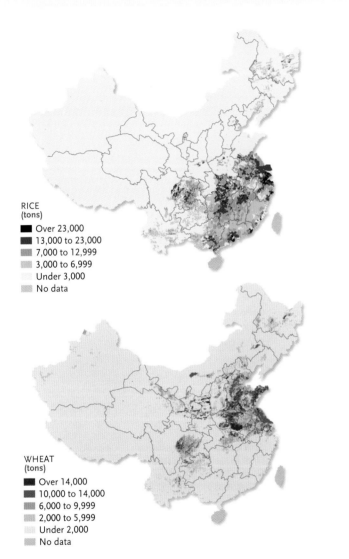

RICE
(tons)

- Over 23,000
- 13,000 to 23,000
- 7,000 to 12,999
- 3,000 to 6,999
- Under 3,000
- No data

WHEAT
(tons)

- Over 14,000
- 10,000 to 14,000
- 6,000 to 9,999
- 2,000 to 5,999
- Under 2,000
- No data

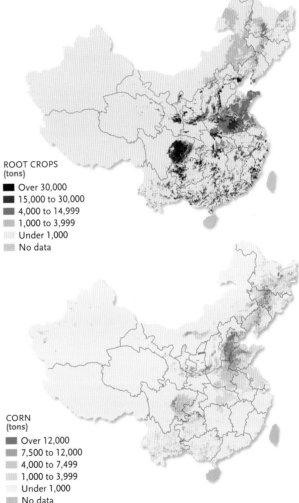

ROOT CROPS
(tons)

- Over 30,000
- 15,000 to 30,000
- 4,000 to 14,999
- 1,000 to 3,999
- Under 1,000
- No data

CORN
(tons)

- Over 12,000
- 7,500 to 12,000
- 4,000 to 7,499
- 1,000 to 3,999
- Under 1,000
- No data

AGRICULTURAL PRODUCTION OVER TIME

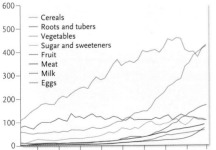

- Cereals
- Roots and tubers
- Vegetables
- Sugar and sweeteners
- Fruit
- Meat
- Milk
- Eggs

1965 1970 1975 1980 1985 1990 1995 2000 2005

The past few decades have seen large jumps in overall agricultural production, and since the early 1980s China has gone from being a net importer to a net exporter of food. Current and future challenges include a continual rise in demand for food and feed, decreases in new arable land, and environmental degradation.

Aquaculture dates back 2,500 years in China, but only in the 1980s did new techniques bring yields far exceeding those of traditional capture fisheries. China now leads the world in aquaculture, which provides not only protein nationwide but employment to several millions.

AQUACULTURE AND FISHING

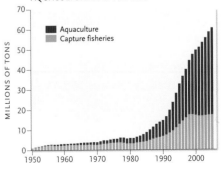

- Aquaculture
- Capture fisheries

MILLIONS OF TONS

1950 1960 1970 1980 1990 2000

Energy

	2005	AT A GLANCE
TOTAL ENERGY SUPPLY	2,232,130,000	TCE*
TOTAL ENERGY CONSUMPTION	2,246,820,000	TCE
ENERGY IMPORTS	269,520,000	TCE
ENERGY EXPORTS	114,470,000	TCE
CARBON EMISSIONS, 2004	4,707,280,000	TONS

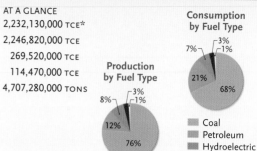

Production by Fuel Type
3%
1%
8%
12%
76%

Consumption by Fuel Type
3%
1%
7%
21%
68%

- Coal
- Petroleum
- Hydroelectric
- Natural gas
- Nuclear

*Tons of coal equivalent

CHINA IS THE WORLD'S SECOND LARGEST energy system after the United States, and it is the largest economy on Earth powered mainly by coal. It has extensive domestic reserves of coal, oil, hydropower, and natural gas, but the rapid continued growth of the economy has outpaced the ability of the country to supply itself. In early 2007, China became a net coal importer, despite domestic production of over 2.3 billion tons.

In contrast to most developed countries, industry is the dominant energy consumer, at over 60 percent of the total; as industrial production has boomed in recent years, this proportion has been rising. Transportation oil demand, though growing quickly, stems less from personal ownership of private cars than from the tremendous demand from railroads and trucks to move coal, oil, cement, grain, and millions of tons of raw materials and manufactured goods around the country and to coastal ports. Economic growth and urbanization are two long-term drivers of China's energy growth, and as incomes rise, demand for automobiles and larger living spaces and greater ownership of household appliances will spur energy demand.

China's reliance on coal results in high levels of carbon dioxide (CO_2) emissions. According to the International Energy Agency, China is likely to surpass the U.S. in CO_2 emissions by 2010, although preliminary estimates indicate it may be as early as 2007. China is now acting to limit growth in emissions. If successful, this program would slow emissions growth by 1.56 billion tons of CO_2.

China currently has 2.6 gigawatts of wind power, located mainly in Nei Mongol and along the eastern coast. Plans are to raise renewable energy capacity—hydropower, wind, solar, geothermal, tidal, biomass—to 20% of total power generation capacity by 2020.

ENERGY CONSUMPTION BY SECTOR

— Industry   — Transportation
— Residential — Commercial
— Agriculture

MILLIONS OF TONS OF COAL EQUIVALENT

1,600
1,200
800
400
0
1980   1985   1990   1995   2000   2005

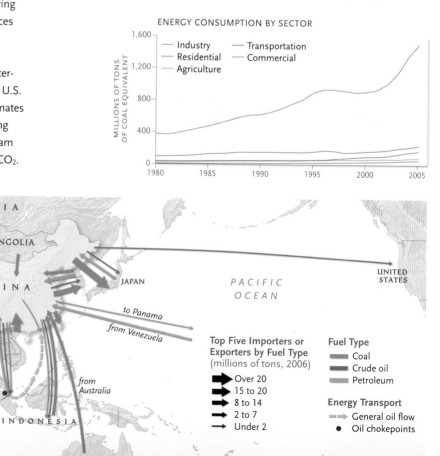

Top Five Importers or Exporters by Fuel Type
(millions of tons, 2006)
- Over 20
- 15 to 20
- 8 to 14
- 2 to 7
- Under 2

Fuel Type
- Coal
- Crude oil
- Petroleum

Energy Transport
- General oil flow
- Oil chokepoints

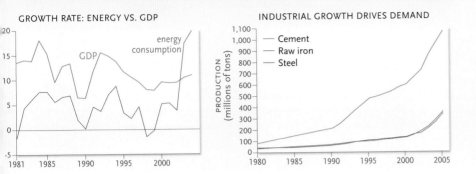

GROWTH RATE: ENERGY VS. GDP

GDP

energy consumption

1981 1985 1990 1995 2000

INDUSTRIAL GROWTH DRIVES DEMAND

PRODUCTION (millions of tons)

— Cement
— Raw iron
— Steel

1,100
1,000
900
800
700
600
500
400
300
200
100

1980 1985 1990 1995 2000 2005

After 20 years in which GDP grew at twice the rate of energy consumption, energy demand began soaring after 2000 to nearly 50% higher than GDP growth. This boom in demand was underpinned by enormous increases in the output of cement, steel, and other heavy industrial materials, primarily for China's extensive infrastructure and urban construction programs. China now produces nearly half of the world's cement and one-third of its steel. Efficiency gains in the industrial sector will be the key to increasing overall efficiency.

HEILONGJIANG

JILIN

LIAONING

XINJIANG UYGUR

NEI MONGOL

HEBEI

BEIJING SHI

TIANJIN SHI

NINGXIA HUIZU

SHANXI

SHANDONG

QINGHAI

GANSU

SHAANXI

HENAN

JIANGSU

SHANGHAI SHI

XIZANG (TIBET)

HUBEI

ANHUI

ZHEJIANG

CHONGQING SHI

SICHUAN

HUNAN

JIANGXI

FUJIAN

GUIZHOU

YUNNAN

GUANGXI ZHUANGZU

GUANGDONG

TAIWAN

HONG KONG S.A.R.

HAINAN

China plunged into an electricity crisis in 2003 after years of underinvesting in generation capacity. Power plant construction has soared and capacity is now running at triple the level since the crisis.

In 2006, China produced 2.3 billion tons of coal — up from 1 billion tons in 2000. The industry employs millions of coal miners, many of whom work in small locally-run mines, which produce nearly half of the nation's coal.

ENERGY CONSUMPTION

Tons of Coal Equivalent per Capita (2005)

- Over 4
- 3 to 4
- 2 to 2.9
- 1.5 to 1.9
- Under 1.5
- No data

COAL AND PETROLEUM*

(millions of tons)

100
90
80
60
40
20
0

Coal production

Coal consumption

■ Petroleum production**
(100,000 barrels/day)

■ Petroleum consumption
(100,000 barrels/day)

ENERGY RESERVES

- Coal
- Gas
- Oil

Production and consumption statistics are shown for all provinces for which data are available in the China Energy Statistical Yearbook.

**Crude oil*

Transportation

AUTOMOBILES IN CHINA

PRIVATE VEHICLE OWNERSHIP (millions of vehicles)

From having an output of nearly nothing in the late 1970s to being a full-grown domestic enterprise with its own "Big Three" (and producing foreign autos under joint agreements), China's auto industry has reached the point of entry into world markets. The Chery brand, owned by the city of Wuhu, markets its QQ model with the slogan "It is like you, peppy and cool."

gas consumption

trucks

passenger vehicles

1982 1986 1990 1994 1998 2002 2006

THIRTY MILLION BICYCLES were built in 1994 for domestic use in China. By 1999 the number was down to one million. Some 470 million bikes are still in use, but automobile production has accelerated ahead with the speed of a drag racer. China is the second largest car market in the world and headed for first by 2015. With its huge contingent of novice drivers, China already has the world's highest rate of fatal auto accidents.

It is still cheaper to fly to Shanghai from Beijing than to drive on the new toll expressway. Internal air travel has grown significantly, as have international routes; for instance, the number of flights to and from the U.S. will double by 2012. Trains also remain a backbone of transport. Lines are being modernized, and 3,355 miles (5,400 kilometers) of high-speed track will be laid and 24,855 miles (40,000 kilometers) of other railways built or reconditioned by 2010 to relieve congestion in the transport of coal, minerals, produce, and people.

China will spend $50 billion on developing container and commodities ports by 2010. The nation is not only a major exporter but also the largest importer of iron ore and coal. Inland shipping, especially along the Yangtze River, supplies another major vein of transport for bulk commodities.

TRANSPORTATION NETWORKS

— Superhighway (complete)
---- Superhighway (under construction)
— Major road
— Railroad
— Major inland waterway
— Navigable section of other major rive
✈ Major international airport
✈ Other important airport
Seaports: container traffic
One box = 2,000,000 TEUs, 2005
(twenty-foot equivalent units: standard 20' x 8' x 8'6" container)

GROWING DEMAND

PASSENGER TRAFFIC (billions of passenger-miles)

1,100 1,000 900 800 700 600 500 400 300 200 100 0
1980 1985 1990 1995 2000 2005

Mode of Transportation
■ Airways
■ Waterways
■ Highways
■ Railways

FREIGHT TRAFFIC (billions of ton-miles)

2,500 2,250 2,000 1,750 1,500 1,250 1,000 750 500 250 0
1980 1985 1990 1995 2000 2005

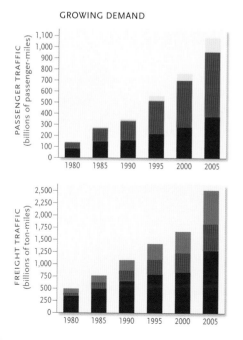

While all sectors of transport have shown significant growth in recent years, passengers traveling highways and cargo moving along inland waterways stand out. The overall rate of increase points to China's transformation from a rather static society to a highly dynamic one. The effective movement of people and goods requires that transport be increasingly integrated, efficient, and rapid.

Qinghai-Tibet Railway: Connecting Tibet to the rest of China, much of this line was built atop permafrost. Other new rail projects include 280 bullet trains. In China, 25% of the world's transport is carried on 6% of the world's track.

Seaports: Each of China's 10 major ports has a capacity of more than 50 million tons yearly. All ports together have a capacity of about three billion tons, and by 2010 35% of the world's shipping is expected to originate from China.

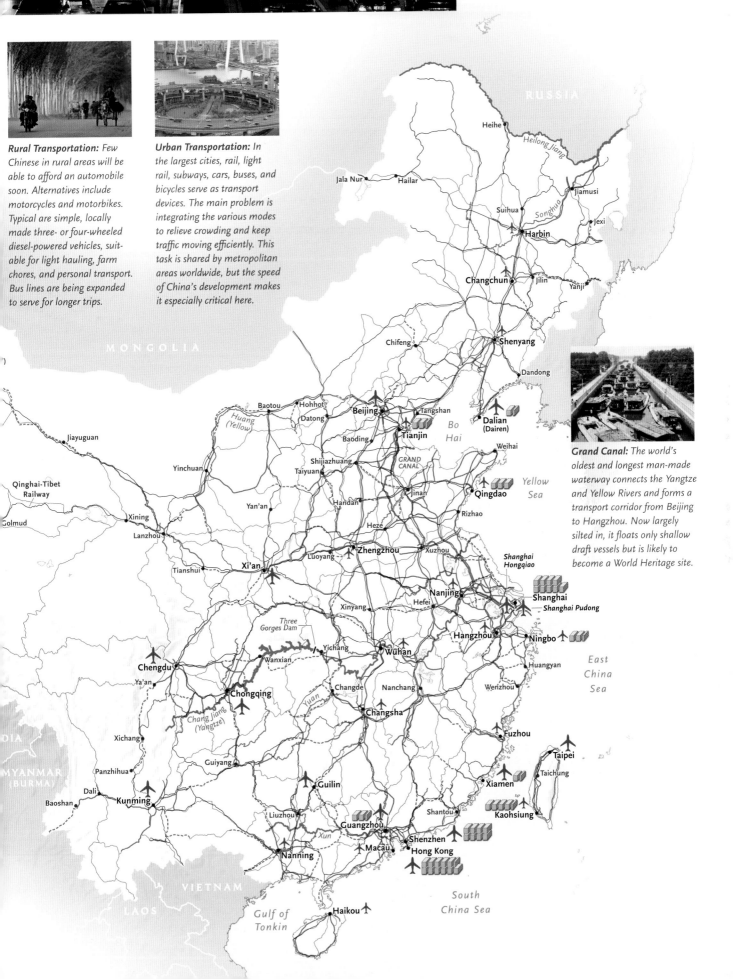

Rural Transportation: Few Chinese in rural areas will be able to afford an automobile soon. Alternatives include motorcycles and motorbikes. Typical are simple, locally made three- or four-wheeled diesel-powered vehicles, suitable for light hauling, farm chores, and personal transport. Bus lines are being expanded to serve for longer trips.

Urban Transportation: In the largest cities, rail, light rail, subways, cars, buses, and bicycles serve as transport devices. The main problem is integrating the various modes to relieve crowding and keep traffic moving efficiently. This task is shared by metropolitan areas worldwide, but the speed of China's development makes it especially critical here.

Grand Canal: The world's oldest and longest man-made waterway connects the Yangtze and Yellow Rivers and forms a transport corridor from Beijing to Hangzhou. Now largely silted in, it floats only shallow draft vessels but is likely to become a World Heritage site.

RUSSIA

MONGOLIA

Heihe

Heilong Jiang

Jala Nur   Hailar

Suihua   Jiamusi

Songhua   Jexi

Harbin

Changchun   Jilin   Yanji

Chifeng   Shenyang

Jiayuguan   Dandong

Baotou   Hohhot   Beijing   Tangshan   Bo
Datong   Tianjin   Hai   Dalian
(Dairen)

Yinchuan   Baoding   Weihai

Qinghai-Tibet   Shijiazhuang   GRAND
Railway   Yan'an   Taiyuan   CANAL   Yellow
Sea

Xining   Jinan   Qingdao

Golmud   Lanzhou   Handan   Rizhao
Heze

Luoyang   Zhengzhou   Xuzhou

Tianshui   Xi'an   Shanghai
Hongqiao

Xinyang   Hefei   Nanjing   Shanghai

Three   Shanghai Pudong
Gorges Dam   Yichang   Wuhan   Hangzhou   Ningbo

Wanxian   Huangyan   East
China
Chengdu   Changde   Nanchang   Sea

Ya'an   Chongqing   Wenzhou

Chang Jiang
(Yangtze)   Changsha

Xichang   Fuzhou

Yuan   Taipei

Panzhihua   Guiyang   Taichung

Dali   Guilin   Xiamen

Baoshan   Kunming   Liuzhou   Shantou   Kaohsiung

Xun   Guangzhou

INDIA   Nanning   Macau   Shenzhen
MYANMAR   Hong Kong
(BURMA)

VIETNAM   South
China
LAOS   Gulf of   Sea
Tonkin   Haikou

Politics

Communist Party of China flag

THE COMMUNIST PARTY OF CHINA (CPC), with a current membership of about 70 million, is by official policy the only political party allowed to exercise power in China. Despite its name, it is now focused on maximizing economic growth and producing a relatively wealthy society within the next 15 years.

For millennia China has been an autocratic state, and the political layers shown at right reflect the authoritarian nature of the current government—with the machinery of the CPC always operating in parallel at all levels. The CPC also controls the People's Liberation Army (PLA), which is the party's ultimate civil enforcer—as evident in 1989 when it crushed the reform movement in Tiananmen Square.

Avenues of advancement for ambitious young Chinese often came with membership in the CPC, the PLA, or state-owned enterprises. Now the nation's economic growth has brought new possibilities for careers under the umbrella of "market socialism" that looks a lot like bureaucratic capitalism. Products are often made under working conditions that resemble those of the 19th century, including long hours, low wages, polluted surroundings, and worker mistreatment.

The government and the CPC have undertaken reforms to combat graft and corruption and reduce confiscation of farmland for manufacturing sites. Those moves, and the acceptance of "advanced social productive forces" (entrepreneurs and the like) with the goal of reaching "a harmonious society," recall the maxims of Confucius, who after 2,500 years has been rehabilitated as a political thinker to admire.

CENTRAL GOVERNMENT

Policy is set by the Communist Party of China but carried out by the state. The president serves as head of state, while in theory, the highest level of state power sits with the 3,000 members of the National People's Congress. The State Council—headed by the premier—leads the administration, and essentially serves as a cabinet. Organizationally, the constitution stipulates a hierarchy that divides China into provinces, cities, counties, and townships. Each of these levels is involved in policy implementation in mainland China today.

省 PROVINCE

22 provinces, 5 autonomous regions, 4 centrally administered municipalities, 2 special administrative regions

Provincial governments hold a great deal of de facto power, particularly in economic matters. Provinces also provide an important basis for cultural identity, as the Chinese tend to be identified by their native province. Provinces and autonomous regions are subdivided into cities, prefectures, or counties.

市 CITY

There are about 650 cities of various sizes and ranks in China today; they bear the burden of implementing many of the social welfare and other changes under way. Many encompass very large surrounding areas.

县 COUNTY

Counties are the level of government in longest continuous existence in China, having been established throughout the country during the Qin Dynasty (221–206 B.C.E.). These are subdivided into townships, ethnic townships, or towns.

乡 TOWNSHIP

Some direct democratic elections have been introduced at the township level, with elections periodically held for local leaders. Most townships are further divided into villages, neighborhoods, or communities.

THE AMERICAN EMBASSY FOLLOWS NATIONALISTS TO TAIWAN, RESULTING IN HOSTILE RELATIONS WITH THE MAINLAND.

THE U.S. AND CHINA HOLD OVER A HUNDRED MEETINGS AT THE AMBASSADORIAL LEVEL, EVENTUALLY DECIDING THAT IMPROVED BILATERAL RELATIONS ARE IN THEIR COMMON INTEREST.

PRESIDENT RICHARD NIXON TRAVELS TO CHINA, AND AT THE CONCLUSION OF HIS TRIP, THE U.S. AND CHINESE GOVERNMENTS ISSUE THE SHANGHAI COMMUNIQUÉ, A STATEMENT OF THEIR FOREIGN POLICY VIEWS.

1950 **1960** **1970**

THE U.S. AND CHINA FIGHT ON OPPOSITE SIDES OF THE KOREAN WAR.

THE ASSISTANT FOR NATIONAL SECURITY AFFAIRS, DR. HENRY KISSINGER, MAKES A SECRET TRIP TO BEIJING TO INITIATE DIRECT CONTACT WITH THE CHINESE LEADERSHIP.

THE U.S. AND CHINA CREATE THE UNITED STATES LIAISON OFFICE IN BEIJING AND A COUNTERPART CHINESE OFFICE IN WASHINGTON, D.C.

THE COMMUNIST PARTY OF CHINA

Founded in 1921 by university professors, the CPC took on many different forms and alliances before becoming the official ruling party with the establishment of the People's Republic of China in 1949. While still self-described as "the vanguard of the Chinese working class," the CPC has in recent years shown a shift from socialism toward pragmatic nationalism—and today, a top goal is to maintain stability while encouraging rapid economic development.

Although the CPC is currently the world's largest political party, only about 5 percent of Chinese are members. (Other parties are permitted as debating societies, but not allowed to share or seek power.) Admission to the party is competitive, and membership requires indoctrination and apprenticeship. Since 2002 the CPC has allowed business owners to join—a signal of change and an acknowledgment of their important role in China's future growth.

In 2005, 19.2% of party members were female, 23% were under 35 years old, and 29% had received a college education.

(Chart: PARTY MEMBERS (millions), 0–70, years 1920–2000)

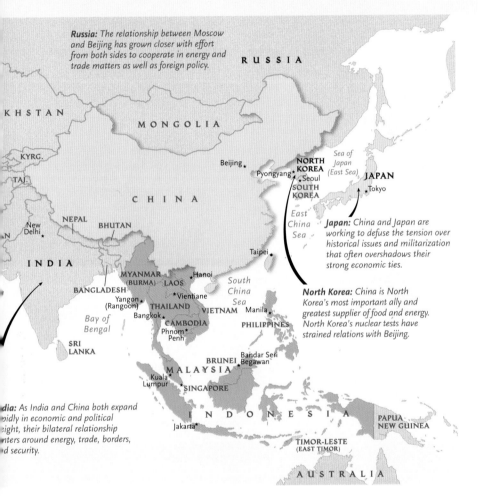

Russia: *The relationship between Moscow and Beijing has grown closer with effort from both sides to cooperate in energy and trade matters as well as foreign policy.*

Japan: *China and Japan are working to defuse the tension over historical issues and militarization that often overshadows their strong economic ties.*

North Korea: *China is North Korea's most important ally and greatest supplier of food and energy. North Korea's nuclear tests have strained relations with Beijing.*

India: *As India and China both expand rapidly in economic and political weight, their bilateral relationship centers around energy, trade, borders, and security.*

Regional Dynamics
- ASEAN member
- ASEAN+3 country

REGIONAL DYNAMICS

China's growing political and economic power in Southeast Asia might be seen in the context of two international organizations, one a failure and the other a success.

The Southeast Asia Treaty Organization (SEATO) of Western powers plus the Philippines, Thailand, and Pakistan was organized as a military bloc in 1954 after the French defeat in North Vietnam. The idea was to stop the spread of communism in Asia. SEATO unraveled as the Vietnam War dragged on, and the alliance was dissolved in 1977.

The Association of Southeast Asian Nations (ASEAN, see map at left) was founded in 1967 to accelerate economic growth, social progress, and cultural development in the context of peace and stability. The addition of the "+3" nations of China, Japan, and South Korea—and later consultative addition of Australia, New Zealand, and India—expanded the group.

Under this cooperative transnational umbrella, spirited competition flourishes between nations and among regions, companies, and individuals. However, no cross-border shooting has broken out since the border clashes between Vietnam and China in 1979.

ON JANUARY 1, 1979, THE U.S. AND CHINESE GOVERNMENTS ESTABLISH FORMAL DIPLOMATIC RELATIONS.

GOVERNMENTAL AND CULTURAL EXCHANGES BETWEEN THE AMERICANS AND CHINESE CONTINUE.

THE ACCIDENTAL BOMBING OF THE CHINESE EMBASSY IN BELGRADE TEMPORARILY STRAINS RELATIONS BETWEEN CHINA AND THE U.S.

A CHINESE FIGHTER JET AND AMERICAN RECONNAISSANCE AIRCRAFT COLLIDE OVER INTERNATIONAL WATERS; THE CHINESE PILOT DIES AND THE AMERICAN CREW MAKES AN EMERGENCY LANDING.

1980 **1990** **2000**

VICE PREMIER DENG XIAOPING VISITS WASHINGTON, D.C., AND VICE PRESIDENT WALTER MONDALE RECIPROCATES WITH A TRIP TO CHINA; THE INTERCHANGE INITIATES A SERIES OF HIGH-LEVEL EXCHANGES THAT LEAD TO NUMEROUS BILATERAL AGREEMENTS.

THE U.S. AND OTHER GOVERNMENTS IMPOSE SANCTIONS AND CALL FOR HUMAN RIGHTS REFORM FOLLOWING THE INFAMOUS TIANANMEN SQUARE INCIDENT.

THE U.S.-CHINA RELATIONSHIP CONTINUES TO GROW IN INTERNATIONAL IMPORTANCE AS CHINA'S ECONOMY BOOMS AND CHINA GAINS REGIONAL POLITICAL CLOUT; CHINA AND THE U.S. WORK WITH OTHER GOVERNMENTS TO ADDRESS TERRORISM AND OTHER SECURITY THREATS.

Military Strength

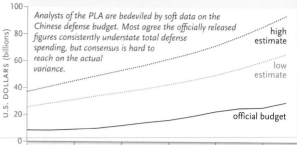

Analysts of the PLA are bedeviled by soft data on the Chinese defense budget. Most agree the officially released figures consistently understate total defense spending, but consensus is hard to reach on the actual variance.

high estimate

low estimate

official budget

U.S. DOLLARS (billions)

100 — 80 — 60 — 40 — 20 — 0

1996   1998   2000   2002   2004

THE CHINESE PEOPLE'S LIBERATION ARMY (PLA) is the official name of all of China's military services. These include the ground forces, the PLA Air Force, the PLA Navy, and the Strategic Missile Force (also known as the Second Artillery Corps), which is the branch of the ground forces responsible for nuclear and conventional missiles. Today, the PLA numbers 2.3 million personnel. This figure does not include the reserves, the paramilitary People's Armed Police, or the People's Militia.

The Communist Party of China (CPC) controls the PLA through the Military Commission of its Central Committee (CMC). The CMC exercises daily control over PLA operations, policies, and programs through four departments: the General Staff Department (operations, training), the General Political Department (personnel, propaganda, CPC organization), the General Logistics Department (supplies and infrastructure), and the General Armaments Department (weapons and ordnance acquisition, maintenance, and research and development).

Below the national level China is divided into seven Military Regions (MR), each encompassing multiple provinces. Each MR is named after the city that serves as the seat of its headquarters. The four general departments at the national level exercise oversight over military units deployed throughout China through the headquarters of their assigned Military Region.

Since the early 1990s the PLA has engaged in a sustained program of modernization and reform unprecedented in its history. It is focusing its weapons acquisitions programs, adjusting its doctrine, and instituting systemic reforms on three fronts:

ORGANIZATIONALLY: to shift from a traditionally ground forces-centric military to one that gives increased emphasis to naval and air forces.

OPERATIONALLY: to transform from a military historically postured to fight long wars of attrition on the mainland to a military that is capable of defending Chinese interests offshore or farther out at sea in short high-intensity maritime and aerospace joint campaigns.

TECHNOLOGICALLY: to retool from a military that previously relied on large numbers of forces (personnel and units) to compensate for technological weakness to a military that is leaner in numbers but that fights with state-of-the-art capabilities.

People's Armed Police: *The People's Armed Police (PAP) is China's national paramilitary police and security force. At 660,000 strong, the principal mission of the PAP is internal security: anti-terrorism, border control, security of key infrastructure, and riot control.*

COMPONENTS OF THE PEOPLE'S LIBERATION ARMY

At 2.3 million personnel the PLA is the world's largest standing military force. Two-year conscripts fill its ranks, but a corps of professional officers and NCOs provide force stability. The Chinese characters on the service flags shown here are the numbers 8 and 1, which commemorate the founding of the PLA on August 1, 1927.

GROUND FORCES *~1,600,000 active members**
The ground forces remains the largest service in terms of personnel. Traditionally, it has also been the dominant service. Infantry, artillery, and armored forces are the mainstays of PLA land power.

AIR FORCE *~400,000 active members**
According to the U.S. Department of Defense, China possesses 1,525 fighters, 775 bombers, and 450 transport aircraft. This includes aircraft belonging to the PLA Navy.

NAVY *~255,000 active members**
The PLA Navy boasts destroyers, frigates, conventional and nuclear submarines, and land-based aircraft. China has not yet fielded an aircraft carrier, despite unconfirmed rumors that one is being developed.

STRATEGIC MISSILE FORCE
~100,000 active members*

(no flag)

The Strategic Missile Force controls China's nuclear and conventional missiles. Although treated as a separate service, technically it is a branch of the ground forces.

**As the People's Liberation Army does not provide official figures for the number of personnel in each service, the estimates shown are based on the assessment of the International Institute for Strategic Studies.*

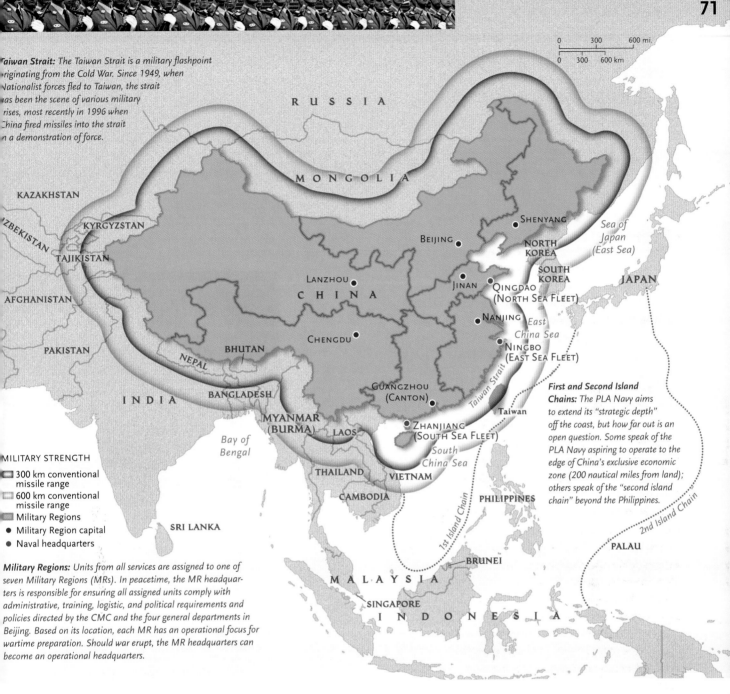

Taiwan Strait: *The Taiwan Strait is a military flashpoint originating from the Cold War. Since 1949, when Nationalist forces fled to Taiwan, the strait has been the scene of various military crises, most recently in 1996 when China fired missiles into the strait in a demonstration of force.*

First and Second Island Chains: *The PLA Navy aims to extend its "strategic depth" off the coast, but how far out is an open question. Some speak of the PLA Navy aspiring to operate to the edge of China's exclusive economic zone (200 nautical miles from land); others speak of the "second island chain" beyond the Philippines.*

MILITARY STRENGTH

- 300 km conventional missile range
- 600 km conventional missile range
- Military Regions
- Military Region capital
- Naval headquarters

Military Regions: *Units from all services are assigned to one of seven Military Regions (MRs). In peacetime, the MR headquarters is responsible for ensuring all assigned units comply with administrative, training, logistic, and political requirements and policies directed by the CMC and the four general departments in Beijing. Based on its location, each MR has an operational focus for wartime preparation. Should war erupt, the MR headquarters can become an operational headquarters.*

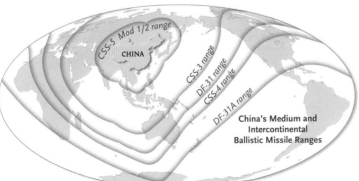

China's Medium and Intercontinental Ballistic Missile Ranges

CHINA'S NUCLEAR REACH

China has been a nuclear power since 1964 when it exploded its first atomic device. Beijing has not released official figures on the size of its nuclear force, but it is commonly believed that China has approximately two dozen intercontinental ballistic missiles with ranges capable of holding portions of the United States at risk. In addition, China possesses about another two dozen nuclear-capable medium-range ballistic missiles dedicated to regional targeting.

A Chinese fighter plane fires at ground targets during a military exercise.

A Chinese submarine sits at the surface with warships gathered for a combined military exercise with Russia.

Telecommunications and Connectivity

AT A GLANCE						
Per 100 People (2005)	CHINA	HONG KONG	JAPAN	ASIA	UNITED STATES	EU-15*
TELEPHONE MAIN LINES	26.6	53.9	45.3	15.5	58.8	52.9
MOBILE PHONE SUBSCRIBERS	29.9	123.5	75.3	23.0	71.4	100.6
INTERNET USERS	8.6	50.1	51.5	9.7	66.3	45.6
PERSONAL COMPUTERS	4.1	59.3	54.2	6.4	76.2	48.6
BROADBAND SUBSCRIBERS (2004)	1.7	21.7	14.6	1.5	12.9	9.8
Compound Annual Growth Rate (2000–2005)	CHINA	HONG KONG	JAPAN	ASIA	UNITED STATES	EU-15*
TELEPHONE MAIN LINES	19.3	-0.7	-1.3	11.9	-1.9	-0.4
MOBILE PHONE SUBSCRIBERS	35.8	9.8	7.6	29.6	14.2	10.1
INTERNET USERS	38.1	13.7	11.7	27.4	9.8	13.8
PERSONAL COMPUTERS	20.8	9.3	11.6	14.9	6.8	11.7
BROADBAND SUBSCRIBERS (2000–2004)	>1000	34.3	116.4	80.6	52.2	122.7

INFORMATION AND COMMUNICATION TECHNOLOGY (ICT) has fast become one of the key engines of China's spectacular economic growth. An intensive program of capacity-building has seen the country add the equivalent of 200 new connections per minute, every hour of every day, for the past decade, growing the nation's combined fixed and mobile networks almost 20-fold.

At the same time, the nation has reinvented itself as the world's largest factory for high-tech goods, overtaking the U.S., Japan, and the EU in 2003 to become the leading global ICT exporter. If much of that prodigious export capability has been built with the help of local subsidiaries of multinational manufacturers, there are now signs that Chinese companies are starting to look beyond low-value-added assembly for foreign buyers toward developing their own world-class products increasingly targeted at China's own market. The steadily rising disposable income of the country's young, educated middle class, coupled with a national passion for electronic gadgets, is beginning to drive the country's high-tech economy in new directions. No longer merely a tech producer, China is becoming a gargantuan tech consumer.

Twisted pair and copper coaxial cable now deliver broadband Internet to 52 million subscribers. Poised to become the world's biggest broadband market in 2007, China is adding high-speed connections at a rate of around five million a month. Yet in terms of penetration, the country still trails far behind far smaller nations like Iceland and South Korea, with its broadband services reaching less than 4% of the population.

TECHNOLOGICAL CONNECTIVITY

Over two million miles of fiber now connect 90% of China's major centers, while high-capacity links, such as a future U.S.-China cable, are dramatically transforming international connectivity. A modest ranking in the global Digital Opportunity Index, which measures grassroots access to technology, belies the highly wired lifestyle of young professionals living in the country's thriving hubs.

Submarine Fiber-optic Cable Systems with Landings in China
(capacity in gigabits per second, 2007)
—— Over 500
—— 100 to 500
—— Under 100

Digital Opportunity Index Value (2005–2006)
- 0.6 to 0.79
- 0.46 to 0.59
- 0.3 to 0.45
- 0.15 to 0.29
- 0.01 to 0.14
- No data

Source: TeleGeography Research

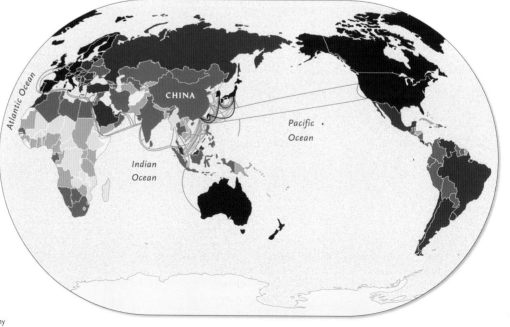

CHINA'S TECH INDUSTRY

Already the world's largest hardware manufacturer, China is now building up its software development capabilities, with Beijing's Zhongguancun district rapidly emerging as a major global hub. While foreign ventures still account for 90% of ICT exports, China's tech industry is starting to invest abroad to gain access to new technologies, premium brands, and broader distribution channels. The challenge: to transition from low-cost producer to leading-edge innovator.

*First fifteen countries to join the European Union

IMPORTS AND EXPORTS OF ICT** GOODS

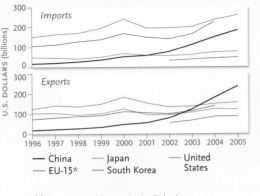

U.S. DOLLARS (billions)

Imports

300 · 200 · 100

Exports

300 · 200 · 100

1996 1997 1998 1999 2000 2001 2002 2003 2004 2005

— China
— EU-15*
— Japan
— South Korea
— United States

**Information and Communication Technology

CHINA'S ICT** BALANCE OF TRADE

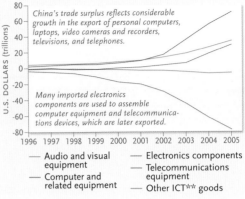

U.S. DOLLARS (trillions)

China's trade surplus reflects considerable growth in the export of personal computers, laptops, video cameras and recorders, televisions, and telephones.

80 · 60 · 40 · 20 · 0 · -20 · -40 · -60 · -80

Many imported electronics components are used to assemble computer equipment and telecommunications devices, which are later exported.

1996 1997 1998 1999 2000 2001 2002 2003 2004 2005

— Audio and visual equipment
— Computer and related equipment
— Electronics components
— Telecommunications equipment
— Other ICT** goods

INTERNET USE

Percent of Population Using the Internet (2007)

- Over 15
- 12 to 15
- 9 to 11
- 6 to 8
- Under 6

China loves the Net. But while users are coming online at a rate of over 25 million each year, growth remains skewed toward young, affluent, urban males. Over 80% of surfers are aged 35 and under, while fewer than 3% of over-40s are online. Away from the boomtowns of the eastern seaboard, Internet use declines rapidly. Over one-third of all users live in four of China's wealthiest industrialized provinces, while the vast agrarian communities of Tibet and Gansu account for less than 1% of the national total. Despite a boom in Chinese-language sites, China's companies have been slow to harness the power of the Net, with fewer than one in four having their own website.

TELEDENSITY

Industrial powerhouses like Beijing, Shanghai, and Guangzhou boast teledensities equal to the world's most wired cities, yet thousands of China's more remote villages still lack a simple phone connection. That picture is now changing, through a combination of government initiatives and market forces. The Cun Cun Tong (Connecting Every Village) program has brought phone service to more than 65,000 remote communities since 2004, targeting two public access lines for every village by 2010. And as urban markets near saturation, operators are looking to rural dwellers to sustain double-digit growth. State-owned China Mobile invested US$1.2 billion to bring service to 26,000 remote villages in 2005; rural areas now generate 50% of new customers.

Mobile and Fixed Line Telephones per 100 People (2006)

- Over 100
- 65 to 100
- 55 to 64
- 45 to 54
- Under 45

INTERNET CONNECTION METHOD

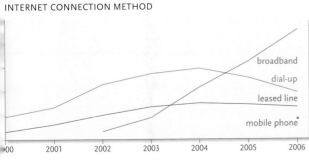

broadband
dial-up
leased line
mobile phone*

00 2001 2002 2003 2004 2005 2006

MOBILE PHONE USAGE

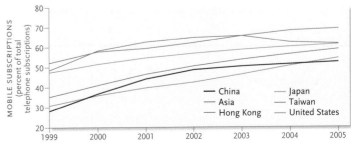

MOBILE SUBSCRIPTIONS (percent of total telephone subscriptions)

80 · 70 · 60 · 50 · 40 · 30 · 20

1999 2000 2001 2002 2003 2004 2005

— China
— Asia
— Hong Kong
— Japan
— Taiwan
— United States

Cities

China counts 51 cities with a population of more than one million people; they are located on the map to the right. The U.S. counts nine such cities. Shenzhen, not as widely known in the West as Beijing, Shanghai, or Hong Kong, has more people than New York City. The massive migration from rural areas to urban ones is among the most profound trends in China during the past 30 years. That trend has not yet run its course. The Chinese cities profiled in the following pages are not necessarily among the most populous. They were chosen to reflect economic diversity and cultural and geographic variety.

KEY TO CITY MAPS

▫ Point of interest		Highway		River
4 Route number		Highway under construction		Ferry route
+ Dhug Ri 4275 Elevation in meters		Primary road		Tram
		Primary road under construction		Park boundary
• • • • Cities/Towns		Secondary road		Lake
Jingan • City region (smaller-scale maps)		Minor road		Selected building footprint
Ⓢ Subway station		Path (city); Minor road (regional)		Park
✈ Airport		Tunnel		Built-up area
XIDAN City region (larger-scale maps)		Railroad		Paved area

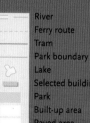

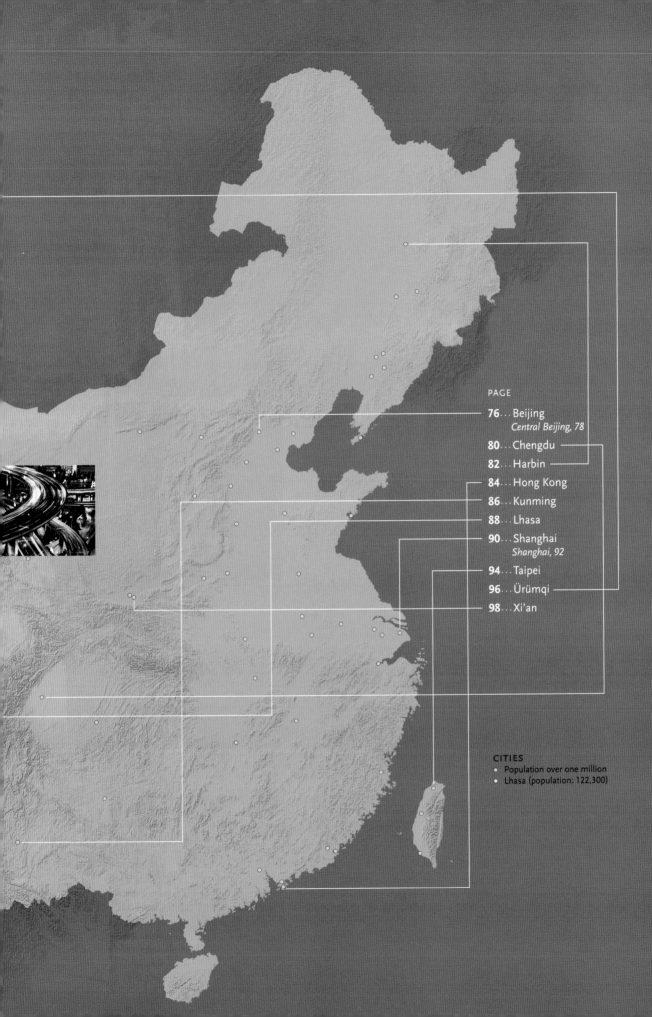

CITIES
○ Population over one million
○ Lhasa (population: 122,300)

Beijing
北京

POPULATION	CITY PROPER 7,724,900
	MUNICIPALITY 15,380,000
AREA	4,569 SQUARE KILOMETERS
	1,764 SQUARE MILES
LATITUDE	39° 55' 44" N
LONGITUDE	116° 23' 18" E
ELEVATION	64 METERS, 209 FEET
TEMPERATURE	DAILY AVERAGE (JANUARY) -4.6°C, 23.7°F
	DAILY AVERAGE (JULY) 26.1°C, 79°F
PRECIPITATION	MONTHLY AVERAGE (JANUARY) 2.8 MILLIMETERS, 0.11 INCHES
	MONTHLY AVERAGE (JULY) 213.0 MILLIMETERS, 8.39 INCHES
TIME ZONE	+8 HOURS UTC (COORDINATED UNIVERSAL TIME)
REGIONAL GOVERNMENT	BEIJING (SHI) MUNICIPALITY

Beijing has taken great pains to cope with another invasion. Preparations to block two earlier on-slaughts failed. Mongols swept around a primitive defense; Manchus attacked through an opening in the later Great Wall of China built during the Ming dynasty of 1368 to 1644. This time the invasion is welcome—the 2008 Olympics—and Beijing is fueling a building frenzy atop an already hectic rush to modernize.

As China's capital, all roads, railroads, and airways point there, and all major political, economic, and industrial decisions flow from Beijing. This centralized system is reflected in the north-south, east-west road grid proceeding from the Ming-era "Forbidden City," home to emperors. Forbidden were commoners and any structure built higher than those of the imperial complex.

Beijing's large-scale modernization began in 1958 when Tiananmen Square was enlarged fourfold, destroying many courtyard houses on the narrow twisting streets of intimate, traditional neighborhoods. Population has tripled since 1949, and swarms of bicycles have become herds of internal combusters creating massive traffic snarls despite extensive widening of roadways and construction of a modern subway system. Huge apartment blocks have risen along with shopping malls, office-complex skyscrapers, and department stores.

With the Olympics come a dozen sports venues, a new subway line, a massive airport terminal, and a worsening housing shortage with escalating prices. Olympic scores also tally nearly 17 billion dollars of investment and two million jobs.

The giant version of Mao Zedong's portrait still looks out on Tiananmen, or "Gate of Heavenly Peace." The much smaller original was to be put up for auction in 2006, but was instead acquired by the National Museum of China—after a storm of protests were registered on the Chinese Internet. Such protests in person would not be looked on with favor.

Cyclists passing Tiananmen Gate at the northern end of Beijing's Tiananmen Square

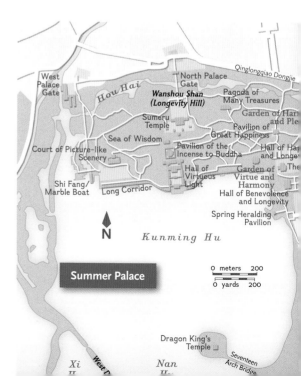

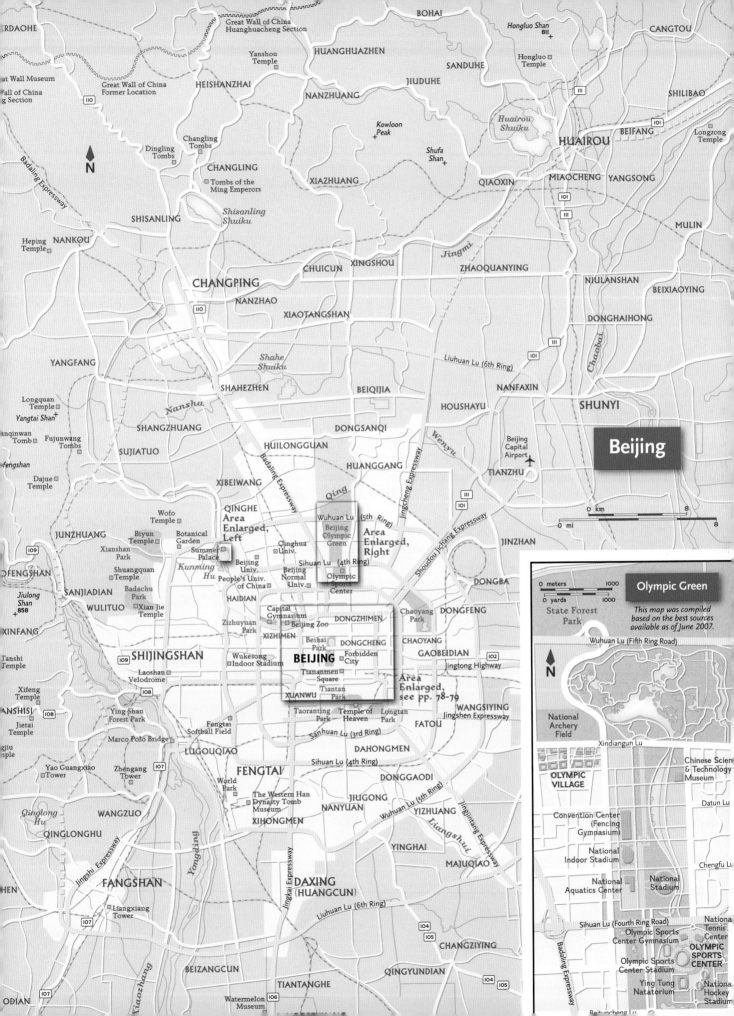

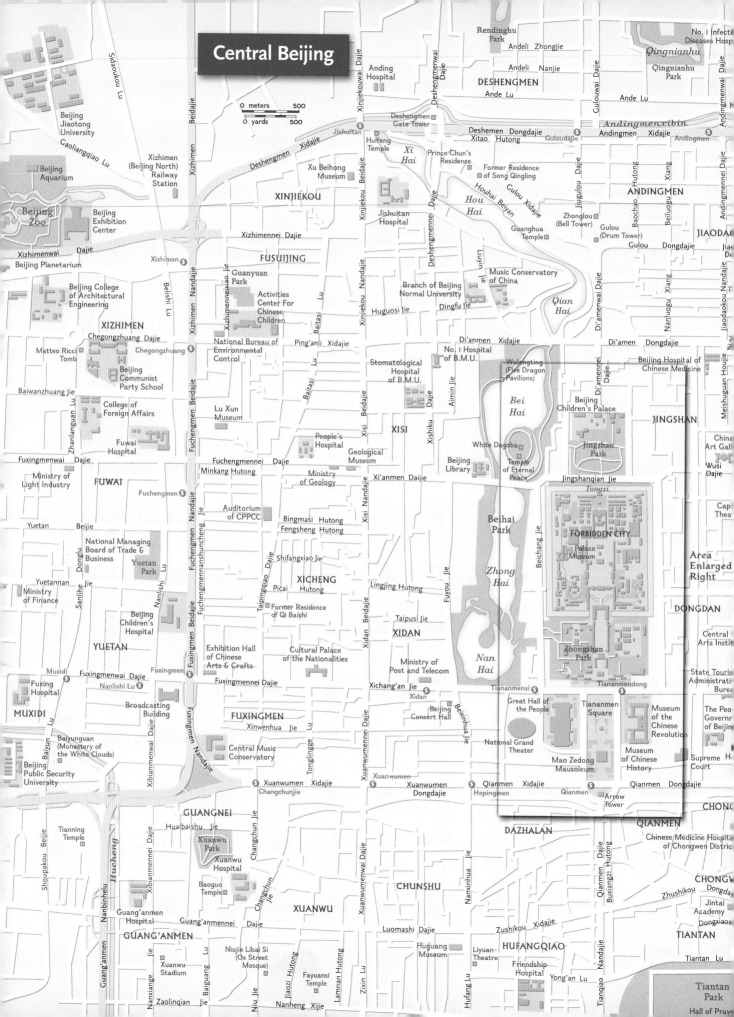

Central Beijing

0 meters 500
0 yards 500

Beijing Jiaotong University

Caoliangqiao Lu

Beijing Aquarium

Beijing Zoo

Xizhimenwai Dajie

Beijing Planetarium

Xizhimen (Beijing North) Railway Station

Beijing Exhibition Center

Shipxouxou Lu

Xizhimen Beidajie

Deshengmen Xidajie

XINJIEKOU

Xu Beihong Museum

Xizhimennei Dajie

Xizhimen

FUSUIJING

Beijing College of Architectural Engineering

Chegongzhuang Dajie

Matteo Ricci Tomb

Belishi Lu

XIZHIMEN

Chegongzhuang

Beijing Communist Party School

Baiwanzhuang Jie

College of Foreign Affairs

Zhanlanguan

Fuwai Hospital

Guanyuan Park

Xizhimennexiao Jie

Activities Center For Chinese Children

Ping'anli Xidajie

National Bureau of Environmental Control

Baitasi Lu

Lu Xun Museum

Xinjiekou Nandajie

Huguosi Jie

Xinjiekou Beidajie

Deshengmennei Dajie

Huifeng Temple

Jishuitan Hospital

Jishuitan

Anding Hospital

Xinjiekouwai Dajie

Deshengmenwai Dajie

DESHENGMEN

Deshengmen Gate Tower

Deshengmen Dongdajie

Xitao Hutong

Xi Hai

Prince Chun's Residence

Former Residence of Song Qingling

Hou Hai

Houhai Beiyan

Liuyin Jie

Branch of Beijing Normal University

Dingfu Jie

Music Conservatory of China

Qian Hai

Guloudajie

Andeli Zhongjie

Andeli Nanjie

Ande Lu

Ande Lu

Zhonglou (Bell Tower)

Gulou (Drum Tower)

Gulou Dongdajie

Jiugoulou Dajie

Gulouwai Dajie

Andingmennei Dajie

Andingmen Xidajie

Andingmen

ANDINGMEN

Baochao Hutong

Beiluogu

Nanluogu Xiang

Jiaodaokou Nandajie

Rendinghu Park

Qingnianhu

Qingnianhu Park

Andingmenwai Dajie

No. 1 Infecti Diseases Hosp

Andingmennei Dajie

Andingmennexibin

JIAODAO

Jia De

Meishuguan Houjie

Di'anmennei Dajie

Di'anmen Xidajie

No. 1 Hospital of B.M.U.

Wulongting (Five Dragon Pavilions)

Bei Hai

Di'anmen Dongdajie

Beijing Hospital of Chinese Medicine

JINGSHAN

Beijing Children's Palace

Jingshan Park

China Art Gal

Wusi Dajie

Cap Thea

Central Arts Insti

State Touris Administrati Burea

The Peo Governn of Beijing

Supreme H Court

Aimin Jie

Stomatological Hospital of B.M.U.

Xisi Beidajie

XISI

People's Hospital

Geological Museum

Xi'anmen Daijie

Xishiku

Beijing Library

White Dagoba

Temple of Eternal Peace

Jingshanqian Jie

Tongzi

FORBIDDEN CITY

Palace Museum

Beichang Jie

Area Enlarged Right

DONGDAN

Fuchengmennei Dajie

Minkang Hutong

Ministry of Geology

Xisi Nandajie

Bingmasi Hutong

Fengsheng Hutong

Shifangxiao Jie

XICHENG

Picai Hutong

Former Residence of Qi Baishi

Taipingqiao Jie

Lingjing Hutong

Taipusi Jie

Fuyou Jie

Beihai Park

Zhong Hai

Nan Hai

Zhongshan Park

Tiananmendong

Fuxingmennei Dajie

FUWAI

Fuchengmen

Ministry of Light Industry

Yuetan Beijie

Donglu

National Managing Board of Trade & Business

Yuetan Park

Yuetan

Yuetannan

Ministry of Finance

Saanlihe Jie

Nanlishi Lu

YUETAN

Beijing Children's Hospital

Muxidi

Fuxing Hospital

Fuxingmenwai Dajie

Nanlishi Lu

MUXIDI

Baiyun Lu

Baiyunguan (Monastery of the White Clouds)

Beijing Public Security University

Fuxingmen

Broadcasting Building

Xibianmenwai Dajie

Fuxingmen Nandajie

Fuxingmennanshuncheng

Fuchengmen Beidajie

Fuchengmen Nandajie

Auditorium of CPPCC

Taipingqiao Lu

Xidan Beidajie

XIDAN

Ministry of Post and Telecom

Xichang'an Jie

Xidan

Exhibition Hall of Chinese Arts & Crafts

Cultural Palace of the Nationalities

Fuxingmennei Dajie

FUXINGMEN

Xinwenhua Jie

Tonglingge

Central Music Conservatory

Xuanwumen Xidajie

Changchunjie

Beijing Concert Hall

Bekxinhua Jie

Beijing

Xuanwumen

Xuanwumennei Dajie

Xuanwumen Dongdajie

Xichang'an Jie

Great Hall of the People

National Grand Theater

Mao Zedong Mausoleum

Tiananmenxi

Tiananmen Square

Museum of the Chinese Revolution

Museum of Chinese History

Qianmen Xidajie

Hepingmen

Qianmen

Qianmen Dongdajie

Arrow Tower

QIANMEN

CHON

GUANGNEI

Huaibaishu Jie

Changchun Jie

Xuanwu Park

Xuanwu Hospital

Baoguo Temple

Tianning Temple

Shoupakou Beijie

Nanbinhelu

Huoheng

Xibianmennei Dajie

Guang'anmennei Dajie

GUANG'ANMEN

Guang'anmen Lu

Guang'anmen Hospital

Xuanwu Stadium

Nanxiange

Zaolinqian Jie

Niujie Libai Si (Ox Street Mosque)

Jiaozi Hutong

Baiguo Jie

Niu Jie

Changchun Jie

Fayuansi Temple

Nanheng Xijie

XUANWU

Luomashi Dajie

Xuanwumennei Dajie

CHUNSHU

Zushikou Xidajie

Nanxinhua Jie

Zixin Lu

Zushikou

Liyuan Theatre

Huguang Museum

Friendship Hospital

HUFANGQIAO

Hufang Lu

Yong'an Lu

DAZHALAN

Qianmen Dajie

Buxiangzi Hutong

Qianmen Dajie

Chinese Medicine Hospita of Chongwen District

Zhushikou

CHONGW

Dongda

Jintai Academy

Dongxiaos

TIANTAN

Tiantan Lu

Tiantan Park

Hall of Pray

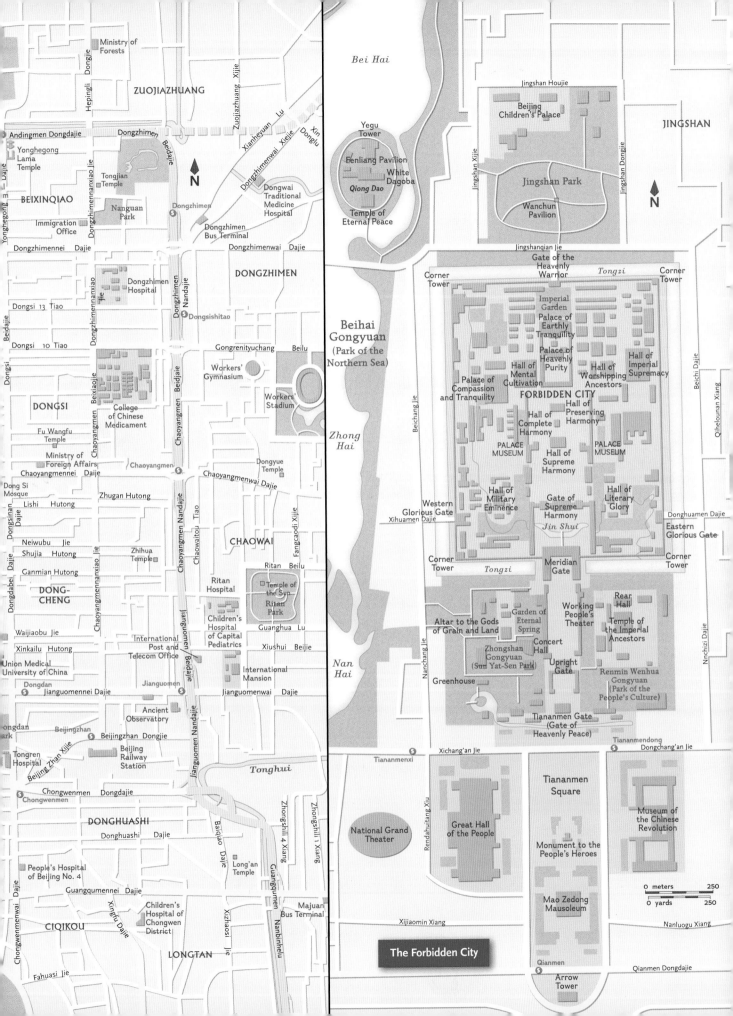

The Forbidden City

Chengdu
成都

POPULATION	CITY PROPER 3,972,500
	METRO AREA 4,648,800
AREA	1,444 SQUARE KILOMETERS
	558 SQUARE MILES
LATITUDE	30° 40' 00" N
LONGITUDE	104° 04' 00" E
ELEVATION	503 METERS, 1,650 FEET
TEMPERATURE	DAILY AVERAGE (JANUARY) 6.2°C, 43.2°F
	DAILY AVERAGE (JULY) 26.3°C, 79.3°F
PRECIPITATION	MONTHLY AVERAGE (JANUARY) 6.7 MILLIMETERS, 0.26 INCHES
	MONTHLY AVERAGE (JULY) 232.8 MILLIMETERS, 9.17 INCHES
TIME ZONE	+8 HOURS UTC (COORDINATED UNIVERSAL TIME)
REGIONAL GOVERNMENT	SICHUAN PROVINCE

A place of settlement since the Bronze Age, Chengdu is the capital of Sichuan Province, famous for its agricultural productivity and fine spicy cuisine. More than 2,000 years ago, a massive irrigation project nearby diverted water from the Min River and sent it into a tunnel bored through a mountain. The Dujiang-yan system is still in daily use and ranks as a United Nations World Heritage site. Flanked by mountains to the west, Chengdu sits on a broad fertile plain, enjoying temperate but damp weather.

Paper money was first circulated here in the 11th century, and financial institutions remain a pillar of the city's economy as do textiles, recalling Chengdu's historic reputation for weaving fine silk brocades.

During World War II, Chengdu became a base for U.S. B-29s that flew from India over the Himalayan "Hump" to China. The bombers launched the first large-scale aerial attacks on Japan, but extreme distances, altitudes, turbulence, and supply difficulties limited their effectiveness. Chengdu has made recent aviation history as the factory site for building the Chinese J-10 jet fighter-bomber.

The last mainland city to fall to the People's Liberation Army in 1949, Chengdu has recently seen rapid modernization in research, industry, and communications, sometimes outrunning the capacity of power supplies to keep up. Nonetheless, in 2007 the city hosted the "Fifth Chinasoft" to "…show the outside world [the] Chinese software industry's resources and development…"

The area is at the center of cutting-edge research in the natural sciences as well. Sichuan boasts the world's largest giant panda population, and the Giant Panda Breeding Research Base about seven miles (11 kilometers) north of Chengdu is one of China's most important centers for captive conservation of the beloved animal.

For all the activity, though, the city's people know how to relax—Chengdu has a greater number of teahouses and bars than Shanghai, which has twice the population.

Bicycle commuters during rush hour, Chengdu

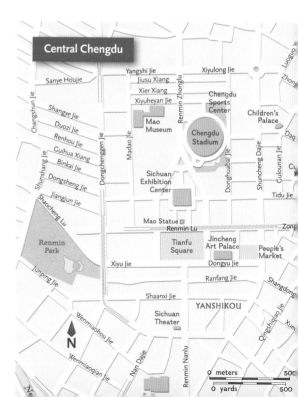

To Chengdu Giant Panda
Breeding Research Base
6 km (3.7 mi)

Chengdu
Zoo
Zhaojue
Temple

Chengdu Juvenile
Science & Technology
Park

Yingmenkou Lu

ZHUGECUN

Southwest Jiaotong
University

Chengdu Railway
Station

Erhuan Lu Beiduan

Simaqiao Lu

WANGJIABEI

TIANXINGQIAO

Jiulidi
Park

Jiulidi Nanlu
Shawan Lu

Fu

Beizhanxier Lu

Renmin Beilu

Chengdu
University

ZHONGSANDONGQIAO

YAOSHANG

Balizhuang Lu

Fuqing Lu Sanduan

SIMAQIAO

Jiefang Lu

ZHANGJIAYUANZI

TEILUXINCUN

BAIMASI

Yihuan Lu Beiduan

XIAOJIACUN

Sanyou Lu

Fuqing Lu

DAOSHIQIAO

HONGLONGMEN

Fuqin Xilu

Xiti Lu

Wudu Lu

Chengbei
Tiyu Park

Ma'an Donglu

CAOJIAXIANG

University Electronic
Science and
Technology

JIANSHE BEILU SANDUAN

SHENGDENGCUN

Lu

Nan Xiangzi

Baixialu
Gymnasium

Wenshu
Temple

Da'an Lu

Xinhui Lu

Jianshe Beilu Erduan

SANDAOYAN

SHIREN

Yongling Lu

Xi Dajie

Jiangshan Lu

Renmin Zhonglu

Chengdu
Theater

Huaxing Lu

Dongjiao
Stadium
Amusement
Park

Jianshe Nanlu

Jianshe Lu

Erhuan Lu Dongduan

BAIGUOLIN

Yongling
Museum

Babao Jie

Wenwu Lu

National Minorities
Institute

Desheng Lu

DONGJIAOCHANG

YANGJIAYUANZI

Qingjiang Donglu

Xi'an Lu

Area
Enlarged,
Left

Dongchengen jie

Chengdu
Sports
Center

Chengdu
Stadium

Shuncheng Dajie

Taisheng Lu

Hongxing Xinhua Dadao

West
Pearl Tower

Xinhong Lu

Shierqiao Lu

Tongren Lu

CHENGDU

Cultural
Palace

Jinjiang
Theater

Culture
Park

Qintai Lu

Jinhe Lu

Sichuan Exhibition
Center

Exhibition
Hall

Hongqi
Theater

Dacisi Lu

Xinhua
Park

Shuanglin Lu

WANNIANCHANG

Qingyang
Palace

Qingyang Jie

Renmin
Park

Renmin Lu

Tianfu Square

Dong'an Nanlu

Dongfeng Lu

Yihuan Lu Dongduan

XIJIAOCHANG

Xiyu Jie

Dongyu Jie

Sun Yat-sen
Statue

Temple of
Mercy

Shuinianhe Lu

Du Fu's
Thatched
Cottage

Caotang Lu

Baihuatan
Park

YANSHIKOU

Huanhua

Gan

LANJIAYUANZI

Yihuan Lu Xiduan

Dashi Donglu

Jinli Lu

SHUANGQIAOZ

Dashi Xilu

NANJIAOCHANG

Nan

LANDONGMEN

NIUWANGMIAO

NIUSHIKOU

Shuanggui Le

LIUJIAYUANZI

Chengdu Sports
College

Nanjiao
Park

Binjiang Lu

LIANHUACHI

Wuhou
Shrine

WuhouCi Dajie

Zhimin Lu

Shuangnan Lu

Physical Cultural
Institute

Xiaojia

YONGFENGXIANG

Jiangxi Jie

Sichuan Institute
of Pedagogics

Huaxi
Medical
University

XINCUN

GONGHECUN

Southwest College
for Nationalities

MOZIQIAO

Xinnan Lu

College of Science
and Technology

Sichuan
University

ZHONGJIAXINFANGZI

Gonglu

Yongfeng Lu

Yihuan Lu Nanduan

Sichuan Museum

Sichuan Incorporated
University

Shunjiang Lu

Wangjianglou
Park

Chuanzang

JIAYUANZI

Provincial
Natatorium

Nanjiao
Stadium

Renmin Nanlu

Kehua Beilu

Laodong Lu

Jingiusi Lu

Sha

DONGJIAWAN

Guyapo

YANGJIAYUANZI

CHENJIAYUANZI

ZHANGJIAYUANZI

DONGJIASHA

LEIJIAYUANZI

Erhuan Lu Nanduan

Fu

Chengdu

0 km   1
0 mi   1

Harbin
哈尔滨

POPULATION	CITY PROPER 3,329,600
	METRO AREA 4,832,100
AREA	1,637 SQUARE KILOMETERS
	632 SQUARE MILES
LATITUDE	45° 45' 00" N
LONGITUDE	126° 39' 00" E
ELEVATION	152 METERS, 500 FEET
TEMPERATURE	DAILY AVERAGE (JANUARY) -19.3°C, -2.7°F
	DAILY AVERAGE (JULY) 23.2°C, 73.8°F
PRECIPITATION	MONTHLY AVERAGE (JANUARY) 4 MILLIMETERS, 0.16 INCHES
	MONTHLY AVERAGE (JULY) 155.7 MILLIMETERS, 6.13 INCHES
TIME ZONE	+8 HOURS UTC (COORDINATED UNIVERSAL TIME)
REGIONAL GOVERNMENT	HEILONGJIANG PROVINCE

Known as the "Ice City" for its brutal winters, Harbin, a northeastern provincial capital (and sister city to Minneapolis), celebrates the cold with the famous Ice and Snow Festival. Gigantic ice blocks are excavated from the flood-prone Songhua River and fashioned into huge illuminated sculptures such as models of the Great Wall and ancient temples.

Here, in the northeast quadrant of China, a failing Mao-era command economy of inefficient and often unsafe state-run mines and industries is giving way to more entrepreneurial and international forces. Harbin's output includes petroleum, coal, chemicals, soybeans, and fertilizer, while its industries produce tractors, turbines, electrical and electronic equipment, and precision instruments.

Harbin rose to prominence with completion of a link to the Trans-Siberian railroad early in the 20th century. With construction came an influx of Russians, who left permanent influences, most notably Saint Sophia, the largest Orthodox church in the Far East. After the 1917 Russian revolution and civil war, many so-called White Russians took refuge in Harbin and reinvigorated Russian influences.

In 1932 Japanese troops occupied Harbin, and in 1935 it was incorporated into the puppet state known as Manchukuo. Soviet troops took the city at the end of World War II. Most Europeans who had remained under Japanese occupation were repatriated. After a period of strained relations between the Soviet Union and China, Russia has reconnected with Harbin, now a center of trade with its old economic partner.

The city is also known for the oldest brewery in China. Harbin beer, the nation's second-biggest seller, is now owned by Anheuser-Busch. The heady brew might be enjoyed at a summer picnic down by the extensive grounds around the Flood Control Monument in Joseph Stalin Park.

Elaborate snow sculptures such as the one pictured above are a regular feature of Harbin's International Ice and Snow Festival.

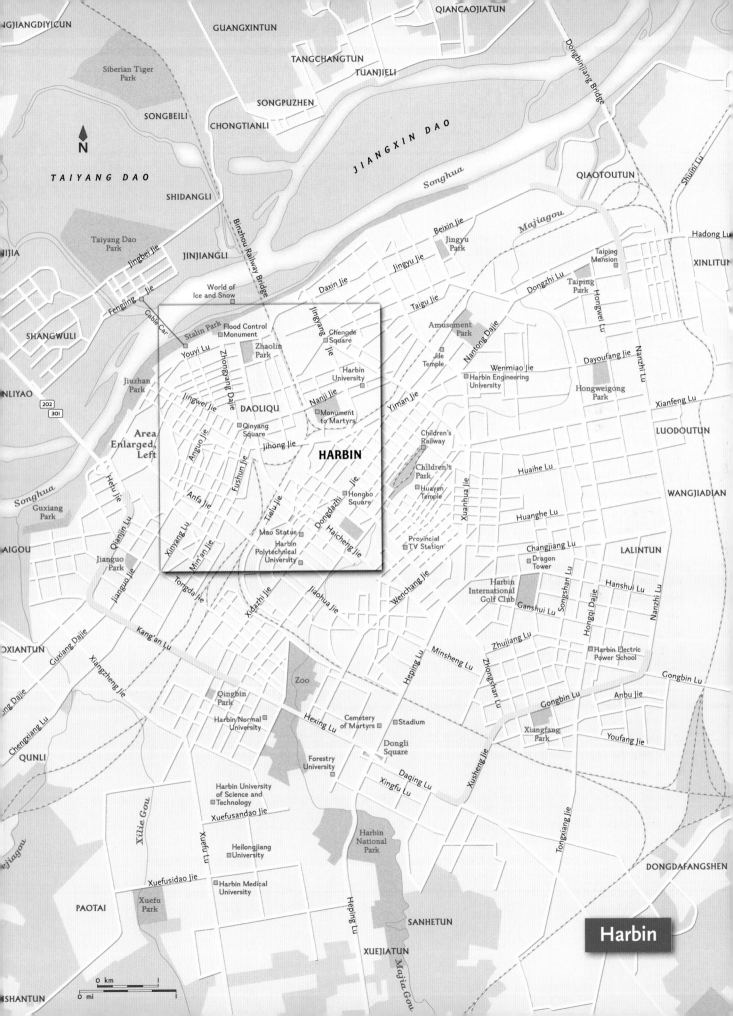

QIANCAOJIATUN

GUANGXINTUN

NGJIANGDIYICUN

TANGCHANGTUN

TUANJIELI

SONGPUZHEN

Siberian Tiger
Park

SONGBEILI

CHONGTIANLI

JIANGXIN DAO

N

Songhua

Dongbinjiang Bridge

Shuini Lu

QIAOTOUTUN

TAIYANG DAO

SHIDANGLI

Hadong Lu

Majiagou

XINLITUN

Beixin Jie

Jingyu Jie

Jingyu
Park

Taiping
Mansion

IJIA

Taiyang Dao
Park

Jingbei Jie

JINJIANGLI

Binzhou Railway Bridge

Daxin Jie

Taigu Jie

Dongzhi Lu

Taiping
Park

Hongwei Lu

Fengling Jie

World of
Ice and Snow

Amusement
Park

Nantong Dajie

Xianfeng Lu

SHANGWULI

Cable Car

Stalin Park

Flood Control
Monument

Jingyang Jie

Chengde
Square

Jile
Temple

Wenmiao Jie

Dayoufang Jie

Nanzhi Lu

Youyi Lu

Zhaolin
Park

Harbin
University

Harbin Engineering
University

Hongweigong
Park

LUODOUTUN

Jiuzhan
Park

Zhongyang Dajie

Nanji Jie

Yiman Jie

202

Jingwei Jie

DAOLIQU

Monument
to Martyrs

Xianfeng Lu

301

Anguo Jie

Qinyang
Square

Children's
Railway

Xuanhua Jie

Huaihe Lu

WANGJIADIAN

Area
Enlarged,
Left

Jihong Jie

Fushun Jie

HARBIN

Children's
Park

Songhua

Guxiang
Park

Anfa Jie

Tielu Jie

Hongbo
Square

Huayen
Temple

Huanghe Lu

Jie

Xinyang Lu

Dongdazhi

Haicheng Jie

Provincial
TV Station

Changjiang Lu

LALINTUN

AIGOU

Helu Jie

Dragon
Tower

Hanshui Lu

Nanzhi Lu

Mao Statue

Qianjin Lu

Min'an Jie

Harbin
Polytechnical
University

Harbin
International
Golf Club

Ganshui Lu

Songshan Lu

Hongqi Dajie

Jianguo
Park

Jianguo Lu

Tongda Jie

Jiaohua Jie

Wenchang Jie

Zhujiang Lu

Harbin Electric
Power School

OXIANTUN

Kang'an Lu

Xidazhi Jie

Zhongshan Lu

Gongbin Lu

Guxiang Dajie

Xiangzheng Jie

Minsheng Lu

Gongbin Lu

Anbu Jie

ng Dajie

Heping Lu

Xiangfang
Park

Youfang Jie

Chengxiang Lu

Qingbin
Park

Zoo

Cemetery
of Martyrs

Stadium

Xusheng Jie

Hexing Lu

Harbin Normal
University

Dongli
Square

Tongxiang Jie

QUNLI

Forestry
University

Daqing Lu

Xingfu Lu

DONGDAFANGSHEN

Harbin University
of Science and
Technology

Xuefusandao Jie

Harbin
National
Park

Xilie Gou

Xuefu Lu

Heilongjiang
University

Xuefusidao Jie

Harbin Medical
University

PAOTAI

Xuefu
Park

SANHETUN

Heping Lu

Majia Gou

XUEJIATUN

0 km   1

SHANTUN

0 mi   1

Harbin

Hong Kong
香港

POPULATION	HONG KONG ISLAND 1,322,800
	S.A.R. 6,935,900
AREA	1,104 SQUARE KILOMETERS
	426 SQUARE MILES
LATITUDE	22° 15' 00" N
LONGITUDE	114° 10' 00" E
ELEVATION	89 METERS, 291 FEET
TEMPERATURE	DAILY AVERAGE (JANUARY) 15.5°C, 59.9°F
	DAILY AVERAGE (JULY) 28.2°C, 82.8°F
PRECIPITATION	MONTHLY AVERAGE (JANUARY) 27.2 MILLIMETERS, 1.07 INCHES
	MONTHLY AVERAGE (JULY) 375.3 MILLIMETERS, 14.78 INCHES
TIME ZONE	+8 HOURS UTC (COORDINATED UNIVERSAL TIME)
REGIONAL GOVERNMENT	SPECIAL ADMINISTRATIVE REGION

Evening view of Hong Kong, Kowloon, and Victoria Harbour from atop Victoria Peak, locally known as "The Peak"

Hong Kong has changed. Time was you could have a fine, cheap suit tailored there. Now you can get a fine suit or a cheap suit. But in the same garment? In this crowded, high-voltage, noisy, worldly, and spectacular city almost anything is possible, but perhaps not that.

Hong Kong Island was ceded "in perpetuity" to Britain in 1842 at the end of the First Opium War. Of the prize, Lord Palmerston harrumphed that it was "a barren island with barely a house on it." At the 1860 end of the Second Opium War, part of the Kowloon Peninsula was likewise ceded. In 1898 Britain received a 99-year-lease for contiguous territory and islands called the New Territories.

The whole became known as Hong Kong and flourished as a major trading port for the British Empire. The colony fell to Japan in World War II. Four years after the war's end the Peoples Republic of China was proclaimed. An enormous Eastern Communist country looked straight at a Western capitalistic colonial enclave right on its shoreline—and nothing happened. China had a doorway to the West, and the West had one to China. Sometimes the door swung more one way than another, but no troops marched through.

With a good supply of labor, Hong Kong became a manufacturer of a whole variety of goods as well as a textile center. When those markets waned, it became a financial hub and a pathway for the outside world to invest in China, as that nation opened its commercial opportunities.

Negotiations begun in 1982 led to the 1997 return of Hong Kong to China's sovereignty—with special exceptions. Under the "Basic Law" following the "one country, two systems" doctrine, Hong Kong would maintain its political, economic, and social freedoms for 50 years. This agreement has not worked perfectly, but the "barren island" is as vital as ever, and in that way Hong Kong has not changed.

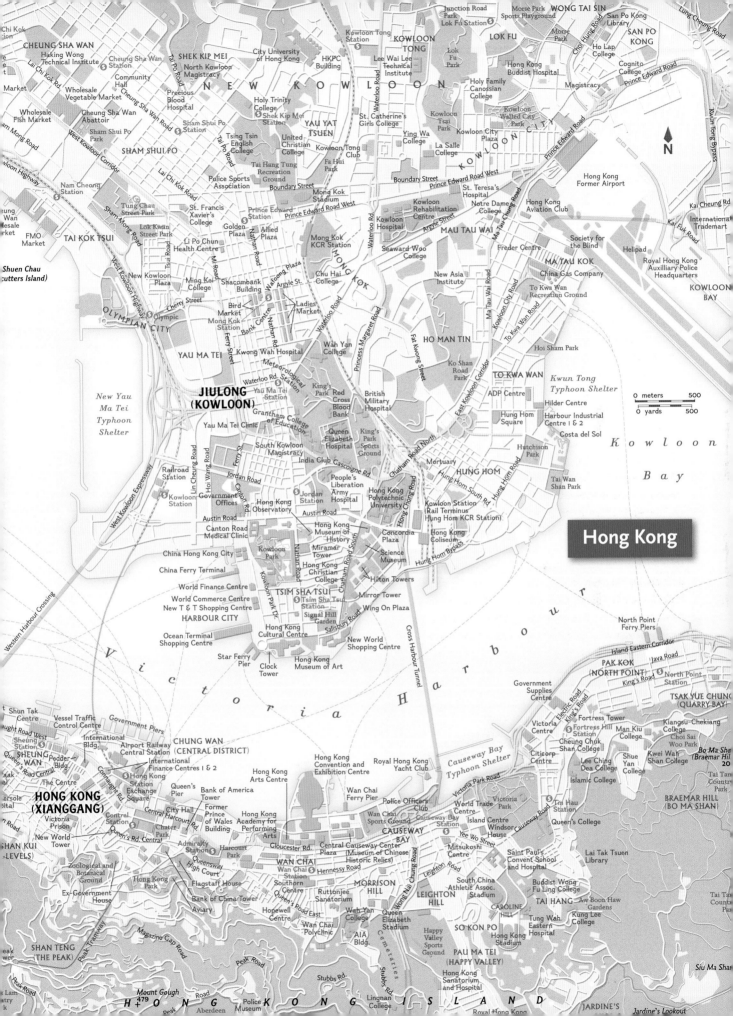

Hong Kong

WONG TAI SIN

Junction Road · Morse Park · San Po Kong Library · Lung Cheung Road

Lok Fu Station · Sports Playground

SAN PO KONG

Morse Park

KOWLOON TONG

Kowloon Tong Station

City University of Hong Kong

HKPC Building

Lee Wai Lee Technical Institute

LOK FU

Lok Fu Station · Lok Fu Park · Hong Kong Buddist Hospital

Ho Lap College · Cognito College · Prince Edward Road

Magistracy

CHEUNG SHA WAN

Haking Wong Technical Institute

Lai Chi Kok Rd.

Cheung Sha Wan Station

Cheung Sha Wan Road

NEW KOWLOON

SHEK KIP MEI

North Kowloon Magistracy

Holy Trinity College

Shek Kip Mei Station

St. Catherine's Girls College

Holy Family Canossian College

Community Hall

Wholesale Vegetable Market

Cheung Sha Wan Abattoir

Sham Shui Po Park

SHAM SHUI PO

Sham Shui Po Station

Tai Po Road

Tsing Tsin English College

United Christian College

YAU YAT TSUEN

Ying Wa College

La Salle College

Kowloon Tsai Park

Kowloon Walled City Park

KOWLOON CITY

Kowloon City Plaza

Hong Kong Former Airport

Kai Cheung Rd

Prince Edward Road

Wholesale Fish Market

Tai Po Road

Fa Hui Park

Kowloon Tong Club

Boundary Street

Prince Edward Road West

St. Teresa's Hospital

Notre Dame College

Kowloon Rehabilitation Centre

Hong Kong Aviation Club

Kai Fuk Road

International Trademart

Am Mong Road

Nam Cheong Station

Tung Chau Street Park

St. Francis Xavier's College

Golden Plaza

Prince Edward Station

Prince Edward Road West

Mong Kok Stadium

Argyle Street

Seaward Woo College

MA TAU WAI

Freder Centre

Society for the Blind

Helipad

Royal Hong Kong Auxilliary Police Headquarters

Wan Wesale Market

FMO Market

TAI KOK TSUI

West Kowloon Highway

Sham Mong Road

Lok Kwan Street Park

Li Po Chun Health Centre

Allied Plaza

Nathan Road

Mong Kok KCR Station

Waterloo Rd

Kowloon Hospital

New Asia Institute

MA TAU KOK

China Gas Company

To Kwa Wan Recreation Ground

KOWLOON BAY

Shuen Chau (Stutters Island)

OLYMPIAN CITY

New Kowloon Plaza

Ming Kei College

Shacombank Building

Cherry Street

Olympic Station

Bird Market

Mong Kok Station

Bank Centre

Ladies Market

MONG KOK

Wah Yan College

HO MAN TIN

Ko Shan Road Park

Hoi Sham Park

Hung Hom South Rd

TO KWA WAN

ADP Centre

Kwun Tong Typhoon Shelter

Hilder Centre

Harbour Industrial Centre I & 2

Chu Hai College

YAU MA TEI

Ferry Street

Kwong Wah Hospital

Meteorological Station

King's Park

Red Cross Blood Bank

British Military Hospital

Hung Hom Square

Costa del Sol

New Yau Ma Tei Typhoon Shelter

JIULONG (KOWLOON)

Yau Ma Tei Station

Grantham College of Education

Yau Ma Tei Clinic

South Kowloon Magistracy

Queen Elizabeth Hospital

King's Park Sports Ground

Hong Kong Polytechnic University

People's Liberation Army Hospital

Mortuary

Tai Wan Shan Park

Hutchison Park

Kowloon Bay

Railroad Station

Lin Cheung Road

Hoi Wang Road

Kowloon Station

Jordan Road

Government Offices

Hong Kong Observatory

Jordan Station

Austin Road

HUNG HOM

Kowloon Station (Rail Terminus) Hung Hom KCR Station)

Hong Kong Coliseum

West Kowloon Expressway

Canton Road

China Hong Kong City

China Ferry Terminal

Austin Road

Canton Medical Clinic

Kowloon Park

Nathan Road

Hong Kong Museum of History

Miramar Tower

Concordia Plaza

Science Museum

Hong Kong Christian College

Hung Hom Bypass

0 meters 500 · 0 yards 500

World Finance Centre

World Commerce Centre

New T & T Shopping Centre

HARBOUR CITY

Kowloon Park Dr.

TSIM SHA TSUI

Tsim Sha Tsui Station

Signal Hill Garden

Chatham Road South

Hilton Towers

Mirror Tower

Wing On Plaza

Cross Harbour Tunnel

Ocean Terminal Shopping Centre

Hong Kong Cultural Centre

Salisbury Road

New World Shopping Centre

Victoria Harbour

Star Ferry Pier

Clock Tower

Hong Kong Museum of Art

North Point Ferry Piers

Island Eastern Corridor

Java Road

North Point Station

PAK KOK (NORTH POINT)

King's Road

TSAK YUE CHUNG (QUARRY BAY)

Western Harbour Crossing

Shun Tak Centre

Vessel Traffic Control Centre

Government Piers

Airport Railway Central Station

CHUNG WAN (CENTRAL DISTRICT)

Hong Kong Convention and Exhibition Centre

Royal Hong Kong Yacht Club

Causeway Bay Typhoon Shelter

Government Supplies Centre

Victoria Centre

Electric Road

King's Road

Fortress Tower

Fortress Hill Station

Man Kiu College

Kiangsu-Chekiang College

Choi Sai Woo Park

SHEUNG WAN

Pedder Bldg.

International Bldg.

International Finance Centres I & 2

Hong Kong Station

Queen's Pier

Hong Kong Arts Centre

Wan Chai Ferry Pier

Victoria Park Road

Cheung Chuk Shan College

Citicorp Centre

Lee Ching Dea College

Shue Yan College

Kwei Wah Shan College

Islamic College

Braemar Hill (Bo Ma Shan) 20

Queen's Road West

Sheung Wan Station

The Centre

Hong Kong Station Exchange Square

Queen's Pier

Bank of America Tower

City Hall

Former Prince of Wales Building

Hong Kong Academy for Performing Arts

Gloucester Rd.

Police Officers' Club

World Trade Centre

Victoria Park

Island Centre

Windsor House

Mitsukoshi Centre

Saint Paul's Convent School and Hospital

Lai Tak Tsuen Library

BRAEMAR HILL (BO MA SHAN)

HONG KONG (XIANGGANG)

Victoria Prison

New World Tower

Central Station

Central Harcourt Rd

Chater Park

Admiralty Station

Queen's Rd. Central

Harcourt Park

Central Causeway Center (Museum of Chinese Historic Relics)

Causeway Bay Station

Yee Wo Street

Queen's College

Tai Hau Station

Causeway Road

SHAN KUI LEVELS)

Zoological and Botanical Ground

Ex-Government House

Hong Kong Park

Queensway

High Court

Flagstaff House

Bank of China Tower

Aviary

Hopewell Centre

WAN CHAI

Wan Chai Station

Southorn Centre

Ruttonjee Sanatorium

MORRISON HILL

Wah Yan College

Queen Elizabeth Stadium

South China Athletic Assoc. Stadium

Buddist Wong Fu Ling College

Aw Boon Haw Gardens

Kung Lee College

TAI HANG

CAROLINE HILL

SO KON PO

Tung Wah Eastern Hospital

Tai Tam Country Park

SHAN TENG (THE PEAK)

Peak Tramway

Magazine Gap Road

Police Museum

Lingnan College

AIA Bldg.

LEIGHTON HILL

Leighton Road

Happy Valley Sports Ground

PAU MA TEI (HAPPY VALLEY)

Hong Kong Sanatorium and Hospital

Siu Ma Shan

Mount Gough 479

HONG KONG ISLAND

Aberdeen

Peak Road

Stubbs Rd

Cemeteries

Royal Hong Kong

JARDINE'S

Jardine's Lookout

Kunming
昆明

POPULATION	CITY PROPER 1,065,400
	METRO AREA 2,402,900
AREA	2,081 SQUARE KILOMETERS
	803 SQUARE MILES
LATITUDE	25° 02' 20" N
LONGITUDE	102° 43' 06" E
ELEVATION	1,897 METERS, 6,224 FEET
TEMPERATURE	DAILY AVERAGE (JANUARY) 8.4°C, 47.1°F
	DAILY AVERAGE (JULY) 20°C, 68°F
PRECIPITATION	MONTHLY AVERAGE (JANUARY) 10.8 MILLIMETERS, 0.43 INCHES
	MONTHLY AVERAGE (JULY) 205.4 MILLIMETERS, 8.09 INCHES
TIME ZONE	+8 HOURS UTC (COORDINATED UNIVERSAL TIME)
REGIONAL GOVERNMENT	YUNNAN PROVINCE

Young by Chinese standards (it was founded in the 8th century), Kunming was late to the 1990s economic fireworks blazing elsewhere in China. Now, its strategic position in the southwest makes the city vital to increasing communications and trade with neighboring countries.

Although known as "Spring City" for a pleasant climate year-round, Kunming's history has been stormy. Overrun by Mongols in the 13th century, it was captured by Manchus in the 17th century and besieged in the 19th century by a Muslim sultan.

During World War II, industries were moved to Kunming to avoid capture by Japanese forces, and American volunteer pilots of the legendary P-40 "Flying Tigers" defended the city and region as the vital terminus of the Burma Road. That road, and a later branch built under command of the American general Joseph Stilwell, was the only land route from the west supplying fuel, material, and munitions to China's forces.

During China's Cultural Revolution, many political victims were exiled to the Kunming region, and many of them decided to remain, mixing with a particularly diverse ethnic population.

Proximity to Vietnam—a rail line was first laid to Hanoi in 1910—Laos, Myanmar (Burma) and nearby Thailand, Malaysia, Singapore, and India bring new opportunities: A six-lane expressway is pointed to junction with a road from India. International air service to Myanmar begins in 2007. Design for a new airport anticipates 60 million passengers by 2035. A rail link to Singapore is scheduled for completion in 2015. New five-star hotels and residential, business, and entertainment developments are planned.

Even with all its frantic new commercial activity, Kunming, surrounded by mountains on three sides and a large lake on the other, is still considered to be one of China's most relaxed and affable cities.

The Jinma-Biji (Golden Horse-Green Rooster) Archway marks one of central Kunming's main commercial districts.

Kunming

Lhasa
拉萨

POPULATION	122,300
AREA	554 SQUARE KILOMETERS
	214 SQUARE MILES
LATITUDE	29° 39' 00" N
LONGITUDE	91° 06' 00" E
ELEVATION	3,600 METERS, 11,812 FEET
TEMPERATURE	DAILY AVERAGE (JANUARY) -1.2°C, 29.8°F
	DAILY AVERAGE (JULY) 16.4°C, 61.5°F
PRECIPITATION	MONTHLY AVERAGE (JANUARY) 0.5 MILLIMETERS, 0.02 INCHES
	MONTHLY AVERAGE (JULY) 129.7 MILLIMETERS, 5.11 INCHES
TIME ZONE	+8 HOURS UTC (COORDINATED UNIVERSAL TIME)
REGIONAL GOVERNMENT	XIZANG (TIBET) AUTONOMOUS REGION

As you ascend toward the Tibetan capital of Lhasa, you will be instructed in the use of supplemental oxygen to prevent altitude sickness. That is, if you are traveling by train—which crosses 340 miles of permafrost and reaches a high point of 16,640 feet, almost a thousand feet higher than Mount Blanc, tallest mountain in western Europe.

Buddhism arrived from India in the 7th century. Elements of Bon, an indigenous religion, were incorporated and influenced Tibetan Buddhism's developing character. At about that time, Songtsen Gampo, the Tibetan ruler in Lhasa, wed one Buddhist from Nepal and one from the Tang court of imperial China. His betrothal was arranged to end hostilities between Tibet and China. Each wife brought a statue of the Buddha as a gift, and the Jokhang Temple was built to house them; it remains the holiest temple in Tibet.

In the 17th century, the fifth Dalai Lama, ruling as the joint political and spiritual leader, rebuilt the Potala Palace in Lhasa. Altogether, the "white" and "red" Potala rises 13 floors and holds almost a thousand rooms supported by some 15,000 columns.

Down through the following centuries, relations between Tibet and China were often contentious. Finally, in 1950 the People's Liberation Army overwhelmed weak Tibetan forces (almost half of Tibet's people were otherwise occupied as monks in monasteries). In 1951 a 17-point agreement ceded Tibet's sovereignty to China but provided for local control of institutions. A 1959 rebellion was quickly suppressed, and the 14th Dalai Lama was forced from the Potala and into exile. In the 1960s, Red Guards of the Cultural Revolution desecrated or destroyed thousands of monasteries.

Now comes Train T27 from Beijing, a 4.2-billion-dollar engineering marvel that brings ever more and more ethnic Hans and their commercial kind of progress to the once-remote land of prayer flags and prayer wheels, artisan industries, intense blue sky—and vast mineral resources.

Now a state museum, Potala Palace once served as the seat of Tibet's government and the chief residence of the Dalai Lama.

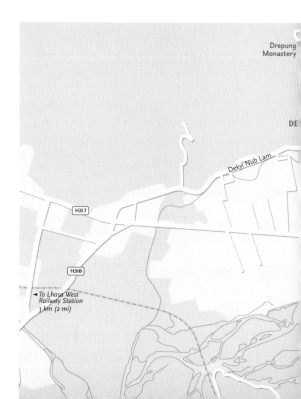

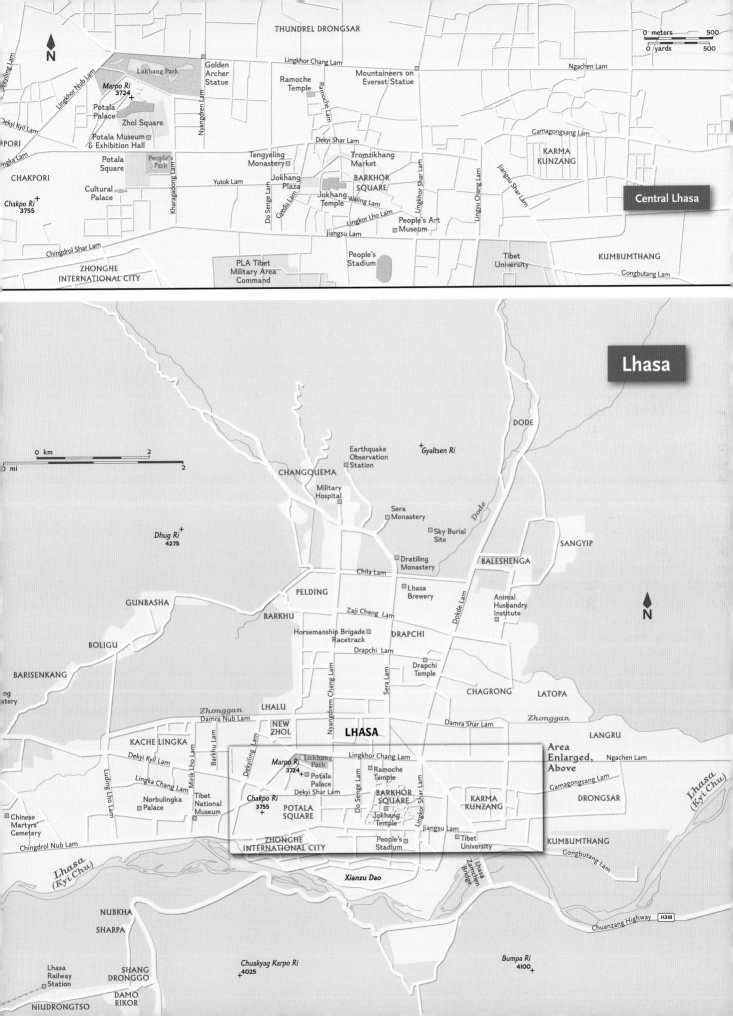

Shanghai
上海

POPULATION	CITY PROPER 15,434,600
	MUNICIPALITY 17,780,000
AREA	6,218 SQUARE KILOMETERS
	2,400 SQUARE MILES
LATITUDE	31° 13' 20" N
LONGITUDE	121° 27' 29" E
ELEVATION	8 METERS, 26 FEET
TEMPERATURE	DAILY AVERAGE (JANUARY) 3.3°C, 37.9°F
	DAILY AVERAGE (JULY) 27.5°C, 81.5°F
PRECIPITATION	MONTHLY AVERAGE (JANUARY) 50.4 MILLIMETERS, 1.98 INCHES
	MONTHLY AVERAGE (JULY) 144 MILLIMETERS, 5.67 INCHES
TIME ZONE	+8 HOURS UTC (COORDINATED UNIVERSAL TIME)
REGIONAL	SHANGHAI (SHI) MUNICIPALITY

The word "shanghaied" once evoked the image of a drunken sailor being hustled aboard a ship to serve as forced labor. The city itself has had more ups and downs than an anchor—from an ancient fishing village to a 17th-century, cotton-processing center to an 18th-century port where British vessels smuggled opium for a trade later enforced by gunboat. That status became a foreign occupation by the 19th century, and the narcotic behind it may have addicted as much as 10 percent of China's population. Foreign settlement, architecture, and commerce continued into the 1920s, when the city was known as "The Paris of the Orient," but also as the "Whore of the Orient" for its high prostitution rate and general decadence.

The first congress of the communist party met in Shanghai in 1921, delegate Mao Zedong attending. The city survived Japanese occupation, the Great Leap Forward, and the Cultural Revolution. Yet it was not until in the early 1990s that, empowered by new economic freedoms, Shanghai took off as fast and high as one of its local products, the Long March rocket.

China's largest city, port, and industrial base has grown furiously in the past few years. Some 6,000 skyscrapers shot up, new highways and rail systems were built (traffic is still horrendous); the world's fastest train—270 mph—runs to the airport. Once a marshland, Pudong was transformed into a futuristic metropolis of office towers and modern factories (one made both refrigerators and rockets). Shanghai city pulses day and night with workers, managers, bureaucrats, and entrepreneurs. It draws billions of dollars in foreign investments and millions more from tourists eager to shop, eat fine Asian cuisine, and marvel (or shudder) at the city's transformation.

Shanghai's Nanjing Lu—one of the world's busiest shopping streets

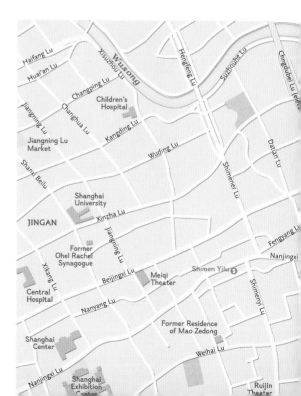

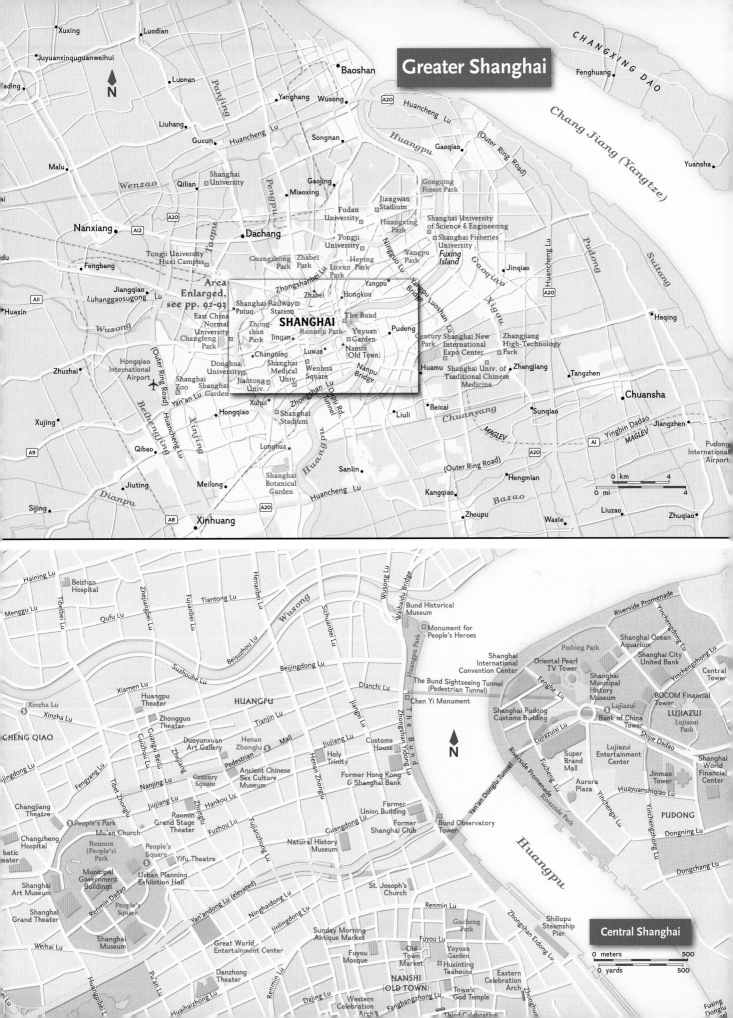

HONGKOU

Zhongqing Lu
ngbaoxing Lu

Yujingpu

Children's Park
Baoxing Lu
Liyang Lu
Lipping Lu

Siping Lu
Linping Lu
Shahong Lu
Gaoyang Lu
Wuhua Lu

Zhoujiazui Lu
Dantu Lu
Gaoyang Lu

Yangshupu
Meizhou Lu
Ninguo Lu
Lanzhou Lu

Xuchang Lu
Changyang Lu
Qiqihaer Lu

Tongbei Lu
Jiangpu Lu
Huimin Lu
Tongbei Lu
Pingliang Lu
Yangzhou Lu

Liaoyang Lu
Huoshan Lu
Dalian Lu

Anguo Lu
Tangshan Lu
Kunming Lu
Changyang Lu

Zhoushan Lu
Huoshan Lu

Qiujiang Lu
Siping Lu
Jiulong Lu
Hanyangdong Lu · Tangshan Lu
Changzi Lu
Changyang Lu
Yangshupu Lu

Huimin Lu

People's Hospital
Shanghai No. 1
Baoshan Lu
nudong Lu

Haining Lu
Wusong Lu
Ernei Lu

Changzi Lu
Ernei Lu

TILANQIAO
Gongping Harbor

Huangpu

Tangqu Belu

Fudu Commercial Town
People's Hospital Shanghai
Tiantong Lu

Damingdong Lu
International Passenger Terminal

Huangpu

ng Lu
Tangqu Lu

Shanghai Post Office
Beisuzhou Lu

Jiulong Lu

Area Enlarged see pp. 90-91

Wusong
Suzhouhe Lu
Sichuanbei Lu

Zhou Beilu
Beijingdong Lu
npu
eater

Sichuanbei Lu
Zhongshan Yidong Lu

Monument for People's Heroes
Bund Historical Museum
Huangpu Park

Chen Yi Monument

Shanghai Ocean Aquarium
Pudong Park

Oriental Pearl TV Tower
Lujiazui

Yinchengbei Lu
Yinchengzhong Lu

Pudong Dadao

Jinmo Lu
Pudong Dadao

Ru Shang Lu

Yuan Shen Lu

Qixia Lu

Central Henan Lu
Nanjingdong Lu

Nanjing Lu

The Bund
Shanghai Int'l. Conv. Ctr.

Lujiazuixi Lu

Lujiazui Entertainment Center
Jinmao Tower
Yincheng Xixi Lu
Yinchengzhong Lu

Lujiazui Park

Shijie Dadao
Dongchang Lu

Ru Shang Lu

Pudong Da Dao

Zhangyang Lu

Customs House
Guangdong Lu

Central Hospital

Yan'andong Lu
Fujian Lu

Bund Observatory Tower

Yan'andong Tunnel

Dongning Lu
Dongchang Lu

Pucheng Lu

Pudongnan Lu

PUDONG

Zhangyang Lu

Dongfang Lu

Punan Stadium

Natural History Museum

Jinlindong Lu

Zhongshan Erdong Lu

Huangpu

Riverside Park

Pumin Lu

Shijie Dadao

Yuan Shen Lu

min
ople's
ople's
quare
nghai
useum

Yan'andong Lu
Jinlindong Lu

Renmin Lu
Gucheng Park
Fuyou Mosque
Yuyuan Garden
Town's God Temple

Zhongshannan Lu

Shiliupu Steamship Pier

Zhangyang Lu

Weifangxi Lu
Dongfang Lu

zhong Lu
aizhou Lu

Sunday Morning Antique Market
Huxinting Teahouse

Fangbangzhong Lu

aihai Park
gpi Nanlu

Tibetan Lu
Renmin Lu

NANSHI (OLD TOWN)
Xueyuan Lu

Waixiangua Jie
Zhonghua

Fuxingdong Tunnel

YANGJIADU

Binjiang Dadao

Pudian Lu

Central Yanggao Lu

of the 1st
nal Congress of the
se Communist
aipingqiao
Park
clandi

Fuxingdong Lu
Zhonghua Theater
Xiaotaoyuan Mosque

Wangyun Lu
Henannan Lu

Dongshi Jie
Warma Lu

Science and Technology Museum

LAOXIMEN

Confucius Temple

Penglai Lu
Zhonghua Lu · Daxing Jie

Guanganan Lu
Ninghe Lu

Wangjiamatou Lu

van

Baiyun Taoist Temple
xingzhong Lu
Shuchang Lu
Zhaozhou Lu

Zhongua Lu

Dongjiadu Lu

DONGJIADU

Pudian Lu

Hua Tai Lu
Hua Tai Lu

abang Lu
pinan Lu

Hunan Stadium

Tibetan Lu
Nanchezhan Lu

Zhongua
Jiangyin Jie
Dongjiangyin Jie
Lujiabang Lu

People's Hospital Shanghai No. 2

Pudong Nanlu

TANGQIAO

an Lu

Zhizoju Lu

Nanpudaqiao

Quxi Lu
Penglai Park

Nanpu Bridge

Pujian Lu

Pudongnan Lu

Dongfang Lu

Pujian Lu

Xietu Lu
Jumen Lu

Xietudong Lu

Folk Collection Exhibition Hall

Zhongshannan Lu

Bansongyuan Lu

Nanpu Square Park

Longyang Lu
Yanggaozhong Lu

Zhongshan Lu
People's Hospital Shanghai No. 9

Huangpu

Linyi Lu

Mengzi Lu
uban Lu
Quxi Lu

NANMATOU

Sanliqiaodong Lu

Shanghai

N

Taipei
台北

POPULATION	CITY PROPER 2,468,700
	METRO AREA 8,241,400
AREA	272 SQUARE KILOMETERS
	105 SQUARE MILES
LATITUDE	25° 02' 21" N
LONGITUDE	121° 31' 30" E
ELEVATION	6 METERS, 20 FEET
TEMPERATURE	DAILY AVERAGE (JANUARY) 15.1°C, 59.2°F
	DAILY AVERAGE (JULY) 28.3°C, 82.9°F
PRECIPITATION	MONTHLY AVERAGE (JANUARY) 89.2 MILLIMETERS, 3.51 INCHES
	MONTHLY AVERAGE (JULY) 240.9 MILLIMETERS, 9.48 INCHES
TIME ZONE	+8 HOURS UTC (COORDINATED UNIVERSAL TIME)
REGIONAL GOVERNMENT	TAIWAN

Where is the tallest building in the world? For the years 2004 through 2007, the answer is Taipei. The pagoda-style skyscraper "Taipei 101" tops out at 1,667 feet.

In the 1970s Taipei's commercial, financial, and industrial growth had raced ahead with little concern for the environment or for the normal needs of daily living. Traffic was so horrendous that major changes to the transportation infrastructure became essential. Boulevards were widened and bus lanes introduced. A mass rapid transit rail system was constructed to ease movement throughout the city. Parks were added for a sense of open space and public recreation. Taipei expanded eastward into a semi-rural area that became a new center for finance and commerce set in glass-and-steel skyscrapers. Museums, memorials, temples, and markets preserve the past amidst all the flash and glitter.

Taipei's past is bound to Taiwan's, a tale of turmoil. When farmers from mainland China began to settle along the Dansheui River in the early 1700s, Taiwan had already seen pirates, Portugese, Dutch, and Spanish traders and incorporation of the island into China by the Qing dynasty. In the next 200 years more than a hundred local uprisings and revolts protested actions of undisciplined soldiers and corrupt officials.

In 1895 China lost a war to Japan, which occupied Taiwan until 1945. In 1949 National forces under Chiang Kai-shek lost a civil war to Communists under Mao Zedong and retreated to Taiwan, taking China's gold reserves with them. Chiang's rule was brutal but laid the foundations for change from an agricultural to a commercial economy.

In recent decades Taiwan's internal politics have evolved into a much more democratic system. The overwhelming question remains. What will be Taiwan's relationship to China? A small but telling hint: China has designated the Taiwan leg of the Olympic flame relay in 2008 as a "domestic route." Taiwan strongly protests that wording.

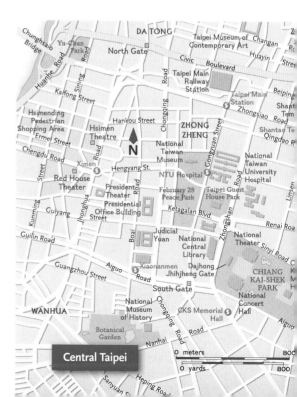

Named for its 101 stories, the Taipei 101 office tower, above, became the world's tallest building upon its completion in 2004.

Ürümqi
乌鲁木齐

POPULATION	1,569,800
AREA	835 SQUARE KILOMETERS
	322 SQUARE MILES
LATITUDE	43° 48' 00" N
LONGITUDE	87° 35' 00" E
ELEVATION	838 METERS, 2,750 FEET
TEMPERATURE	DAILY AVERAGE (JANUARY) -14.3°C, 6.3°F
	DAILY AVERAGE (JULY) 24.2°C, 75.6°F
PRECIPITATION	MONTHLY AVERAGE (JANUARY) 7.9 MILLIMETERS, 0.31 INCHES
	MONTHLY AVERAGE (JULY) 21.2 MILLIMETERS, 0.83 INCHES
TIME ZONE	+8 HOURS UTC (COORDINATED UNIVERSAL TIME)
REGIONAL GOVERNMENT	XINJIANG UYGUR AUTONOMOUS REGION

Ürümqi

Ürümqi has the unique distinction of being, of all the world's cities, the one most distant from an ocean. Even so, in 1992 it was declared a "port" like Shanghai to qualify for a low tax rate to lure investment.

As far from Beijing as Las Vegas is from Chicago, this oasis settlement in a desert region was long a stopping place and fortified position on the northern route of the Silk Road, which connected China to Europe and regions in between 2,000 years ago and again 700 to 900 years ago.

As recently as the early 1950s, the population of Ürümqi and surrounding Xinjiang Uygur Autonomous Region was home to 12 times as many Uygurs, a native ethnic Muslim minority, as Hans, the nationwide ethnic majority. In Ürümqi today, Hans outnumber Uygurs by almost six to one, and many Uygurs resent the loss of their traditional Islamic cultural influence and the commercial successes of Han newcomers.

The dusty trade goods town of a generation ago is now a major metropolis—one that literally sits on a major coalfield surrounded by a hundred mines and choked by pollution. The region produces 30 percent of China's petroleum and natural gas and a third of the energy produced by wind turbines.

This and more all adds up to an annual economic growth rate of 17 percent, nearly twice the rate of China's already hyper growth. In the far countryside horsemen may still gallop hard in "sheep tussling," chasing each other to grab away a fresh carcass, but that's far from the skyscraper skyline of Ürümqi.

High-rises loom over a poor, mostly Uygur neighborhood in Ürümqi.

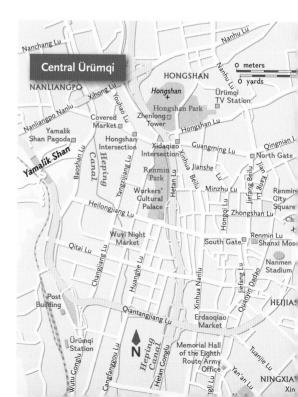

Central Ürümqi

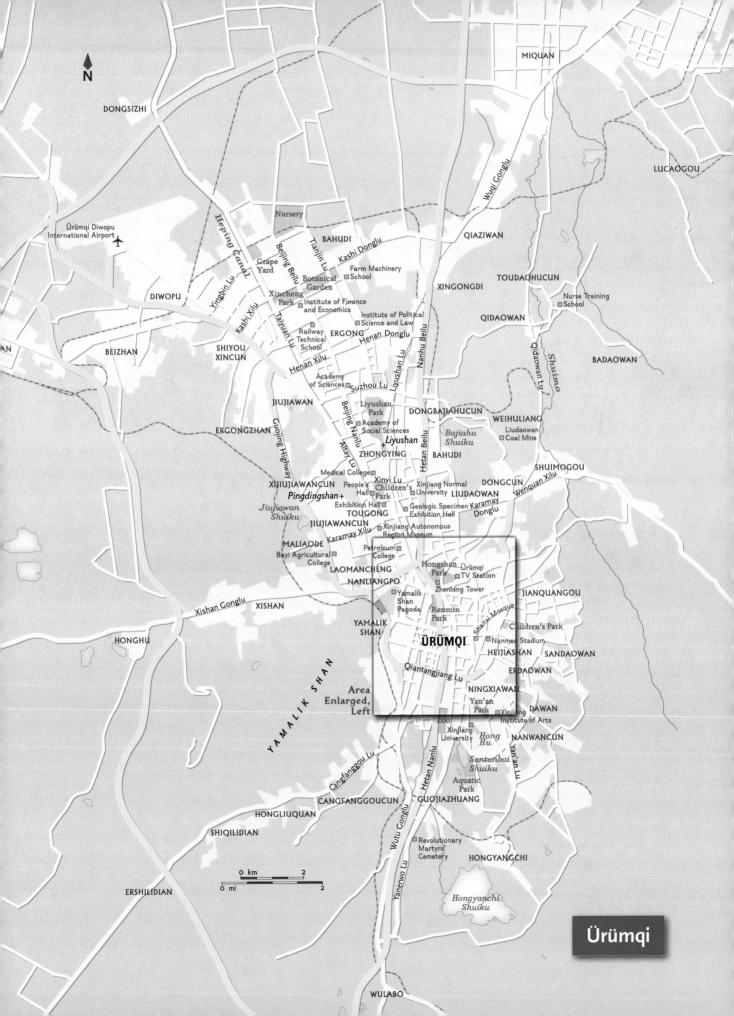

N

DONGSIZHI

MIQUAN

LUCAOGOU

Ürümqi Diwopu
International Airport

Heping Canal

Nursery

BAHUDI

QIAZIWAN

Grape
Yard

Tianjin Lu

Kashi Donglu

Botanical
Garden

Farm Machinery
School

XINGONGDI

TOUDAOHUCUN

Yingbin Lu

Beijing Beilu

Xincheng
Park

Institute of Finance
and Economics

Institute of Political
Science and Law

QIDAOWAN

Nurse Training
School

DIWOPU

Kashi Xilu

Taiyuan Lu

Railway
Technical
School

Henan Donglu

Nanhu Beilu

Shuimo

Qidaowan Lu

BADAOWAN

BEIZHAN

SHIYOU
XINCUN

Henan Xilu

ERGONG

Academy
of Sciences

Suzhou Lu

Liyushan Lu

JIUJIAWAN

Beijing Nanlu

Liyushan
Park

DONGBAJIAHUCUN

WEIHULIANG

Liudaowan
Coal Mine

ERGONGZHAN

Guojing Highway

Academy of
Social Sciences

Liyushan

ZHONGYING

*Bajiahu
Shuiku*

BAHUDI

Hetan Beilu

Altay Lu

Medical College

SHUIMOGOU

XIJIUJIAWANCUN

Xinyi Lu

People's
Hall

Children's
Park

Xinjiang Normal
University

DONGCUN

Pingdingshan

*Jiujiawan
Shuiku*

Exhibition Hall

Geologic Specimen
Exhibition Hall

Karamay
Donglu

LIUDAOWAN

Wenquan Xilu

TOUGONG

MALIAODE

JIUJIAWANCUN

Karamay Xilu

Xinjiang Autonomous
Region Museum

Bayi Agricultural
College

Petroleum
College

LAOMANCHENG

Hongshan
Park

Ürümqi
TV Station

JIANQUANGOU

NANLIANGPO

Yamalik
Shan
Pagoda

Zhenlong Tower

Renmin
Park

Shanxi Mosque

Children's Park

Xishan Gonglu

XISHAN

YAMALIK
SHAN

ÜRÜMQI

Nanmen Stadium

SANDAOWAN

HONGHU

HEIJIASHAN

Qiantangjiang Lu

ERDAOWAN

YAMALIK SHAN

Area
Enlarged,
Left

NINGXIAWAN

Yan'an
Park

DAWAN

Xinjiang
Institute of Arts

Zoo

Xinjiang
University

*Hong
Hu*

NANWANCUN

Cangfanggou Lu

Hetan Nanlu

*Santunbai
Shuiku*

Yan'an Lu

CANGFANGGOUCUN

Wutu Gonglu

GUOJIAZHUANG

Aquatic
Park

HONGLIUQUAN

SHIQILIDIAN

Yanerwo Lu

Revolutionary
Martyrs'
Cemetery

HONGYANGCHI

0 km 2

0 mi 2

ERSHILIDIAN

*Hongyanchi
Shuiku*

WULABO

Ürümqi

Xi'an
西安

POPULATION	CITY PROPER 4,235,200
	METRO AREA 4,931,100
AREA	1,066 SQUARE KILOMETERS
	412 SQUARE MILES
LATITUDE	34° 15' 30" N
LONGITUDE	108° 55' 43" E
ELEVATION	400 METERS, 1,311 FEET
TEMPERATURE	DAILY AVERAGE (JANUARY) -0.6°C, 30.9°F
	DAILY AVERAGE (JULY) 27°C, 80.6°F
PRECIPITATION	MONTHLY AVERAGE (JANUARY) 6.7 MILLIMETERS, 0.26 INCHES
	MONTHLY AVERAGE (JULY) 91.7 MILLIMETERS, 3.61 INCHES
TIME ZONE	+8 HOURS UTC (COORDINATED UNIVERSAL TIME)
REGIONAL GOVERNMENT	SHAANXI PROVINCE

Known as one of the four great cities of the ancient world in company with Athens, Rome, and Cairo, Xi'an is the capital of Shaanxi province and one of China's great magnets for tourism.

With more than 3,000 years of history behind it, and having served as capital for 13 imperial dynasties, Xi'an and nearby sites have seen the entire sweep of Chinese civilization. In 221 B.C.E. Qin Shi Huang Di unified China by subjugating lesser states. A book-burning tyrant, he nevertheless reformed politics, commerce, farming, and culture and began linking existing forts with stone barriers—the forerunner of the Great Wall.

Emperor Qin planned to have an army accompany him to the afterlife and commissioned some 6,000 full-size terra-cotta statues of warriors and their mounts, uncovered in 1974 in a great archaeological find. (For all his preparation, Qin's dynasty fell after only 15 years.)

Then followed the Han Dynasty, 206 B.C.E. to 220 C.E., a time when the Roman Republic and later Empire were at their height. As the eastern terminus of the Silk Road, Xi'an supplied wealthy Romans with lustrous robes and other luxuries. Trade came from the west, and over time many other peoples arrived, including persecuted Nestorian Christians, Buddhists, and Muslims, who still maintain a presence in the city.

Temples, mausoleums, towers, walls, pagodas, and more draw many visitors who may pay little attention to the vitality of daily life. Yet the city is a musical, artistic, and intellectual center. It houses an economic and technological development zone. The world's second-largest petroleum company is greatly expanding its solar research and development activities in Xi'an. An international seminar on propellants, explosives, and pyrotechnics is scheduled. (China invented black powder and has long been expert in fireworks.) A local farmer has put masks on his goats so that when he herds them into the city for milking they won't eat plants and garbage on their way. Ingenuity finds a way in Xi'an.

Xi'an's Bell Tower and main square at dusk

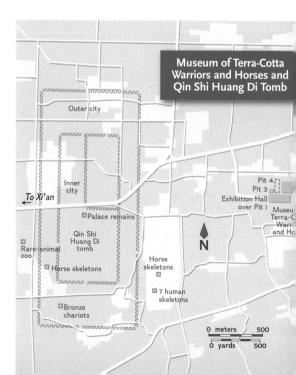

Museum of Terra-Cotta Warriors and Horses and Qin Shi Huang Di Tomb

Outer city

Inner city

To Xi'an

Palace remains

Qin Shi Huang Di tomb

Rare-animal zoo

Horse skeletons

Horse skeletons

7 human skeletons

Bronze chariots

Pit 4
Pit 3
Exhibition Hall over Pit I
Museu Terra-C Warr and Ho

N

| 0 meters | 500 |
| 0 yards | 500 |

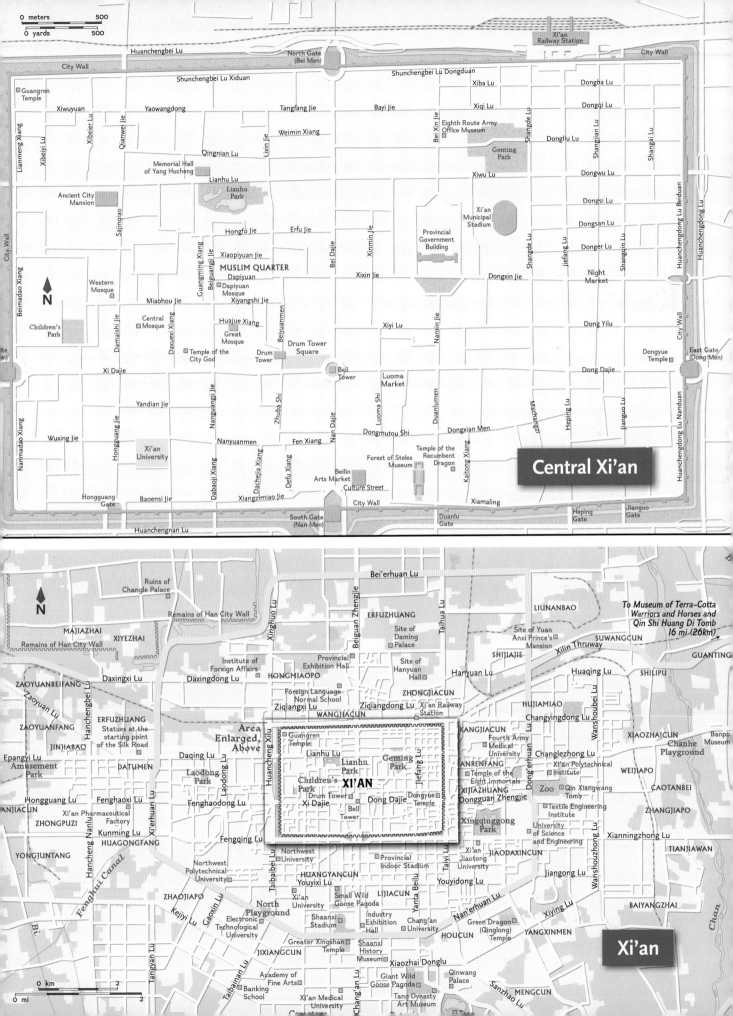

Central Xi'an

0 meters 500
0 yards 500

City Wall · Huanchengbei Lu · North Gate (Bei Men) · Xi'an Railway Station · City Wall

Guangren Temple · Xiwuyuan · Yaowangdong · Shunchengbei Lu Xiduan · Tangfang Jie · Bayi Jie · Xiba Lu · Dongba Lu

Lianmeng Xiang · Xibeiyi Lu · Xibeier Lu · Qianwei Jie · Weimin Xiang · Bei Xin Jie · Xiqi Lu · Dongqi Lu · Shangde Lu · Dongliu Lu · Shangjian Lu · Shangai Lu

Qingnian Lu · Lixin Jie · Eighth Route Army Office Museum

Memorial Hall of Yang Hucheng · Lianhu Lu · Geming Park · Xiwu Lu · Dongwu Lu

Ancient City Mansion · Lianhu Park · Dongsi Lu · Dongsan Lu

Sajinqiao · Hongfu Jie · Erfu Jie · Bei Dajie · Xinmin Jie · Provincial Government Building · Xi'an Municipal Stadium · Donger Lu

Beimdao Xiang · Xiaopiyun Jie · MUSLIM QUARTER · Guangming Xiang · Beiguangji Jie · Dapiyuan · Xixin Jie · Jiefang Lu · Shangde Lu · Shangqin Lu · Huanchengdong Lu Beiduan · Huanchendong Lu

Western Mosque · Dapiyuan Mosque · Dongxin Jie · Night Market

Children's Park · Miaohou Jie · Xiyangshi Jie · Central Mosque · Daxuexi Xiang · Damaishi Jie · Huajue Xiang · Beiyuanmen · Xiyi Lu · Nanxin Jie · Dong Yilu

Great Mosque · Temple of the City God · Drum Tower · Drum Tower Square · City Wall · Dongyue Temple · East Gate (Dong Men)

Xi Dajie · Bell Tower · Luoma Market · Dong Dajie

Yandian Jie · Nanguangji Jie · Zhuba Shi · Nan Dajie · Luoma Shi · Duanlumen · Machangzi · Heping Lu · Jianguo Lu

Nanmdao Xiang · Hongguang Jie · Honggang Jie · Nanyuanmen · Fen Xiang · Dongmutou Shi · Dongxian Men

Wuxing Jie · Nanyuanmen · Dachejia Xiang · Defu Xiang · Xi'an University

Honggguang Gate · Baoensi Jie · Dabaoji Xiang · Xiangzimiao Jie · Beilin Arts Market · Culture Street · Forest of Steles Museum · Temple of the Recumbent Dragon · Kaitong Xiang · Xiamaling · City Wall · Heping Gate · Jianguo Gate

South Gate (Nan Men) · Duanlu Gate

Huanchengnan Lu

Xi'an

0 km 2
0 mi 2

N

Bei'erhuan Lu

Ruins of Changle Palace · Remains of Han City Wall · Xinghuo Lu · Beiguan Zhengjie · ERFUZHUANG · Taihua Lu · LIUNANBAO · To Museum of Terra-Cotta Warriors and Horses and Qin Shi Huang Di Tomb 16 mi (26km)

MAJIAZHAI · XIYEZHAI · Remains of Han City Wall · Site of Daming Palace · Site of Yuan Anxi Prince's Mansion · SUWANGCUN · Xilin Thruway · GUANTING

Institute of Foreign Affairs · Site of Hanyuan Hall · SHIJIAJIE · SHILIPU

ZAOYUANBEIFANG · Daxingxi Lu · Daxingdong Lu · HONGMIAOPO · Provincial Exhibition Hall · Hanyuan Lu · Huaqing Lu

Hanchengbei Lu · Foreign Language Normal School · ZHONGJIACUN · HUJIAMIAO · Changyingdong Lu

ZAOYUANFANG · ERFUZHUANG Statues at the starting point of the Silk Road · Ziqiangxi Lu · Ziqiangdong Lu · Xi'an Railway Station · KANGJIACUN · XIAOZHAICUN · Chanhe Playground · Banpo Museum

JINHABAO · Daqing Lu · WANGJIACUN · Fourth Army Medical University · Changlezhong Lu · Xi'an Polytechnic Institute · WEIJIAPO

Epangyi Lu · Amusement Park · DATUMEN · Laodong Park · Area Enlarged, Above · Guangren Temple · Lianhu Lu · Lianhu Park · Geming Park · Tiefang Lu · NANRENFANG · Temple of the Eight Immortals · Zoo · Qin Xiangwang Tomb · CAOTANBEI

Honggguang Lu · Fenghaoxi Lu · Laodong Lu · Children's Park · XI'AN · Dongwu Lu · XIJIAZHUANG · Dongguan Zhengjie · University of Science and Engineering · ZHANGJIAPO

ANJIACUN · Xi'an Pharmaceutical Factory · Fenghaodong Lu · Drum Tower · Xi Dajie · Dong Dajie · Dongyue Temple · Xingqinggong Park · Textile Engineering Institute

ZHONGPUZI · Kunming Lu · HUAGONGFANG · Bell Tower · Jiaodaxincun · Xianningzhong Lu · TIANJIAWAN

YONGJUNTANG · Fengqing Lu · Northwest University · Xi'an Jiaotong University · Jiangong Lu

Hancheng Nanlu · Xierhuan Lu · Taibaibei Lu · HUANGYANCUN · Youyixi Lu · Provincial Indoor Stadium · Taiyi Lu · Youyidong Lu · Nan'erhuan Lu · XIYING Lu · BAIYANGZHAI

Fenghui Canal · ZHAOJIAPO · Gaoxin Lu · Xi'an University · LIJIACUN · Yanta Beilu

Kejiyi Lu · North Playground · Small Wild Goose Pagoda · Chang'an University · Green Dragon (Qinglong) Temple · YANGXINMEN

Tangyan Lu · Electronic Technological University · Shaanxi Stadium · Industry Exhibition Hall · HOUCUN

JIXIANGCUN · Greater Xingshan Temple · Shaanxi History Museum · Giant Wild Goose Pagoda · MENGCUN

Taibainan Lu · Academy of Fine Arts · Banking School · Xi'an Medical University · Xiaozhai Donglu · Qinwang Palace · Tang Dynasty Art Museum · Sanzhao Lu · Chan

Chang'an Lu

History

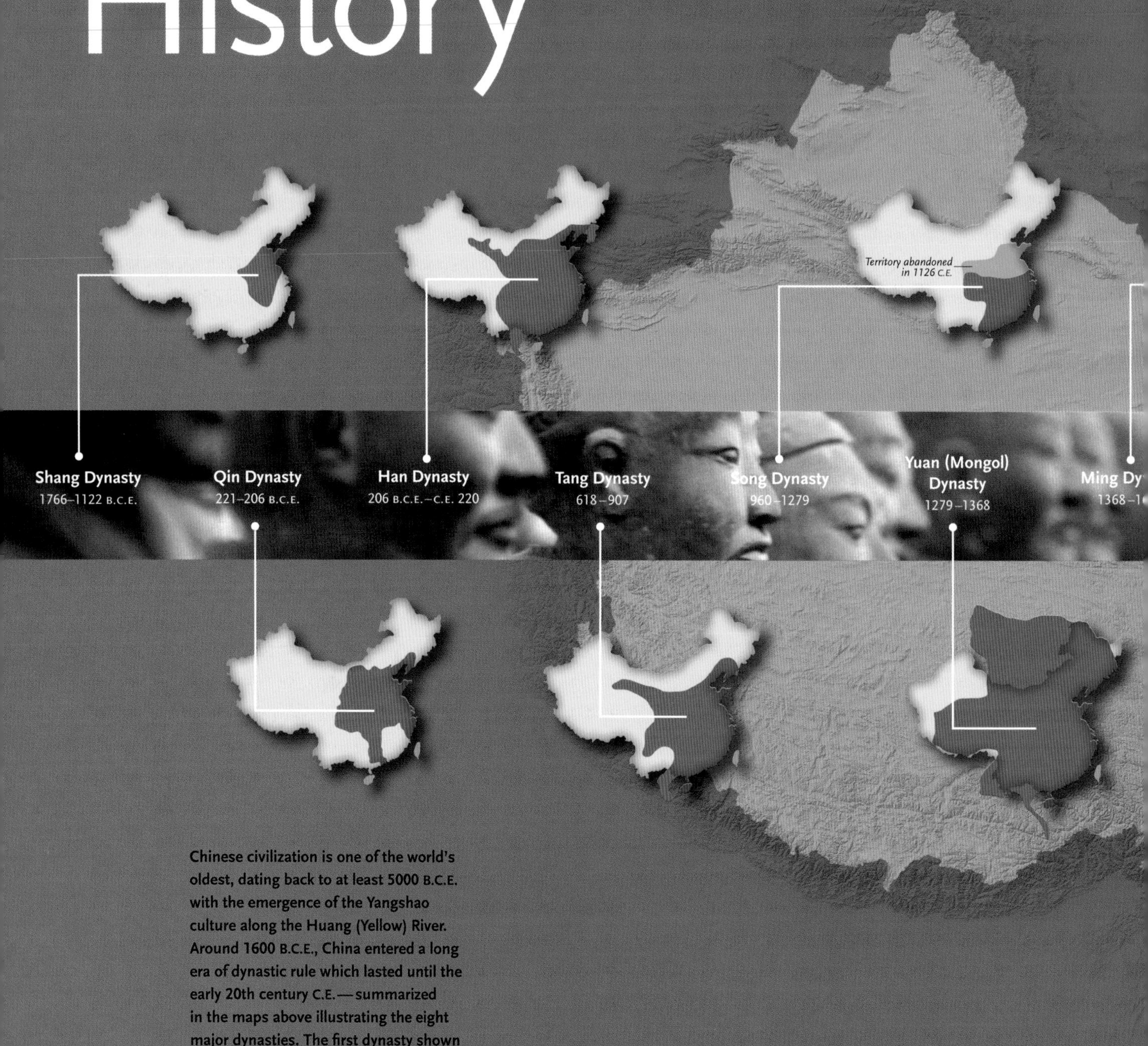

Shang Dynasty
1766–1122 B.C.E.

Qin Dynasty
221–206 B.C.E.

Han Dynasty
206 B.C.E.–C.E. 220

Tang Dynasty
618–907

Song Dynasty
960–1279

Yuan (Mongol) Dynasty
1279–1368

Ming Dy
1368–1

Territory abandoned in 1126 C.E.

Chinese civilization is one of the world's oldest, dating back to at least 5000 B.C.E. with the emergence of the Yangshao culture along the Huang (Yellow) River. Around 1600 B.C.E., China entered a long era of dynastic rule which lasted until the early 20th century C.E.—summarized in the maps above illustrating the eight major dynasties. The first dynasty shown here, the Shang, is the oldest for which scholars have found an accurate written history.

A more detailed time line on pages 102 to 105 covers China's recent history, beginning with the Boxer Rebellion in 1900 and continuing to the present.

Above: Terra-cotta warriors buried with the Emperor of Qin, ca 210 B.C.E., Xi'an

g (Manchu)
Dynasty
1644–1912

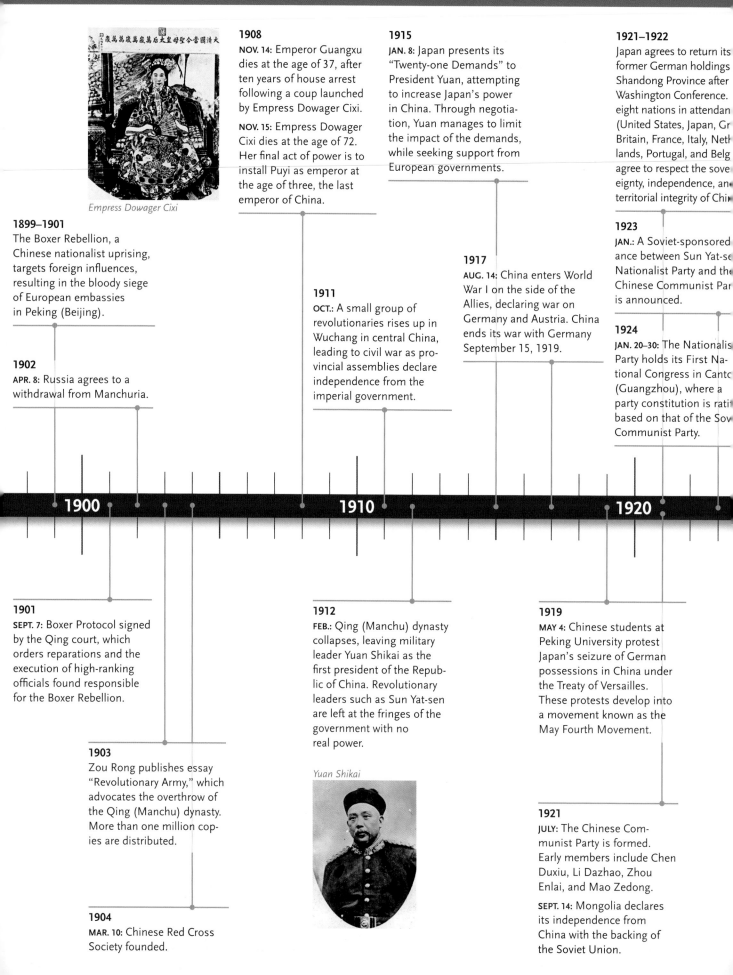

Empress Dowager Cixi

1908

NOV. 14: Emperor Guangxu dies at the age of 37, after ten years of house arrest following a coup launched by Empress Dowager Cixi.

NOV. 15: Empress Dowager Cixi dies at the age of 72. Her final act of power is to install Puyi as emperor at the age of three, the last emperor of China.

1915

JAN. 8: Japan presents its "Twenty-one Demands" to President Yuan, attempting to increase Japan's power in China. Through negotiation, Yuan manages to limit the impact of the demands, while seeking support from European governments.

1921–1922

Japan agrees to return its former German holdings Shandong Province after Washington Conference. eight nations in attendan (United States, Japan, Gr Britain, France, Italy, Neth lands, Portugal, and Belg agree to respect the sove eignty, independence, an territorial integrity of Chi

1899–1901

The Boxer Rebellion, a Chinese nationalist uprising, targets foreign influences, resulting in the bloody siege of European embassies in Peking (Beijing).

1911

OCT.: A small group of revolutionaries rises up in Wuchang in central China, leading to civil war as provincial assemblies declare independence from the imperial government.

1917

AUG. 14: China enters World War I on the side of the Allies, declaring war on Germany and Austria. China ends its war with Germany September 15, 1919.

1923

JAN.: A Soviet-sponsored ance between Sun Yat-se Nationalist Party and the Chinese Communist Par is announced.

1902

APR. 8: Russia agrees to a withdrawal from Manchuria.

1924

JAN. 20–30: The Nationalis Party holds its First National Congress in Canto (Guangzhou), where a party constitution is rati based on that of the Sov Communist Party.

1900   **1910**   **1920**

1901

SEPT. 7: Boxer Protocol signed by the Qing court, which orders reparations and the execution of high-ranking officials found responsible for the Boxer Rebellion.

1912

FEB.: Qing (Manchu) dynasty collapses, leaving military leader Yuan Shikai as the first president of the Republic of China. Revolutionary leaders such as Sun Yat-sen are left at the fringes of the government with no real power.

Yuan Shikai

1919

MAY 4: Chinese students at Peking University protest Japan's seizure of German possessions in China under the Treaty of Versailles. These protests develop into a movement known as the May Fourth Movement.

1903

Zou Rong publishes essay "Revolutionary Army," which advocates the overthrow of the Qing (Manchu) dynasty. More than one million copies are distributed.

1921

JULY: The Chinese Communist Party is formed. Early members include Chen Duxiu, Li Dazhao, Zhou Enlai, and Mao Zedong.

SEPT. 14: Mongolia declares its independence from China with the backing of the Soviet Union.

1904

MAR. 10: Chinese Red Cross Society founded.

12: Sun Yat-sen, founder
e Nationalist Party
mintang), dies at the age
. Leadership of the party
fers to Chiang Kai-shek.

30: British police fire
Chinese students
ged in an anti-imperialist
onstration, killing 12.

23: French and Brit-
narines in Canton
ngzhou) fire upon an
imperialist parade of
ents and military cadets,
g 52. This and earlier
nes prompt a strike and
ott against Britain.

*Chiang Kai-shek and
Sun Yat-sen, 1924*

1927

APR.: After the joint Nationalist-
Communist Northern Expe-
dition's seizure of Shanghai,
Chiang Kai-shek launches a
coup against his Communist
allies, rounding up and execut-
ing thousands of leftists and
labor leaders.

1934

More than 100,000 Chinese
Communists begin a 6,000-
mile trek through some
of China's most difficult
terrain that has come to be
known as the Long March.
Only about 8,000 ultimately
reach the central province
of Shaanxi. The Long March
results in the emergence of
Mao Zedong as the undis-
puted party leader.

1941

American Volunteer Group
nicknamed "The Flying
Tigers" is established, defending China against
Japanese forces.

DEC. 7: Japan attacks Pearl
Harbor, drawing the United
States into the war in the
Pacific.

DEC. 25: Japan captures Hong
Kong, drawing Great Britain
into the war in the Pacific.

1945

SEPT. 2: Japan formally surren-
ders the war. Nationalist Chinese troops race to take over
Japanese-controlled areas
before the Communists.

1950

JUNE: Agrarian Reform Law
passes, formally redistributing land from landlords to
the peasants. It also makes
provisions for redistributing
the wealth of many of the
families central to the
Nationalist movement.

OCT.: China enters the
Korean War against United
Nations forces in defense
of North Korea.

OCT.: China invades Tibet.

1930 — **1940** — **1950**

---

rge of peasant revolts,
y Communists and Na-
alist Party leftists, widens
within the party.

10: Chiang Kai-shek
Nationalist Party leaders
ally establish a new
onal Government of
Republic of China,
its capital at Nanking
njing).

1931

NOV. 7: Chinese Communists
establish a rival government
in central China, the Jiangxi
Soviet. Through the practice
of redistributing land, they
gain the support of the
poorer classes.

1936

DEC. 12: Chiang Kai-shek is
detained by Communists
and his own general in
Sian (Xi'an). He is released
when he agrees to an alliance against the Japanese
invaders.

1937

JULY 7: Marco Polo Bridge
Incident marks the begin-
ning of World War II in Asia.

NOV.–DEC.: Japanese take
Shanghai and the capital city
of Nanking (Nanjing), killing
hundreds of thousands of
civilians. The bombing of
Shanghai is the first instance
of an aerial bombing of an
urban population in World
War II.

1946

U.S.-mediated negotiations
between the Communists
and the Nationalist government result in failure. Civil
war spreads throughout
the country.

Mao Zedong, 1950

1949

APR. 24: Communist forces
occupy the capital city of
Nanking (Nanjing).

OCT. 1: Mao Zedong declares
the establishment of the
People's Republic of China
in Peking (Beijing), which
becomes the new capital.

Nationalist government
retreats to the island of
Taiwan, where it imposes
martial law for the next
38 years.

Dalai Lama

1958
The Great Leap Forward, a campaign aimed at rapid industrialization and collectivization of agriculture, begins. Its aim is to achieve the level of economic development of Western countries by mobilizing China's large population to increase output under the leadership of political cadres.

1953
China's first modern census shows the population to be approximately 583 million.

1959
MAR.: People in Tibet revolt against the Chinese occupation but are defeated. The Dalai Lama, Tibet's spiritual and temporal leader, flees to India.

1954
SEPT.: The first constitution of the People's Republic of China is adopted at the first meeting of the National People's Congress.

1959–1961
Millions of people starve to death due to a combination of natural disasters and the policies of the Great Leap Forward campaign.

1966–1976
Mao Zedong launches the Cultural Revolution, a movement aimed at reviving China's revolutionary spirit and opposing efforts at reform and "revisionism." China is thrown into upheaval, as groups of Red Guards seize power from local officials and harass and abuse those thought to be disloyal to Mao's vision of socialism.

1966
AUG.–NOV.: Responding to Mao's call to "Bombard the Headquarters," students form groups of Red Guards to seize power in schools and government offices. Ten million youths attend rallies in Peking (Beijing) and spread the revolution throughout the country. Classes are suspended and schools and universities closed.

1967
JUNE 14: China detonates its first hydrogen bomb.

1971
JULY: Henry Kissinger secretly meets with Mao Zedong in Beijing in an effort to diffuse tensions between the U.S. and China.

SEPT.: Lin Biao, Minister of Defense, dies in a plane crash while trying to flee the country after an apparent coup plot was uncovered.

OCT.: The UN General Assembly votes to give the People's Republic of China the seat held by the rival government in Taiwan, the Republic of China.

1975
Zhou Enlai outlines a program of Four Modern[tions (agriculture, indust][national defense, science

1976
SEPT. 9: Mao Zedong dies[the age of 82. Hua Guof[is elevated to the positio[premier.

1950   **1960**   **1970**

1956
"Hundred Flowers" campaign launched, encouraging free debate and inquiry in an apparent effort to repair ties with the intellectual class. This is quickly reversed, and the party turns against those who speak out and others deemed "anti-revolutionary" in the "Anti-Rightist Campaign" of 1957–58.

1962
NOV.: Chinese troops cross into India's Himalayan territory following a border dispute. After a swift victory, China pulls back across the border and establishes a demilitarized zone.

1964
MAY: *Quotations of Chairman Mao* is first published, later dubbed *Little Red Book* in the West.

OCT. 16: China performs its first successful nuclear test at Lop Nur in western China.

1969
MAR.: The government directs that all schools be reopened.

1970
APR. 24: China launches its first successful satellite.

SEPT.: Universities finally reopen, four years after they were closed at the start of the Cultural Revolution.

1972
FEB. 21–28: Richard Nixon[the first U.S. President t[visit the People's Republ[China, meets with Chair[Mao Zedong.

1974
Archaeologists uncover t[terra cotta army, a group[about 8,000 life-size Terra[cotta figures of warriors a[horses, near Sian (Xi'an).[They were buried with the[first Emperor of Qin in[210–209 B.C.E.

Red Army soldiers reading from Quotations of Chairman Mao

Terra-cotta warriors

1984

APR.: China designates 14 more special economic zones in large coastal cities, opening them to foreign trade and investment.

1997

FEB. 19: Deng Xiaoping dies at the age of 92.

JULY 1: Hong Kong becomes a Special Administrative Region of China after being controlled by the U.K. for more than 150 years.

2003

MAR.: China experiences an outbreak of severe acute respiratory syndrome (SARS), an atypical pneumonia, which ultimately infects more than 8,000 people and kills more than 750 worldwide.

OCT. 15: China sends its first manned spacecraft into orbit.

[

...munist Party leaders ...e economic and tech-...gical development their ...priorities, abandoning ...Maoist emphasis on ...ical orthodoxy and ...tarian principles.

...979

...policy penalizing married ...ouples for having more than ...ne child is adopted in an ef-...ort to address overpopulation.

...pecial economic zones are ...reated in the cities of ...henzhen, Zhuhai, Shantou, ...nd Xiamen to encourage ...oreign investment.

...he U.S. switches its official ...ecognition of the government ...f China from the Republic of ...hina to the People's Republic ...f China. Congress passes ...he Taiwan Relations Act in an ...ttempt to maintain unofficial ...es with the ROC.

1989

APR.–JUNE: Students demanding civil liberties and measures to curb corruption occupy Tiananmen Square in Beijing. As Mikhail Gorbachev arrives in Beijing, the foreign press displays the protests for the world to see.

JUNE 3–4: The government orders the army to use force to quell the demonstrations, resulting in hundreds of deaths, mostly among ordinary residents of Beijing who attempt to resist the military action.

Jiang Zemin succeeds Zhao Ziyang as the General Secretary of the Communist Party of China.

Chinese activist blocks tanks, Tiananmen Square, 1989

2006

MAY: The main wall of the Three Gorges Dam on the Yangtze River is completed. When fully operational in 2009, it should produce more than 18,000 megawatts of electricity and allow larger vessels to travel upriver. It has flooded more than 1,200 towns and villages, displaced more than one million people, and caused widespread water contamination.

1980 **1990** **2000**

...–1980

...by Deng Xiaoping, ...ical reformers release ...ons of political ...oners from forced-...r camps.

...reform movement gains ...nentum, forcing many ...ists (including Premier ...Guofeng) out of office.

Deng Xiaoping

1990

DEC. 19: Shanghai Stock Exchange opens, the first in China since the Communist takeover.

1982

China's population exceeds one billion.

1983–1986

Mass arrests and swift trials result in an estimated 10,000 executions as officials carry out an anti-crime campaign.

1999

DEC. 20: Macau reverts to China, as a Special Administrative Region, after more than 400 years of Portuguese rule.

1995

MAR.: Jiang Zemin elected President of China.

Jiang Zemin

2001

JULY 13: Beijing is announced as the host of the 2008 Summer Olympics.

2002

Jiang Zemin steps down as President and General Secretary of the Communist Party and is succeeded by Hu Jintao.

DEC. 11: China is admitted to the World Trade Organization.

2005

OCT. 12: China's second manned space mission takes off from the Jiuquan Satellite Launch Center in Nei Mongol province.

2007

JAN. 11: China shoots down one of its own aging weather satellites, proving its capability of destroying enemy spy satellites.

Appendix

Pronunciation Guide, Currency, Abbreviations, and Metric Conversions

GUIDE TO PRONOUNCING PLACE-NAMES IN CHINA

A VISITOR TO China will often see signs identifying places in Chinese characters as well as in the Roman, or Latin, alphabet. There are two systems for transliterating Chinese words into Roman letters: Pinyin and Wade-Giles. Pinyin was developed in the People's Republic of China in the 1950s to romanize Chinese and minority languages, superseding the Wade-Giles system developed in the mid-19th century. Pinyin is now used internationally, even supplanting the traditional use of Wade-Giles on Taiwan. Use of both Pinyin and Wade-Giles is common on Taiwan, where Taipei, in Wade-Giles, is known as Taibei in Pinyin.

The word Pinyin literally means "putting together the sounds." Pinyin more closely represents the spoken sounds of standard Mandarin Chinese, giving it an advantage over the Wade-Giles method. This is why we use "Beijing" (Pinyin name) and not "Peking" because Chinese call the city "bay-JING," not "pay-KING." Fortunately, many letters are pronounced as they are in English, and there are fixed rules, for example "g" always sounds like "good," never like "germ." Unfortunately, the sounds chosen for some letters do not correspond to the usual English sounds: "X" in Xinjiang has a "sh" sound to produce "shin-JEEAHNG." Below are guides to help pronounce certain letters to match Chinese Pinyin sounds:

GEOGRAPHIC NAMES

中国

The Chinese script (at left) consists of two characters that are the two syllables for Zhongguo, the Pinyin name for China. Zhongguo (meaning "central state") is pronounced **JAWNG-gwo**. The following list provides a pronunciation guide for some major geographic names in China:

CITIES

Beijing **bay-JING** (means "northern capital")

Chengdu **chung-DOO**

Chongqing **chong-CHING**

Guangzhou **gwahng-JOH**

Guilin **gway-LIN**

Hangzhou **hahng-JOH**

Kunming **koon-MING**

Lanzhou **lahn-JOH**

Nanjing **nahn-JING** (means "southern capital")

Qingdao **ching-DOW**

Shanghai **shang-HYE**

Shenzhen **shun-JUHN**

Shenyang **shun-YAHNG**

Tianjin **tyahn-JEEN**

Wuhan **woo-HAHN**

Xi'an **shee-AHN**

Xianggang **SHYAHNG-gahng** (Pinyin name for Hong Kong)

RIVERS

Chang Jiang **chang-JEEAHNG** (means "long river," Pinyin name for Yangtze River)

Huang **HWAWNG** (means "yellow")

Lancang **LAHN-TSAHNG** (Pinyin name for Mekong River)

Xi **SHEE** (means "west")

MOUNTAINS

Qomolangma **cho-mo-LAHNG-mah** (Pinyin name for Mount Everest)

Tian Shan **TYAHN SHAHN** (means "heavenly mountains")

PROVINCES & REGIONS

Anhui **ahn-HWAY**

Fujian **foo-JYAN**

Gansu **gahn-SOO**

Guangdong **gwahng-DONG** (means "eastern expanses")

Guangxi **gwahng-shee** (means "western expanses")

Guizhou **gway-JOH**

Hainan **HYE-NAHN**

Hebei **huh-BAY**

Heilongjiang **hay-long-JEEAHNG**

Henan **heh-NAHN**

Hubei **hoo-BAY**

Hunan **hoo-NAHN**

Jiangsu **jeeahng-SOO**

Jiangxi **jeeahng-SHEE**

Jilin **jee-LIN**

Liaoning **leeau-NING**

Nei Mongol **nay MONG-goal** (Pinyin name for Inner Mongolia)

Ningxia **NING-sheeah**

Qinghai **ching-HYE**

Shaanxi **shahn-SHEE**

Shandong **shahn-DONG**

Shanxi **shahn-SHEE**

Sichuan **seh-CHWAHN** (Pinyin spelling for Szechwan)

Xinjiang **shin-JEEAHNG**

Xizang **shee-ZAHNG** (Pinyin name for Tibet, means "western reserve")

Yunnan **yoon-NAHN**

Zhejiang **juh-JEEAHNG**

VOWELS

a ah sound as in father

ai long i sound as in die

ao ow sound as in cow

e uh sound as in but

ei ay sound as in day, or ei in weigh

i a long e sound as in he—not the sound of eye, or the i in sir after the letters c, ch, r, s, sh, z, zh

ian pronounced yen as in Tiananmen Square

o o sound as in or

ou oa sound as in boat, or oe in Joe

u u as in flute

ui way sound

CONSONANTS

c ts sound as in tsar or bats

q ch sound as in cheek

x sh sound as in show

zh j sound as in jump

*Symbol
for yuan*

CHINA'S CURRENCY

The currency of the People's Republic of China is the renminbi, or RMB (people's currency), but it is commonly called the yuan (pronounced YOU-ahn). Hong Kong uses the Hong Kong dollar, Macau the pataca, and Taiwan the new Taiwan dollar.

ABBREVIATIONS

Afghan.	*Afghanistan*	m	*meters*
B.C.E.	*Before Common Era*	mi	*miles*
C.E.	*Common Era*	Mt.-s.	*Mount-ain-s*
ft	*feet*	NT$	*new Taiwan dollar*
F	*female*	NA	*Not Available*
GDP	*Gross Domestic Product*	Pak.	*Pakistan*
Ha	*hectares*	Pen.	*Peninsula*
HK$	*Hong Kong dollar*	Ra.	*Range*
int.	*integrated*	R.	*River*
I.-s.	*Island-s*	S.A.R.	*Special Administrative Region*
km	*kilometers*	sq	*square*
Kyrg.	*Kyrgyzstan*	Taj.	*Tajikistan*
MOP	*Macanese pataca*	Univ.	*University*
M	*male*	Uzb.	*Uzbekistan*

CONVERSION FROM METRIC MEASURES

SYMBOL	WHEN YOU KNOW	MULTIPLY BY	TO FIND	SYMBOL
LENGTH				
m	meters	3.28	feet	ft
km	kilometers	0.62	miles	mi
AREA				
km²	square kilometers	0.39	square miles	mi²
ha	hectares	2.47	acres	—
TEMPERATURE				
°C	degrees Celsius (Centigrade)	9/5 then add 32	degrees Fahrenheit	°F

CONVERSION TO METRIC MEASURES

SYMBOL	WHEN YOU KNOW	MULTIPLY BY	TO FIND	SYMBOL
LENGTH				
ft	feet	0.30	meters	m
mi	miles	1.61	kilometers	km
AREA				
mi²	square miles	2.59	square kilometers	km²
—	acres	0.40	hectares	ha
TEMPERATURE				
°F	degrees Fahrenheit	5/9 after subtracting 32	degrees Celsius (Centigrade)	°C

China by the Numbers

AT A GLANCE

TOTAL AREA	3,705,407 SQ MI (9,596,960 SQ KM)
POPULATION	1,313,424,000 PEOPLE
GDP PER CAPITA	$7,700
LITERACY RATE	91%
LIFE EXPECTANCY	70/73 YEARS (MALE/FEMALE)

China's land area is approximately 119% of the contiguous (lower 48) United States. The map below illustrates the comparable sizes of both countries. China and the U.S. also share a similar range of latitude, roughly 20°N to 50°N.

Geographic Comparisions and Superlatives

NATURAL FEATURES

1 **HIGHEST POINT:** Qomolangma [Mt. Everest], Xizang [Tibet] (29,035 feet/8,850 meters)

2 **LOWEST POINT:** Turpan Depression, Xinjiang Uygur (505 feet/154 meters below sea level)

3 **LENGTH OF COASTLINE:** 9,010 miles/14,500 kilometers

4 **LONGEST RIVER:** Chang Jiang [Yangtze] (3,964 mi/6,379 km)

5 **LARGEST WATERSHED:** Chang Jiang [Yangtze] (698,266 sq mi/1,808,500 sq km)

6 **LARGEST FRESHWATER LAKE:** Poyang Lake, Jiangxi (1,384 sq mi/3,585 sq km)

7 **LARGEST SALTWATER LAKE:** Qinghai Lake, Qinghai (1,790 sq mi/4,635 sq km)

8 **LARGEST WETLAND:** Sanjiang Pingyuan, Heilongjiang (208 sq mi/539 sq km)

9 **LARGEST ISLAND:** Taiwan (13,823 sq mi/35,801 sq km)

10 **HIGHEST PLATEAU:** Plateau of Tibet (average elevation 15,000 feet/4,572 meters)

11 **HIGHEST RIVER:** Yarlung Zangbo, Xizang [Tibet] (average elevation 13,000 feet/3,962 meters)

12 **DEEPEST VALLEY:** Yarlung Zangbo Grand Canyon, Xizang [Tibet] (17,657 feet/5,382 meters)

13 **LARGEST PLAIN:** North China Plain (158,000 sq mi/409,220 sq km)

14 **LARGEST WATERFALL:** Huangguoshu Falls, Guizhou (243 feet/74 meters tall; 266 feet/81 meters wide)

15 **LARGEST DESERTS:** Taklimakan, Xinjiang Uygur (125,000 sq mi/323,750 sq km); Gobi [partially in Mongolia] (500,000 sq mi/1,295,000 sq km)

16 **LARGEST CAVE:** Teng Long Dong [Soaring Dragon Cave], Hubei (1.4 billion cubic feet/40 million cubic meters)

17 **HOTTEST RECORDED TEMPERATURE:** Turpan Depression, Xinjiang Uygur (121.3°F/49.6°C)

18 **COLDEST RECORDED TEMPERATURE:** Mohe, Heilongjiang (-62.1°F/-52.3°C)

19 **HOTTEST AVERAGE TEMPERATURE:** Sanya, Hainan (77.7°F/25.4°C)

20 **COLDEST AVERAGE TEMPERATURE:** summit of Qomolangma [Mt. Everest], Xizang [Tibet] (-20.2°F/-29°C)

HUMAN FEATURES

1 **MOST POPULOUS ADMINISTRATIVE REGION:** Henan Province (93,800,000 people)

2 **MOST DENSELY POPULATED ADMINISTRATIVE REGION:** Macau, S.A.R. (44,780 per sq mi/17,309 per sq km)

3 **MOST POPULOUS CITY:** Shanghai (17,780,000 people)

4 **FASTEST GROWING CITY:** Shenzhen, Guangdong (from 337,000 in 1979 to 8,460,000 in 2006)

5 **LARGEST ADMINISTRATIVE REGION:** Xinjiang Uygur Autonomous Region (642,820 sq mi/1,664,900 sq km)

6 **SMALLEST ADMINISTRATIVE REGION:** Macau, S.A.R. (10.9 sq mi/28.2 sq km)

7 **LARGEST DEFENSE WALL:** Great Wall of China (Ming Dynasty section 1,700 mi/2,736 km long)

8 **LONGEST CANAL:** Grand Canal (1,115 mi/1,794 km)

9 **HIGHEST PAVED ROAD:** Karakoram Highway (15,397 feet/4,693 meters); "Everest Highway" [planned] (17,060 feet/5,200 meters)

10 **HIGHEST RAILROAD:** Qinghai-Tibet Railway (16,640 feet/5,072 meters)

11 **TALLEST BUILDINGS:** Taipei 101, Taiwan (1,667 feet/508 meters); Shanghai World Financial Center [under construction] (1,614 feet/492 meters)

12 **LARGEST HYDROELECTRIC DAM:** Three Gorges Dam, Hubei (22.5 gigawatt planned capacity)

13 **LONGEST BRIDGE:** Hangzhou Bay Bridge, between Shanghai and Ningbo (22.4 mi/36 km)

14 **LONGEST ROAD TUNNEL:** Zhongnanshan Tunnel, Shaanxi (11.2 mi/18.0 km)

15 **LONGEST RAIL TUNNEL:** Wushaoling Tunnel, Gansu (13.1 mi/21.1 km)

16 **LARGEST PROTECTED AREA:** Qiangtang Nature Reserve, Xizang [Tibet] (115,058 sq mi/298,000 sq km)

LAND COMPARISON

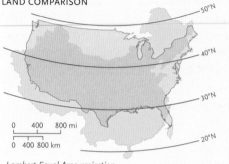

Lambert Equal Area projection

White lines represent administrative boundaries

Flags of China

9

NATIONAL FLAGS

CHINA MAY BE considered the "Mother of Flags." Thousands of years ago the Chinese developed silk, which until modern times was the most common fabric for flags — uncomplicatedly dyed and embroidered, light weight for flying easily, and durable. Although silk flags were developed by the Chinese, they used them largely for decorative, religious, and military banners because China had no national flag until the 19th century.

NATIONAL FLAGS

China long considered itself the center of the earth, believing that only foreigners needed to identify themselves. In 1863 China finally obtained a naval flag **(1)**. In 1872 that European-designed ensign was replaced by one **(2)** with traditional Chinese colors and symbols. A later version **(3)** was in use until its 1911 revolution turned China into a republic.

Several flags vied for supremacy — a red war flag with a black nine-pointed

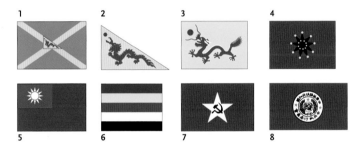

1 2 3 4

5 6 7 8

star **(4)**, the party flag of the Kuomintang/Nationalists **(5)**, and the Five-Bar Flag **(6)** flown by the republic 1912–1928. The five flag colors referred to China's main peoples — the Han (Chinese), Manchu, Mongol, Tibetan, and Muslim (Turkistani). Yellow, a Chinese dynastic color, recalled the Yellow River, one of the country's chief resources. In the civil wars from the early 1930s on, Communists, Nationalists, and others often used red flags. Among these were the military flag **(7)** and the national flag **(8)** of the Soviet Republic of China (1932–1935).

Finally on 1 October 1949 Mao Zedong proclaimed the newly unified People's Republic of China. The red and yellow of its flag **(9)** represented the revolution and the unity of the people. The symbolism of the five stars has been interpreted differently over the years. At first it was said that the large star stood for the leadership of the Communist Party. The four smaller stars were for workers, peasants, petty bourgeoisie, and "patriotic capitalists." Later the large star was interpreted as standing for the Han people and the small ones for other nationalities. Thus its current symbolism is similar to that of the national flag of 1912–1928.

OTHER CHINESE FLAGS

Almost all Chinese flags today are red and yellow. The Communist Party banner **(10)** has the traditional hammer and sickle. The star, which for many Communists symbolizes world unity, is absent. The Youth League flag **(11)** is clearly based on that of the party. The Young Pioneers has a golden flame on its flag **(12)** standing for its commitment to a Communist future for the country.

10 11 12

ADDITIONAL FLAGS

Maintaining national unity across its far flung territories has often been a problem for China. Local people have sometimes created flags and attempted to assert independence. Chinese rulers, regardless of political philosophies, have sought to unite everyone under one symbol and one ruler. Chinese recognition of special flags for Hong Kong **(13)** and for Macau **(14)** in 1997 and 1999 was considered a major concession. No other cities or units of government have that privilege. Chinese centralist policies today place an unofficial ban on distinctive flags for cities, provinces, and even organizations.

Based on religious symbols found in its military banners, Tibet created its own national flag **(15)**, in use from 1947 until 1959. Forbidden in China today, it is widely displayed abroad by those seeking to re-establish Tibetan independence. Some nationalists in Xinjiang (East Turkistan) illegally use a blue flag with a white crescent **(16)**. Mongolia and Manchuria had their own national flags as Japanese puppet states in 1932–1945.

In 1895 the island of Taiwan briefly had a national flag. When the

Chinese Communists failed to capture Taiwan in 1949, the flag of "Nationalist China" **(17)** remained in use. However, few countries today recognize Taiwan and its flag. Taiwanese favoring independence for their island have promoted various flags for a Taiwan Republic. The flag of China's People's Liberation Army (PLA) **(18)** is red with a star and the Chinese symbols for 8 and 1 commemorating its August 1st establishment in 1928.

13 14 15

16 17 18

For more military flags, see Military Strength on p. 70.

China Facts

CHINA'S ADMINISTRATIVE DIVISIONS. Currently, there are 34 province-level divisions in China, and like U.S. states, they tend to be smaller in the east and larger in the west. Four different types of province-level divisions exist:

PROVINCES (SHENG, IN CHINESE). The People's Republic of China claims 23 provinces, including Taiwan. The island of Hainan, established as a province in 1988, is China's newest province.

AUTONOMOUS REGIONS (ZIZHIQU, IN CHINESE). Five autonomous regions exist in China for the purpose of ethnic regional autonomy. The Zhuang are the most populous ethnic minority, numbering some 16 million, and most live in the Guangxi Zhuangzu Autonomous Region in southern China. Other large ethnic minorities have their own autonomous regions, such as the Hui in Ningxia Huizu, Uygurs in Xinjiang Uygur, and Mongols in Inner Mongolia (Nei Mongol, in Chinese). The newest region, Tibet (Xizang, in Chinese), was created in 1965.

MUNICIPALITIES (SHI, IN CHINESE). Four cities report directly to the central government in Beijing with province-level status: Beijing, Tianjin, Shanghai, and Chongqing. The newest municipality, Chongqing, was carved from eastern Sichuan Province in 1997.

SPECIAL ADMINISTRATIVE REGIONS (S.A.R.). Hong Kong and Macau constitute China's two special administrative regions, which are designed to provide a high degree of political and economic autonomy. Hong Kong became the first S.A.R. in 1997 when it was restored to Chinese sovereignty, after more than 150 years of British rule. Macau followed in 1999, ending more than 400 years of Portuguese administration.

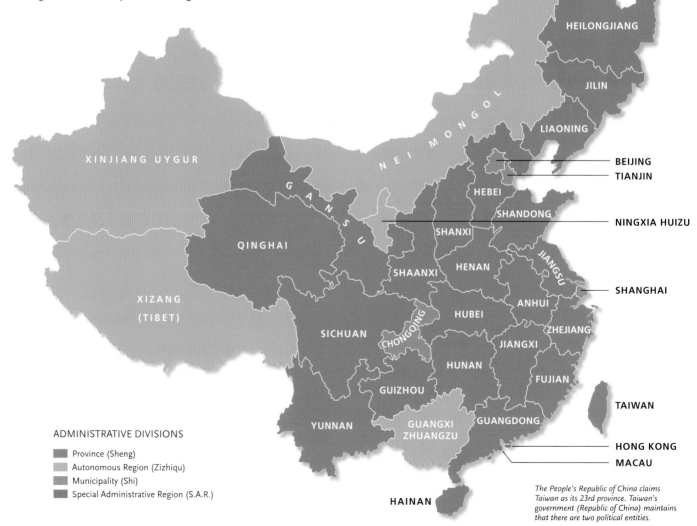

ADMINISTRATIVE DIVISIONS

- Province (Sheng)
- Autonomous Region (Zizhiqu)
- Municipality (Shi)
- Special Administrative Region (S.A.R.)

The People's Republic of China claims Taiwan as its 23rd province. Taiwan's government (Republic of China) maintains that there are two political entities.

ANHUI

Land area	140,126 sq km (54,103 sq mi)
Population	61,200,000
Capital	Hefei 1,424,800
Population density (per sq km)	437
Population growth 2000-05 (%)	2.2
Life expectancy	M 70.2, F 73.6
Ethnic minorities (% of counties)	0.0
GDP per capita	8,675 yuan (1,055 US$)
Area as cropland (%)	65.5
Leading agriculture	rapeseed, hemp, sesame
Leading industry	refrigerators, washing machines
Change in vehicles 2000-05 (%)	126.1
Water use per capita (cubic m)	340.9
College students per 1,000 people	11.1
Foreign tourist visits	410,600

BEIJING

Land area	16,411 sq km (6,336 sq mi)
Population	15,380,000
Capital	Beijing 7,724,900
Population density (per sq km)	937
Population growth 2000-05 (%)	11.3
Life expectancy	M 74.3, F 78.0
Ethnic minorities (% of counties)	0.0
GDP per capita	45,444 yuan (5,526 US$)
Area as cropland (%)	19.4
Leading agriculture	apples, pears
Leading industry	mobile phones, motor vehicles
Change in vehicles 2000-05 (%)	200.2
Water use per capita (cubic m)	225.0
College students per 1,000 people	65.8
Foreign tourist visits	3,116,200

CHONGQING

Land area	82,269 sq km (31,764 sq mi)
Population	27,980,000
Capital	Chongqing 4,306,900
Population density (per sq km)	340
Population growth 2000-05 (%)	-9.4
Life expectancy	M 69.8, F 73.9
Ethnic minorities (% of counties)	10.0
GDP per capita	10,982 yuan (1,336 US$)
Area as cropland (%)	41.9
Leading agriculture	tubers, tobacco
Leading industry	motor vehicles, air conditioners
Change in vehicles 2000-05 (%)	300.5
Water use per capita (cubic m)	255.1
College students per 1,000 people	14.7
Foreign tourist visits	418,100

FUJIAN

Land area	124,016 sq km (47,883 sq mi)
Population	35,350,000
Capital	Fuzhou 1,224,800
Population density (per sq km)	285
Population growth 2000-05 (%)	1.8
Life expectancy	M 70.3, F 75.1
Ethnic minorities (% of counties)	0.0
GDP per capita	18,646 yuan (2,268 US$)
Area as cropland (%)	20.0
Leading agriculture	citrus, tea, bananas
Leading industry	hydropower, chemical fiber
Change in vehicles 2000-05 (%)	177.3
Water use per capita (cubic m)	530.2
College students per 1,000 people	14.3
Foreign tourist visits	723,600

GANSU

Land area	404,091 sq km (156,020 sq mi)
Population	25,940,000
Capital	Lanzhou 1,444,400
Population density (per sq km)	64
Population growth 2000-05 (%)	1.2
Life expectancy	M 66.8, F 68.3
Ethnic minorities (% of counties)	24.4
GDP per capita	7,477 yuan (909 US$)
Area as cropland (%)	9.2
Leading agriculture	beetroots, tubers, apples
Leading industry	int. circuits, hydropower
Change in vehicles 2000-05 (%)	59.8
Water use per capita (cubic m)	475.5
College students per 1,000 people	12.1
Foreign tourist visits	172,000

GUANGDONG

Land area	179,757 sq km (69,405 sq mi)
Population	91,940,000
Capital	Guangzhou 3,162,200
Population density (per sq km)	511
Population growth 2000-05 (%)	6.4
Life expectancy	M 70.8, F 75.9
Ethnic minorities (% of counties)	2.5
GDP per capita	24,435 yuan (2,972 US$)
Area as cropland (%)	26.8
Leading agriculture	bananas, sugarcane, citrus
Leading industry	televisions, air conditioners
Change in vehicles 2000-05 (%)	186.1
Water use per capita (cubic m)	500.7
College students per 1,000 people	14.6
Foreign tourist visits	4,765,300

GUANGXI ZHUANGZU

Land area	237,558 sq km (91,722 sq mi)
Population	46,600,000
Capital	Nanning 807,400
Population density (per sq km)	196
Population growth 2000-05 (%)	3.8
Life expectancy	M 69.1, F 73.8
Ethnic minorities (% of counties)	100
GDP per capita	8,788 yuan (1,069 US$)
Area as cropland (%)	27.3
Leading agriculture	sugarcane, cocoons, bananas
Leading industry	refined sugar, motor vehicles
Change in vehicles 2000-05 (%)	123.2
Water use per capita (cubic m)	673.4
College students per 1,000 people	9.9
Foreign tourist visits	886,600

GUIZHOU

Land area	176,152 sq km (68,013 sq mi)
Population	37,300,000
Capital	Guiyang 1,195,600
Population density (per sq km)	212
Population growth 2000-05 (%)	5.8
Life expectancy	M 64.5, F 67.6
Ethnic minorities (% of counties)	52.3
GDP per capita	5,052 yuan (614 US$)
Area as cropland (%)	27.3
Leading agriculture	tobacco, tubers, rapeseed
Leading industry	sulfuric acid, coal
Change in vehicles 2000-05 (%)	213.6
Water use per capita (cubic m)	261.4
College students per 1,000 people	8.4
Foreign tourist visits	92,600

HAINAN

Land area	35,354 sq km (13,650 sq mi)
Population	8,280,000
Capital	Haikou 646,800
Population density (per sq km)	234
Population growth 2000-05 (%)	5.2
Life expectancy	M 70.7, F 75.3
Ethnic minorities (% of counties)	30.0
GDP per capita	10,871 yuan (1,322 US$)
Area as cropland (%)	22.0
Leading agriculture	bananas, sugarcane
Leading industry	refined sugar, natural gas
Change in vehicles 2000-05 (%)	169.0
Water use per capita (cubic m)	533.6
College students per 1,000 people	11.3
Foreign tourist visits	269,400

HEBEI

Land area	188,434 sq km (72,755 sq mi)
Population	68,510,000
Capital	Shijiazhuang 2,171,700
Population density (per sq km)	364
Population growth 2000-05 (%)	1.6
Life expectancy	M 70.7, F 74.6
Ethnic minorities (% of counties)	3.5
GDP per capita	14,782 yuan (1,798 US$)
Area as cropland (%)	46.6
Leading agriculture	pears, grapes, wheat
Leading industry	plate glass, steel
Change in vehicles 2000-05 (%)	157.8
Water use per capita (cubic m)	295.4
College students per 1,000 people	14.4
Foreign tourist visits	573,900

HEILONGJIANG

Land area	452,645 sq km (174,767 sq mi)
Population	38,200,000
Capital	Harbin 3,329,600
Population density (per sq km)	84
Population growth 2000-05 (%)	3.6
Life expectancy	M 70.4, F 74.7
Ethnic minorities (% of counties)	0.8
GDP per capita	14,434 yuan (1,755 US$)
Area as cropland (%)	22.3
Leading agriculture	beans, fiber crops, beetroots
Leading industry	crude oil, beer
Change in vehicles 2000-05 (%)	156.5
Water use per capita (cubic m)	712.9
College students per 1,000 people	18.9
Foreign tourist visits	764,200

HENAN

Land area	165,536 sq km (63,914 sq mi)
Population	93,800,000
Capital	Zhengzhou 2,032,500
Population density (per sq km)	567
Population growth 2000-05 (%)	1.3
Life expectancy	M 69.7, F 73.4
Ethnic minorities (% of counties)	0.0
GDP per capita	11,346 yuan (1,380 US$)
Area as cropland (%)	84.1
Leading agriculture	wheat, sesame, hemp
Leading industry	coal, chemical fertilizer
Change in vehicles 2000-05 (%)	140.1
Water use per capita (cubic m)	211.5
College students per 1,000 people	11.2
Foreign tourist visits	347,300

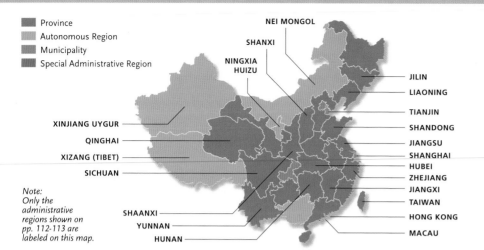

- Province
- Autonomous Region
- Municipality
- Special Administrative Region

NEI MONGOL
SHANXI
NINGXIA HUIZU
JILIN
LIAONING
TIANJIN
SHANDONG
JIANGSU
SHANGHAI
HUBEI
ZHEJIANG
JIANGXI
TAIWAN
HONG KONG
MACAU

XINJIANG UYGUR
QINGHAI
XIZANG (TIBET)
SICHUAN
SHAANXI
YUNNAN
HUNAN

Note:
Only the administrative regions shown on pp. 112-113 are labeled on this map.

HONG KONG

Land area	1,104 sq km (426 sq mi)
Population	6,935,900
Capital	NA
Population density (per sq km)	6,283
Population growth 2000-05 (%)	4.1
Life expectancy	M 78.8, F 84.5
Ethnic minorities (% of counties)	NA
GDP per capita	199,261 HK$ (25,622 US$)
Area as cropland (%)	5.7
Leading agriculture	fish, vegetables
Leading industry	textiles, tourism
Change in vehicles 2000-05 (%)	2.9
Water use per capita (cubic m)	139.5
College students per 1,000 people	53.7
Foreign tourist visits	23,359,400

HUBEI

Land area	185,888 sq km (71,772 sq mi)
Population	57,100,000
Capital	Wuhan 4,287,700
Population density (per sq km)	307
Population growth 2000-05 (%)	-5.3
Life expectancy	M 69.3, F 73.0
Ethnic minorities (% of counties)	9.8
GDP per capita	11,431 yuan (1,390 US$)
Area as cropland (%)	39.2
Leading agriculture	rapeseed, sesame, rice
Leading industry	hydropower, sulfuric acid
Change in vehicles 2000-05 (%)	195.3
Water use per capita (cubic m)	445.1
College students per 1,000 people	21.8
Foreign tourist visits	626,800

HUNAN

Land area	211,855 sq km (81,798 sq mi)
Population	63,260,000
Capital	Changsha 2,190,700
Population density (per sq km)	299
Population growth 2000-05 (%)	-1.8
Life expectancy	M 69.1, F 72.5
Ethnic minorities (% of counties)	12.3
GDP per capita	10,426 yuan (1,268 US$)
Area as cropland (%)	37.7
Leading agriculture	rice, citrus, tobacco
Leading industry	cigarettes, chemical pesticide
Change in vehicles 2000-05 (%)	85.5
Water use per capita (cubic m)	520.7
College students per 1,000 people	14.5
Foreign tourist visits	608,800

JIANGSU

Land area	106,742 sq km (41,213 sq mi)
Population	74,750,000
Capital	Nanjing 3,234,800
Population density (per sq km)	700
Population growth 2000-05 (%)	0.5
Life expectancy	M 71.7, F 76.2
Ethnic minorities (% of counties)	0.0
GDP per capita	24,560 yuan (2,987 US$)
Area as cropland (%)	71.6
Leading agriculture	rice, cocoons, rapeseed
Leading industry	int. circuits, microcomputers
Change in vehicles 2000-05 (%)	477.7
Water use per capita (cubic m)	697.4
College students per 1,000 people	20.1
Foreign tourist visits	2,621,500

JIANGXI

Land area	166,894 sq km (64,438 sq mi)
Population	43,110,000
Capital	Nanchang 1,999,500
Population density (per sq km)	258
Population growth 2000-05 (%)	4.1
Life expectancy	M 68.4, F 69.3
Ethnic minorities (% of counties)	0.0
GDP per capita	9,440 yuan (1,148 US$)
Area as cropland (%)	31.5
Leading agriculture	rice, sesame, citrus
Leading industry	microcomputers, cement
Change in vehicles 2000-05 (%)	222.0
Water use per capita (cubic m)	484.0
College students per 1,000 people	17.7
Foreign tourist visits	136,300

JILIN

Land area	191,124 sq km (73,793 sq mi)
Population	27,160,000
Capital	Changchun 2,669,100
Population density (per sq km)	142
Population growth 2000-05 (%)	-0.4
Life expectancy	M 71.4, F 75.0
Ethnic minorities (% of counties)	18.3
GDP per capita	13,348 yuan (1,623 US$)
Area as cropland (%)	25.9
Leading agriculture	corn, beans, sesame
Leading industry	motor vehicles, ethylene
Change in vehicles 2000-05 (%)	156.7
Water use per capita (cubic m)	363.3
College students per 1,000 people	21.4
Foreign tourist visits	306,800

LIAONING

Land area	148,064 sq km (57,168 sq mi)
Population	42,210,000
Capital	Shenyang 3,564,800
Population density (per sq km)	285
Population growth 2000-05 (%)	-0.4
Life expectancy	M 71.5, F 75.4
Ethnic minorities (% of counties)	8.0
GDP per capita	18,983 yuan (2,309 US$)
Area as cropland (%)	25.6
Leading agriculture	pears, grapes, corn
Leading industry	machine tools, steel
Change in vehicles 2000-05 (%)	145.9
Water use per capita (cubic m)	316.7
College students per 1,000 people	21.4
Foreign tourist visits	1,111,100

MACAU

Land area	28 sq km (11 sq mi)
Population	488,100
Capital	NA
Population density (per sq km)	17,310
Population growth 2000-05 (%)	13.1
Life expectancy	79.3
Ethnic minorities (% of counties)	NA
GDP per capita	194,458 MOP (24,274 US$)
Area as cropland (%)	NA
Leading agriculture	fish, crustaceans
Leading industry	tourism, gambling
Change in vehicles 2000-05 (%)	32.8
Water use per capita (cubic m)	120.5
College students per 1,000 people	28.6
Foreign tourist visits	18,711,200

NEI MONGOL

Land area	1,145,121 sq km (442,134 sq mi)
Population	23,860,000
Capital	Hohhot 792,800
Population density (per sq km)	21
Population growth 2000-05 (%)	0.4
Life expectancy	M 68.3, F 71.8
Ethnic minorities (% of counties)	100
GDP per capita	16,331 yuan (1,986 US$)
Area as cropland (%)	5.4
Leading agriculture	beans, beetroots, corn
Leading industry	coal, salt
Change in vehicles 2000-05 (%)	116.2
Water use per capita (cubic m)	734.5
College students per 1,000 people	13.0
Foreign tourist visits	995,600

NINGXIA HUIZU

Land area	51,954 sq km (20,060 sq mi)
Population	5,960,000
Capital	Yinchuan 486,700
Population density (per sq km)	115
Population growth 2000-05 (%)	6.0
Life expectancy	M 68.7, F 71.8
Ethnic minorities (% of counties)	100
GDP per capita	10,239 yuan (1,245 US$)
Area as cropland (%)	21.2
Leading agriculture	apples, wheat
Leading industry	chemical fertilizer, coal
Change in vehicles 2000-05 (%)	107.3
Water use per capita (cubic m)	1314.2
College students per 1,000 people	12.8
Foreign tourist visits	6,600

QINGHAI

Land area	717,481 sq km (277,021 sq mi)
Population	5,430,000
Capital	Xining 774,100
Population density (per sq km)	8
Population growth 2000-05 (%)	4.8
Life expectancy	M 64.6, F 67.7
Ethnic minorities (% of counties)	81.4
GDP per capita	10,045 yuan (1,222 US$)
Area as cropland (%)	0.7
Leading agriculture	rapeseed, wheat
Leading industry	natural gas, hydropower
Change in vehicles 2000-05 (%)	93.6
Water use per capita (cubic m)	565.9
College students per 1,000 people	9.1
Foreign tourist visits	14,600

SHAANXI

Land area	205,795 sq km (79,458 sq mi)
Population	37,200,000
Capital	Xi'an 4,235,200
Population density (per sq km)	181
Population growth 2000-05 (%)	3.2
Life expectancy	M 68.9, F 71.3
Ethnic minorities (% of counties)	0.0
GDP per capita	9,899 yuan (1,204 US$)
Area as cropland (%)	20.4
Leading agriculture	apples, wheat, pears
Leading industry	natural gas, coal
Change in vehicles 2000-05 (%)	139.2
Water use per capita (cubic m)	212.4
College students per 1,000 people	23.5
Foreign tourist visits	745,700

SHANDONG

Land area	157,126 sq km (60,667 sq mi)
Population	92,480,000
Capital	Jinan 2,151,300
Population density (per sq km)	589
Population growth 2000-05 (%)	1.9
Life expectancy	M 71.7, F 76.3
Ethnic minorities (% of counties)	0.0
GDP per capita	20,096 yuan (2,444 US$)
Area as cropland (%)	68.3
Leading agriculture	apples, peanuts, wheat
Leading industry	cement, salt
Change in vehicles 2000-05 (%)	278.9
Water use per capita (cubic m)	228.9
College students per 1,000 people	16.0
Foreign tourist visits	1,247,800

SHANGHAI

Land area	8,239 sq km (3,181 sq mi)
Population	17,780,000
Capital	Shanghai 15,434,600
Population density (per sq km)	2,158
Population growth 2000-05 (%)	6.2
Life expectancy	M 76.2, F 80.0
Ethnic minorities (% of counties)	0.0
GDP per capita	51,474 yuan (6,260 US$)
Area as cropland (%)	49.0
Leading agriculture	citrus, sugarcane
Leading industry	automobiles, ethylene
Change in vehicles 2000-05 (%)	708.8
Water use per capita (cubic m)	684.2
College students per 1,000 people	38.4
Foreign tourist visits	3,799,300

SHANXI

Land area	156,711 sq km (60,506 sq mi)
Population	33,550,000
Capital	Taiyuan 2,782,600
Population density (per sq km)	214
Population growth 2000-05 (%)	1.8
Life expectancy	M 70.0, F 73.6
Ethnic minorities (% of counties)	0.0
GDP per capita	12,495 yuan (1,520 US$)
Area as cropland (%)	24.2
Leading agriculture	apples, corn, beetroots
Leading industry	coal, pig iron
Change in vehicles 2000-05 (%)	150.0
Water use per capita (cubic m)	166.6
College students per 1,000 people	16.1
Foreign tourist visits	254,000

SICHUAN

Land area	484,056 sq km (186,895 sq mi)
Population	82,120,000
Capital	Chengdu 3,972,500
Population density (per sq km)	170
Population growth 2000-05 (%)	-1.4
Life expectancy	M 69.3, F 73.4
Ethnic minorities (% of counties)	28.2
GDP per capita	9,060 yuan (1,102 US$)
Area as cropland (%)	19.6
Leading agriculture	tubers, citrus, rapeseed
Leading industry	natural gas, hydropower
Change in vehicles 2000-05 (%)	321.1
Water use per capita (cubic m)	259.3
College students per 1,000 people	12.0
Foreign tourist visits	682,700

TAIWAN

Land area	36,188 sq km (13,972 sq mi)
Population	22,770,000
Capital	Taipei 2,468,700
Population density (per sq km)	629
Population growth 2000-05 (%)	2.2
Life expectancy	M 73.7, F 79.4
Ethnic minorities (% of counties)	NA
GDP per capita	492,076 NT$ (15,291 US$)
Area as cropland (%)	21.0
Leading agriculture	rice, corn, vegetables
Leading industry	electronics, petroleum refining
Change in vehicles 2001-05 (%)	13.7
Water use per capita (cubic m)	128.6
College students per 1,000 people	56.9
Foreign tourist visits	2,798,200

TIANJIN

Land area	11,917 sq km (4,601 sq mi)
Population	10,430,000
Capital	Tianjin 3,755,200
Population density (per sq km)	875
Population growth 2000-05 (%)	4.2
Life expectancy	M 73.3, F 76.6
Ethnic minorities (% of counties)	0.0
GDP per capita	35,783 yuan (4,352 US$)
Area as cropland (%)	41.9
Leading agriculture	cotton, grapes
Leading industry	mobile phones, crude oil
Change in vehicles 2000-05 (%)	116.0
Water use per capita (cubic m)	222.0
College students per 1,000 people	43.4
Foreign tourist visits	674,600

XINJIANG UYGUR

Land area	1,664,897 sq km (642,820 sq mi)
Population	20,100,000
Capital	Ürümqi 1,569,800
Population density (per sq km)	12
Population growth 2000-05 (%)	4.4
Life expectancy	M 66.0, F 69.1
Ethnic minorities (% of counties)	100
GDP per capita	13,108 yuan (1,594 US$)
Area as cropland (%)	2.2
Leading agriculture	beetroots, cotton, grapes
Leading industry	natural gas, crude oil
Change in vehicles 2000-05 (%)	80.3
Water use per capita (cubic m)	2539.7
College students per 1,000 people	13.3
Foreign tourist visits	290,100

XIZANG (TIBET)

Land area	1,202,072 sq km (464,123 sq mi)
Population	2,770,000
Capital	Lhasa 122,300
Population density (per sq km)	2
Population growth 2000-05 (%)	5.7
Life expectancy	M 62.5, F 66.2
Ethnic minorities (% of counties)	100
GDP per capita	9,114 yuan (1,108 US$)
Area as cropland (%)	0.2
Leading agriculture	rapeseed, wheat
Leading industry	cement, hydropower
Change in vehicles 2000-05 (%)	126.6
Water use per capita (cubic m)	1201.8
College students per 1,000 people	11.4
Foreign tourist visits	111,000

YUNNAN

Land area	383,194 sq km (147,952 sq mi)
Population	44,500,000
Capital	Kunming 1,065,400
Population density (per sq km)	116
Population growth 2000-05 (%)	3.8
Life expectancy	M 64.2, F 66.9
Ethnic minorities (% of counties)	60.5
GDP per capita	7,835 yuan (953 US$)
Area as cropland (%)	15.8
Leading agriculture	tobacco, sugarcane, tea
Leading industry	sulfuric acid, cigarettes
Change in vehicles 2000-05 (%)	151.9
Water use per capita (cubic m)	330.9
College students per 1,000 people	9.0
Foreign tourist visits	996,500

ZHEJIANG

Land area	105,397 sq km (40,694 sq mi)
Population	48,980,000
Capital	Hangzhou 1,911,400
Population density (per sq km)	465
Population growth 2000-05 (%)	4.7
Life expectancy	M 72.5, F 77.2
Ethnic minorities (% of counties)	1.1
GDP per capita	27,703 yuan (3,369 US$)
Area as cropland (%)	26.9
Leading agriculture	tea, cocoons, citrus
Leading industry	washing machines, chemical fiber
Change in vehicles 2000-05 (%)	537.8
Water use per capita (cubic m)	429.8
College students per 1,000 people	18.9
Foreign tourist visits	2,329,200

Place-Name Index

THE FOLLOWING SYSTEM is used to locate a place on a map in the *National Geographic Atlas of China*. The boldface type after an entry refers to the page on which the map is found. The letter-number combination refers to the grid on which the particular place-name is located. The edge of each map is marked horizontally with numbers and vertically with letters. In between, at equally spaced intervals, are index ticks ( ). If these small ticks were connected with lines, each page would be divided into a grid. Take the town of Henan, for example. The index entry reads "Henan, *Qinghai* 29 L17 ." On page 29, Henan is located within the grid square where row L and column 17 intersect (see below).

The name of the administrative region in which a feature lies is shown in italic type. If a feature, such as a mountain range, is in more than one administrative region, all of the regions in which it appears are listed. Entries also include a description, such as "river," "lake," "desert," etc. All entries listed without a description are populated places.

When a feature or place can be referred to by more than one name, both may appear in the index with cross-references. For example, the entry for Kaitong reads "Kaitong see Tongyu, *Jilin* 21 G12." That entry is "Tongyu (Kaitong), *Jilin* 21 G12."

Some place-names have more than one page and grid square listed. Cities which are included on the main China political map (pages 16–17) are indexed to both that map and the regional map on which they appear. For example, the entry for Chengdu reads "Chengdu, *Sichuan* 17 J11; 24 B5," meaning that Chengdu appears in grid square J11 on page 17 and in grid square B5 on page 24. Other labels are indexed more than once if they appear on the China physical map (pages 18–19) as well as on one or more regional maps.

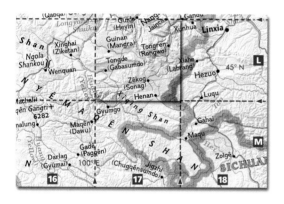

Abbreviations:

mts.	*mountains*
pen.	*peninsula*
plat.	*plateau*
prov.	*province*

Examples:

feature description — *page number / grid square*
Dokog, river, *Sichuan* 22 H1
feature name — *province*
Halahai, *Jilin* 21 H13 — *page number / grid square*

124 Wutai – Yellow

Wutai, *Shanxi* **22 D9**
Wutai, *Xinjiang Uygur* **28 D6**
Wutai Shan, mts., *Shanxi* **22 D9**
Wutongdaquan, *Xinjiang Uygur* **29 F13**
Wutonggou, *Xinjiang Uygur* **29 G10**
Wuwei, *Anhui* **23 K11**
Wuwei, *Gansu* **17 F10; 29 J17**
Wuxi, *Chongqing Shi* **24 B8**
Wuxi, *Jiangsu* **17 H14; 23 J13**
Wuxiang, *Shanxi* **22 E8**
Wuxue, *Hubei* **23 L10**
Wuyang, *Henan* **22 H9**
Wuyiling, *Heilongjiang* **17 B15; 21 D15**
Wuying, *Heilongjiang* **21 E15**
Wuyi Shan, mts., *Fujian-Jiangxi* **15 K14; 25 E13**
Wuyishan, *Fujian* **25 D14**
Wuyuan, *Nei Mongol* **17 E11; 20 K4**
Wuzhai, *Shanxi* **22 D8**
Wuzhen, *Hubei* **22 J8**
Wuzhi, *Henan* **22 G8**
Wuzhi Shan, mts., *Hainan* **24 L8**
Wuzhi Shan, peak, *Hainan* **24 L8**
Wuzhong, *Ningxia Huizu* **17 F11; 22 D5**
Wuzhou, *Guangxi Zhuangzu* **17 L13; 25 H10**

X

Xabart, *Nei Mongol* **21 D11**
Xagquka, *Xizang* **27 E11**
Xaidulla, *Xinjiang Uygur* **28 K3**
Xainza, *Xizang* **16 H7; 26 E9**
Xaitongmoin (Kaika), *Xizang* **26 F8**
Xakur, *Xinjiang Uygur* **28 H5**
Xamal, *Xinjiang Uygur* **28 H4**
Xangda *see* Nangqên, *Qinghai* **27 D13**
Xangdoring, *Xizang* **26 D5**
Xangzha, *Xizang* **27 E13**
Xarag, *Qinghai* **29 K15**
Xar Burd, *Nei Mongol* **17 F11; 20 L3**
Xar Hudag, *Nei Mongol* **20 G8**
Xar Moron, river, *Nei Mongol* **21 J11**
Xar Moron Sum, *Nei Mongol* **20 K6**
Xaxa, *Xizang* **26 D5**
Xayar, *Xinjiang Uygur* **28 G6**
Xebert, *Nei Mongol* **21 H12**
Xêgar *see* Tingri, *Xizang* **26 G8**
Xi, river, *Guangdong* **15 L13; 25 H10**
Xi, river, *Nei Mongol* **29 F16**
Xia Awat, *Xinjiang Uygur* **28 H3**
Xiachuan Dao, island, *Guangdong* **25 J11**
Xiadong, *Gansu* **29 G14**
Xiahe (Labrang), *Gansu* **29 L18**
Xiajin, *Shandong* **23 E10**
Xiamaya, *Xinjiang Uygur* **29 E13**
Xiamen (Amoy), *Fujian* **17 K14; 25 G14**
Xiamen Gang, harbor, *Fujian* **25 G14**
Xi'an, *Shaanxi* **17 G12; 22 G6**
Xianfeng, *Hubei* **22 L6**
Xiang, river, *Hunan* **15 J13; 25 D11**
Xiangcheng, *Henan* **22 H9**
Xiangcheng, *Sichuan* **24 C2**
Xiangdong, *Jiangxi* **25 D11**
Xiangfan, *Hubei* **17 H13; 22 J8**
Xiangfen, *Shanxi* **22 F7**
Xianggang *see* Hong Kong, S.A.R., special administrative region, *China* **17 L13; 25 J12**
Xianghuang Qi (Xin Bulag), *Nei Mongol* **20 J7**
Xiangning, *Shanxi* **22 F7**
Xiangquan, river, *Xizang* **26 E3**
Xiangride, *Qinghai* **29 L15**
Xiangshan, *Zhejiang* **25 C16**
Xiangshui, *Jiangsu* **23 G12**
Xiangtan, *Hunan* **17 J13; 25 D11**
Xiangxi, *Hubei* **22 K7**
Xiangyin, *Hunan* **25 D11**
Xiangyuan, *Shanxi* **22 F8**
Xiangyun, *Yunnan* **24 F3**
Xiangzhou, *Guangxi Zhuangzu* **24 G8**
Xianju, *Zhejiang* **25 C15**
Xianning, *Hubei* **17 J13; 22 L9**
Xianshui *see* Dawu, *Sichuan* **24 B3**
Xiantao, *Hubei* **17 J13; 22 K8**
Xianyang, *Shaanxi* **17 G12; 22 G6**
Xianyou, *Fujian* **17 K14; 25 F14**
Xiao, river, *Hunan* **25 F10**
Xiaoba *see* Qingtongxia, *Ningxia Huizu* **17 F11; 22 D4**
Xiaochang, *Hubei* **22 K9**
Xiaogan, *Hubei* **17 H13; 22 K9**
Xiaoguai, *Xinjiang Uygur* **28 D8**
Xiaohezi, *Hebei* **23 B10**
Xiao Hinggan Ling, mts., *Heilongjiang* **17 B15; 21 D14**
Xiaojiang, *Zhejiang* **25 D15**
Xiaojin, *Sichuan* **24 B4**
Xiaolan, *Guangdong* **25 H11**
Xiaonanchuan, *Qinghai* **29 L13**
Xiao Qaidam, *Qinghai* **29 K13**
Xiao Shan, mts., *Henan* **22 G7**
Xiaoshan, *Zhejiang* **25 B15**
Xiaoshi, *Liaoning* **21 K13**
Xiaoxian (Longcheng), *Anhui* **23 G11**
Xiaoyang Shan, island, *Zhejiang* **23 K14; 25 B16**
Xiaoyi, *Shanxi* **22 E8**
Xiapu, *Fujian* **17 J15; 25 E15**
Xiawa, *Nei Mongol* **21 J11**
Xiawazi, *Jilin* **21 G13**
Xiaxian, *Shanxi* **22 G7**
Xiayi, *Henan* **23 G10**
Xibu *see* Dongshan, *Fujian* **25 G14**
Xichang, *Sichuan* **17 K10; 24 D4**
Xichang Satellite Launch Center, site, *Sichuan* **24 D4**
Xichong, *Sichuan* **24 B6**
Xichuan, *Henan* **22 H7**
Xide, *Sichuan* **24 D4**
Xieyang Dao, island, *Guangxi Zhuangzu* **24 K8**
Xifeng, *Gansu* **17 G11; 22 F5**
Xifeng, *Guizhou* **24 E6**
Xifeng, *Heilongjiang* **21 E17**
Xifeng, *Liaoning* **21 J13**
Xigangzi, *Heilongjiang* **21 C14**
Xigazê, *Xizang* **16 J7; 26 G9**
Xihan, river, *Gansu* **22 H4**
Xihe (Hanyuan), *Gansu* **22 G4**
Xihu, *Gansu* **29 G13**
Xihua, *Henan* **22 H9**
Xiji, *Ningxia Huizu* **22 F4**
Xijir, *Qinghai* **29 M12**
Xijir Ulan Hu, lake, *Qinghai* **29 M11**
Xikouzi, *Nei Mongol* **21 A11**
Xil, *Nei Mongol* **20 J7**
Xiliangzi, *Qinghai* **29 J13**
Xiliao, river, *Nei Mongol* **21 H12**
Xilin, river, *Nei Mongol* **20 H9**
Xilin, *Guangxi Zhuangzu* **24 G5**
Xilin, *Heilongjiang* **21 E15**
Xilinhot, *Nei Mongol* **17 D13; 20 H9**
Xilinji *see* Mohe, *Heilongjiang* **21 A12**
Xilin Qagan Obo, *Nei Mongol* **20 H6**
Ximeng, *Yunnan* **24 H2**
Ximing, *Shanxi* **22 E8**
Xin, river, *Jiangxi* **25 D13**
Xin'an *see* Lai'an, *Anhui* **23 J12**
Xin'an, *Henan* **22 G8**
Xin'an *see* Guannan, *Jiangsu* **23 H12**
Xin'anjiang Shuiku, reservoir, *Zhejiang* **25 C14**
Xin'anzhen, *Jilin* **21 H13**
Xin Barag Youqi (Altan Emel), *Nei Mongol* **17 C13; 20 E9**
Xin Barag Zuoqi (Amgalang), *Nei Mongol* **17 C13; 21 E10**
Xinbin, *Liaoning* **21 K14**
Xinbo, *Hebei* **23 A11**
Xin Bulag *see* Xianghuang Qi, *Nei Mongol* **20 J7**
Xin Bulag Dong, *Nei Mongol* **21 E10**
Xincai, *Henan* **22 J9**
Xincheng, *Guangxi Zhuangzu* **24 G8**
Xincheng, *Ningxia Huizu* **17 F11; 22 D4**
Xincheng, *Shanxi* **22 D8**
Xinchengzi, *Liaoning* **21 K13**
Xincun, *Hainan* **24 L9**
Xincun, *Hebei* **23 D11**
Xindianzi, *Nei Mongol* **20 L6**
Xindu, *Sichuan* **24 B5**
Xin'e, *Heilongjiang* **21 D14**
Xinfeng, *Guangdong* **25 G12**
Xinfeng, *Jiangxi* **25 F12**
Xinfengjiang Shuiku, reservoir, *Guangdong* **25 G12**
Xing'an, *Guangxi Zhuangzu* **24 F9**
Xingcheng, *Liaoning* **21 L11**
Xingdi, *Xinjiang Uygur* **28 G9**
Xingdong, *Heilongjiang* **21 E16**
Xingguo, *Jiangxi* **25 E12**
Xinghai (Ziketan), *Qinghai* **29 L16**
Xinghe, *Nei Mongol* **20 L7**
Xinghua, *Heilongjiang* **21 B13**
Xinghua, *Jiangsu* **17 G14; 23 H13**
Xinghua Wan, bay, *Fujian* **25 F15**
Xingkai Hu (Ozero Khanka), lake, *Heilongjiang* **15 C16; 21 G17**
Xinglong, *Hainan* **24 L9**
Xinglong, *Hebei* **23 C11**
Xinglong, *Heilongjiang* **21 B13**
Xinglongzhen, *Heilongjiang* **21 F14**
Xingning, *Guangdong* **25 G13**
Xingping, *Shaanxi* **22 G6**
Xingren, *Guizhou* **24 F5**
Xingshan, *Hubei* **22 K7**
Xingtai, *Hebei* **17 F13; 22 E9**
Xingtang, *Hebei* **22 D9**
Xingwen, *Sichuan* **24 D6**
Xingxian, *Shanxi* **22 D7**
Xingxingxia, *Xinjiang Uygur* **16 E8; 29 G13**
Xingyang, *Henan* **22 G8**
Xingyi, *Guizhou* **17 K11; 24 F5**
Xingzi, *Jiangxi* **25 C13**
Xinhe (Toksu), *Xinjiang Uygur* **16 E6; 28 G6**
Xin Hot *see* Abag Qi, *Nei Mongol* **20 H8**
Xinhuang, *Hunan* **24 E8**
Xinhui, *Guangdong* **25 H11**
Xining, *Qinghai* **17 G10; 29 K17**
Xinji, *Hebei* **23 E10**
Xinjian, *Jiangxi* **25 D12**
Xinjiang, *Shanxi* **22 F7**
Xinjiang Uygur (Sinkiang), autonomous region, *China* **16 E6; 28 G6**
Xinjie, *Nei Mongol* **20 M5**
Xinjieji, *Heilongjiang* **21 B14**
Xinjin, *Sichuan* **24 B5**
Xinlin, *Heilongjiang* **21 B13**
Xinlincun, *Heilongjiang* **21 E17**
Xinlitun, *Heilongjiang* **21 F17**
Xinlong (Rulong), *Sichuan* **17 J10; 24 B3**
Xinmi, *Henan* **22 G8**
Xinmiao, *Jilin* **21 G13**
Xinmin, *Liaoning* **21 K12**
Xinning, *Hunan* **24 E9**
Xinping, *Yunnan* **24 G3**
Xinpu *see* Lianyungang, *Jiangsu* **17 G14; 23 G12**
Xinqing, *Heilongjiang* **17 B15; 21 D15**
Xinshao, *Hunan* **17 K13; 25 E10**
Xinshi, *Hunan* **25 E11**
Xintai, *Shandong* **17 G14; 23 F11**
Xintian, *Hunan* **25 F10**
Xinxiang, *Henan* **17 G13; 22 G9**
Xinyang, *Henan* **17 H13; 22 J9**
Xinye, *Henan* **22 J8**
Xinyi, *Guangdong* **24 J9**
Xinyi, *Jiangsu* **23 G12**
Xinying, *Hainan* **24 K8**
Xinyu, *Jiangxi* **17 J13; 25 D12**
Xinyuan *see* Tianjun, *Qinghai* **29 K16**
Xinyuan (Künes), *Xinjiang Uygur* **16 D6; 28 E7**
Xinzhangfang, *Nei Mongol* **21 C12**
Xinzheng, *Henan* **22 G9**
Xinzhou, *Hainan* **24 L8**
Xinzhou, *Shanxi* **17 F12; 22 D8**
Xiong'er Shan, mts., *Henan* **22 G7**
Xiongyuecheng, *Liaoning* **21 L12**
Xiongzhou, *Hebei* **23 D10**
Xiping, *Henan* **22 H9**
Xiping *see* Datong, *Shanxi* **22 C9**
Xiqing Shan, mts., *Qinghai* **29 M17**
Xiqu, *Gansu* **29 H18**
Xireg *see* Ulan, *Qinghai* **29 K15**
Xishui, *Guizhou* **24 D6**
Xi Taijnar Hu, lake, *Qinghai* **29 K12**
Xi Ujimqin Qi (Bayan Ul Hot), *Nei Mongol* **21 H10**
Xiushan, *Chongqing Shi* **24 D8**
Xiushui, *Jiangxi* **25 C12**
Xiuwen, *Guizhou* **24 E6**
Xiuwu, *Henan* **22 F8**
Xiuyan, *Liaoning* **21 L13**
Xiuying, *Hainan* **24 K9**
Xiwopu, *Nei Mongol* **21 J10**
Xiwu, *Qinghai* **27 D14**
Xixabangma Feng, peak, *Xizang* **26 G7**
Xixia, *Henan* **22 H7**
Xixian, *Henan* **22 J9**
Xixiang, *Shaanxi* **22 H5**
Xiyang, *Shanxi* **22 E9**
Xizang (Tibet), autonomous region, *China* **16 H6; 26 D5**
Xizhong Dao, island, *Liaoning* **21 M12**
Xizhou Shan, mts., *Shanxi* **22 D8**
Xobando, *Xizang* **27 E13**
Xoka, *Xizang* **27 F12**
Xorkol, *Xinjiang Uygur* **16 F7; 29 J11**
Xortang, *Xinjiang Uygur* **28 K7**
Xuan'en, *Hubei* **22 L6**
Xuanhan, *Sichuan* **24 B7**
Xuanhua, *Hebei* **17 E13; 23 B10**
Xuanwei, *Yunnan* **17 K11; 24 E5**
Xuanzhou, *Anhui* **23 K12**
Xuchang, *Henan* **22 H9**
Xuelian Feng, peak, *Xinjiang Uygur* **28 F5**
Xueshuiwen, *Heilongjiang* **21 D15**
Xugin, river, *Qinghai* **29 L14**
Xugui, *Qinghai* **29 L14**
Xun, river, *Guangxi Zhuangzu* **24 H9**
Xun, river, *Shaanxi* **22 H6**
Xundian, *Yunnan* **24 F4**
Xungru, *Xizang* **26 G6**
Xunhe, *Heilongjiang* **21 D15**
Xunhua, *Qinghai* **29 L18**
Xunke, *Heilongjiang* **17 B15; 21 D15**
Xunwu, *Jiangxi* **25 F12**
Xunxian, *Henan* **22 F9**
Xunyang, *Shaanxi* **22 H6**
Xunyi, *Shaanxi* **22 G6**
Xupu, *Hunan* **24 D9**
Xur, *Qinghai* **29 L14**
Xuru Co, lake, *Xizang* **26 F7**
Xuwen, *Guangdong* **17 M12; 24 K9**
Xuyi, *Jiangsu* **23 H12**
Xuyong, *Sichuan* **24 D6**
Xuzhou, *Jiangsu* **17 G14; 23 G11**

Y

Ya'an, *Sichuan* **17 J10; 24 C4**
Yabrai Shan, mts., *Nei Mongol* **29 H17**
Yabrai Yanchang, *Nei Mongol* **20 L1**
Yabuli, *Heilongjiang* **21 G15**
Yacheng, *Hainan* **24 M8**
Yachi, river, *Guizhou* **24 E6**
Yadong (Chomo), *Xizang* **16 J7; 26 H9**
Yag, river, *Qinghai* **29 M13**
Yagan, *Nei Mongol* **29 F17**
Yaggain Canco, lake, *Xizang* **26 D9**
Yagra, *Xizang* **26 E5**
Yagradagzê Shan, peak, *Qinghai* **29 M14**
Yajiang (Hekou), *Sichuan* **24 B3**
Yakatograk, *Xinjiang Uygur* **28 J8**
Yakeshi, *Nei Mongol* **17 B14; 21 D11**
Yalong, river, *Sichuan* **15 J10; 24 C3**
Yalu, river, *Jilin-Liaoning* **15 E16; 21 K14**
Yalu, river, *Nei Mongol* **21 E12**
Yamansu, *Xinjiang Uygur* **29 F12**
Yamzho Yumco, lake, *Xizang* **27 G10**
Yan, river, *Shaanxi* **22 F7**
Yan'an, *Shaanxi* **17 G12; 22 E6**
Yanbian, *Sichuan* **24 E3**
Yanchang, *Shaanxi* **22 E6**
Yancheng, *Jiangsu* **17 G14; 23 H13**
Yanchi, *Ningxia Huizu* **22 D5**
Yanchi, *Xinjiang Uygur* **28 B9**
Yanchi, *Xinjiang Uygur* **29 E13**
Yanchuan, *Shaanxi* **22 E7**
Yandu, *Jiangsu* **23 H13**
Yandun, *Xinjiang Uygur* **29 F13**
Ya'ngamdo, *Xizang* **27 E12**
Yangbajain, *Xizang* **27 F10**
Yangcheng, *Shanxi* **22 F8**
Yangchun, *Guangdong* **25 J10**
Yanggao, *Shanxi* **22 C9**
Yanggu, *Shandong* **23 F10**
Yang Hu, lake, *Xizang* **26 B6**
Yangjiang, *Guangdong* **17 L13; 25 J10**
Yangkang, *Qinghai* **29 J15**
Yangmei, *Taiwan* **25 F16**
Yangming Shan, peak, *Hunan* **25 F10**
Yangmingshan, *Taiwan* **25 F16**
Yangpu Gang, harbor, *Hainan* **24 L8**
Yangqu, *Shanxi* **22 D8**
Yangquan, *Shanxi* **22 E8**
Yangshan, *Guangdong* **25 G10**
Yangshuo, *Guangxi Zhuangzu* **24 G9**
Yangtze *see* Chang Jiang, Jinsha, Tongtian, river, *China* **15 H14; 25 B13; 27 C13**
Yangtze, Mouth of the, delta, *Jiangsu* **15 H15; 23 J14**
Yangtze, Source of the, source, *Qinghai* **14 H7**
Yangtze Gorges, gorges, *Chongqing Shi-Hubei* **15 H12; 24 B8**
Yangxian, *Shaanxi* **22 H5**
Yangxin, *Hubei* **23 L10**
Yangxin, *Shandong* **23 E11**
Yangyuan, *Hebei* **22 C9**
Yangzhou, *Jiangsu* **23 J12**
Yanhe, *Guizhou* **24 D8**
Yanhu, *Xinjiang Uygur* **28 E9**
Yanhu (Caka), *Xizang* **26 D5**
Yanji, *Jilin* **17 D16; 21 J16**
Yanjin, *Yunnan* **24 D5**
Yanjing *see* Yanyuan, *Sichuan* **24 D3**
Yanliang, *Shaanxi* **22 G6**
Yanling, *Hunan* **25 E11**
Yanqi, *Xinjiang Uygur* **16 E7; 28 F8**
Yan Shan, mts., *Hebei* **23 C11**
Yanshan, *Jiangxi* **25 D14**
Yanshan, *Yunnan* **24 G5**
Yanshiping, *Qinghai* **27 C11**
Yanshou, *Heilongjiang* **21 G15**
Yantai, *Shandong* **17 F14; 23 E13**
Yantongshan, *Jilin* **21 J14**
Yanyuan (Yanjing), *Sichuan* **24 D3**
Yanzhou, *Shandong* **23 F11**
Yao'an, *Yunnan* **24 F3**
Yaoxian, *Shaanxi* **22 G6**
Yaoxiaoling, *Heilongjiang* **21 E14**
Yarkant, river, *Xinjiang Uygur* **14 F4; 28 H4**
Yarkant *see* Shache, *Xinjiang Uygur* **28 J3**
Yarlung Zangbo (Brahmaputra), river, *Xizang* **14 J7; 27 G11**
Yawatongguz, river, *Xinjiang Uygur* **28 K6**
Yawatongguzlangar, *Xinjiang Uygur* **28 K6**
Yecheng (Kargilik), *Xinjiang Uygur* **16 F4; 28 J3**
Yellow *see* Huang, river, *China* **15 F13; 23 F10; 29 L16**
Yellow, Mouth of the, delta, *Shandong* **15 F14**

Acknowledgments

General Consultants/Reviewers

Howard Giskin
Appalachian State University

Youqin Huang
SUNY-Albany

Yehua Dennis Wei
University of Utah

Contributing Writers

Daniel Brito, Kam Wing Chan, Christopher Daly, Paul Davis, David Finkelstein, David G. Fridley, Daniel Griswold, David Jeffery, Matthew J. Jewell, K. M. Kostyal, Ruth Levine, David B. Miller, Clifton W. Pannell, Sarah Parkes, Carmen Revenga, Whitney Smith

Primary Reference Sources

China Statistical Yearbook 2006.
National Bureau of Statistics of the People's Republic of China; World Gazetteer: www.world-gazetteer.com

Country Themes: Natural

LANDFORMS, pp. 32–33

CONSULTANT

Peng Gong, *University of California, Berkeley*

GRAPHICS

CHINA'S LANDFORMS: *National Physical Atlas of China.* China Cartographic Publishing House, Beijing, China, 1999; supported by the Chinese Academy of Sciences, and the National Bureau of Surveying and Mapping; compiled and edited by the Institute of Geography, Chinese Academy of Sciences.

LAND COVER, pp. 34–35

CONSULTANT

Paul Davis, *The Global Land Cover Facility, University of Maryland*

GRAPHICS

LAND COVER TYPES: M. Hansen, R. De-Fries, J.R.G. Townshend, and R. Sohlberg. 1998. "Global land cover classification at 1km spatial resolution using a classification tree approach." 1 km Land Cover Classification Derived from AVHRR; College Park, Maryland: The Global Land Cover Facility. (Data derived from NOAA AVHRR and NASA Landsat imagery.) **LAND COVER DISTRIBUTION:** Analysis by Bill Buckingham of land cover data from UMIACS (University of Maryland Institute for Advanced Computer Studies).

FRESH WATER, pp. 36–37

CONSULTANT

Carmen Revenga, *Freshwater Policy Analyst*

GRAPHICS

AT A GLANCE: AQUASTAT. Land and Water Development Division of the Food and Agriculture Organization (FAO). **ACCESS TO SAFE DRINKING WATER:** WHO & UNICEF Joint Monitoring Programme for Water Supply &

Sanitation. **MAIN MAP:** Lehner, B., Verdin, K., Jarvis, A. (2006): Hydro-SHEDS Technical Documentation. World Wildlife Fund U.S., Washington, D.C. (available at hydrosheds.cr.usgs.gov). • *Groundwater Resources of the World: Transboundary Aquifer Systems.* BGR Hannover/UNESCO Paris, 2006.

CLIMATE, pp. 38–39

CONSULTANT

Christopher Daly, *PRISM Group, Oregon State University*

GENERAL REFERENCES

Spatial climate data provided courtesy of the PRISM Group, Oregon State University: www.prismclimate.org.

BIODIVERSITY, pp. 40–41

CONSULTANTS

Daniel Brito & Naamal De Silva, *Conservation International*

John Morrison, *World Wildlife Fund*

GENERAL REFERENCES

Fishbase, 2007: www.fishbase.org; International Union for Conservation of Nature and Natural Resources (IUCN): www.iucnredlist.org; World Resources Institute: www.wri.org.

GRAPHICS

ALLIANCE FOR ZERO EXTINCTION AND HOTSPOTS: Alliance for Zero Extinction (AZE): www.zeroextinction.org; Conservation International, Biodiversity Hotspots: www.biodiversityhotspots.org. **BIOMES AND ECOREGIONS OF CHINA:** Terrestrial Ecoregions of the World were developed by D.M. Olson, E. Dinerstein, E.D. Wikramanayake, N.D. Burgess, G.V.N. Powell, E.C. Underwood, J.A. D'Amico, I. Itoua, H.E. Strand, J.C. Morrison, C.J. Loucks, T.F. Allnutt, T.H. Ricketts, Y. Kura, J.F. Lamoreux, W.W. Wettengel, P. Hedao, K.R. Kassem, World Wildlife Fund: www.nationalgeographic.com/wildworld. Marine Ecoregions of the World (MEOW) were developed by the MEOW Working Group, co-chaired by The Nature Conservancy and the World Wildlife Fund (Mark Spalding, Helen Fox, Gerald Allen, Nick Davidson, Zach Ferdana, Max Finlayson, Ben Halpern, Miguel Jorge, Al Lombana, Sara Lourie, Kirsten Martin, Edmund McManus, Jennifer Molnar, Kate Newman, Cheri Recchia, James Robertson): www.worldwildlife.org/MEOW.

PROTECTED AREAS, pp. 42–43

CONSULTANT

Frank Biasi, *National Geographic Maps; additional thanks to* **Lucy Fish,** **Charles Besançon,** *and* **Timothy Johnson,** *UNEP-WCMC*

GRAPHICS

AT A GLANCE: World Resources Institute: www.wri.org. **CHINA'S PROTECTED AREAS:** China Protected Areas Data Set extracted from the World Database on Protected Areas (WDPA), May 2007 by UNEP World Conservation Monitoring Centre, Cambridge, U.K.

ENVIRONMENTAL ISSUES, pp. 44–45

CONSULTANT

Jinhua Zhang, *United Nations Environment Programme (UNEP)*

GENERAL REFERENCES

www.unep.org; *2005 Report on the State of the Environment in China.* State Environmental Protection Administration.

GRAPHICS

GLOBAL IMPACT OF POLLUTION: National Aeronautics and Space Administration (NASA) Goddard Space Flight Center. **CARBON DIOXIDE EMISSIONS:** *International Energy Annual 2004.* Energy Information Administration: www.eia.doe.gov/iea. **ACCESS TO SAFE DRINKING WATER:** *Millennium Development Goals: China's Progress, 2003.* United Nations. **MAIN MAP:** "Most polluted cities in China blacklisted." China Daily: www.chinadaily.com.cn. • *GEO-2000 Environment Outlook.* UNEP.

Country Themes: Human

POPULATION, pp. 46–47

CONSULTANTS

Carl Haub, *Population Reference Bureau (PRB)*

Youqin Huang, *SUNY-Albany*

GENERAL REFERENCES

Center for International Earth Science Information Network (CIESIN), Columbia University: www.ciesin.org; U.S. Census Bureau; *World Urbanization Prospects* and *World Population Prospects.* Division of the Department of Economic and Social Affairs of the United Nations Secretariat: esa.un.org.

GRAPHICS

FAMILY PLANNING AND THE DEMOGRAPHIC TRANSITION: Heilig, G.K. (1999): *China Food. Can China Feed Itself?* IIASA, Laxenburg (CD-ROM Vers. 1.1). **POPULATION STRUCTURE:** *Midyear Population, by Age and Sex.* U.S. Census Bureau, International Data Base: www.census.gov/ipc/www/idbnew.html. **POPULATION DENSITY:** Center for International Earth Science Information Network (CIESIN), Columbia University, and Centro Internacional de Agricultura Tropical (CIAT), 2005. Gridded Population of the World Version 3 (GPWv3): Population Density Grids—World Population Density, 2005 [map]. Palisades, New York: Socioeconomic Data and Applications Center (SEDAC), Columbia University. Accessed December 2006. Available at http://sedac.ciesin.columbia.edu/gpw. **URBAN POPULATION:** World Gazetteer: www.world-gazetteer.com.

URBANIZATION, pp. 48–49

CONSULTANTS

Kam Wing Chan, *University of Washington*

Annemarie Schneider, *University of California, Santa Barbara*

GENERAL REFERENCES

World Urbanization Prospects: The 2005 Revision. Population Division of the Department of Economic and Social Affairs of the United Nations Secretariat: esa.un.org/unup.

GRAPHICS

DEGREE OF URBANIZATION: 1950–1990: from NBS official data; 1990–2000 from *Urbanization in China in the 1990s: New Definition, Different Series, and Revised Trends,* The China Review, 3(2), pp. 49–71; 2005–2010 by Kam Wing Chan. **DONGGUAN'S URBAN GROWTH:** Image courtesy of Karen Seto, Stanford University. **GROWTH OF MAJOR CITIES:** *Urban and Regional Development Statistics, 2006.* ROC Executive Yuan. **INTER-PROVINCIAL MIGRATION:** Based on Census 2000 data, see Kam Wing Chan (forthcoming). Internal Migration and Rural Migrant Labor: Trends, Geography, and Policies. • *The Labor of Reform in China.* Mary Gallagher, Ching Kwan Lee, and Albert Park, eds.

HUMAN DEVELOPMENT INDICATORS, pp. 50–51

CONSULTANTS

Ruth Levine, *Center for Global Development*

Yehua Dennis Wei, *University of Utah*

GENERAL REFERENCES

UNDP Human Development Report 2005 and 2006. United Nations Development Programme (UNDP): hdr.undp.org.

GRAPHICS

AT A GLANCE: World Development Indicators database, World Bank. • UNICEF China: www.unicef.org/infobycountry/china_statistics.html#12. **ILLITERACY:** Pinyin News: www.pinyin.info/news/2005/illiteracy-in-taiwan. **INFANT MORTALITY:** Ministry of Health: www.moh.gov.cn/2.htm. *Hong Kong and Taiwan: The Statesman's Yearbook: The Politics, Cultures, and Economies of the World (2006).* Barry Turner, ed. Palgrave Macmillan. **EPIDEMIOLOGIC TRANSITION:** *The Global Burden of Disease: A Comprehensive Assessment of Mortality and Disability from Diseases, Injuries, and Risk Factors in 1990 and Projected to 2020.* Christopher J.L. Murray and Alan D. Lopez, eds. • *Revised Global Burden of Disease (2002) Estimates.* World Health Organization: www.who.int/healthinfo/bodgbd2002revised/en/index.html.

RELIGION, PHILOSOPHY, AND LANGUAGE, pp. 52–53

CONSULTANTS

Lawrence Crissman, *Griffith University*

Meng Yeh, *Center for the Study of Languages, Rice University*

Chun-fang Yu, *Columbia University*

GRAPHICS

CHINESE CHARACTERS: Meng Yeh
SACRED SITES: *Cultural Atlas of China*,
Caroline Blunden, Mark Elvin, Stone-
henge Press/Time-Life Inc., 1991;
www.travelchinaguide.com; www.
wadsworth.com; www.mapsofchina.net
**MINORITY LANGUAGES, CHINESE DIA-
LECTS AND NUMBER OF SPEAKERS:**
Language Atlas of China, Australian
Academy of the Humanities and the
Chinese Academy of Social Sciences
in collaboration with, and assisted by,
the Department of Linguistics, the
Research School of Pacific Studies,
The Australian National University,
Australian Academy of the Humanities
and the Longman Group, Hong Kong,
1987. (Used with permission from
Lawrence W. Crissman, Director, Spa-
tial Data Projects Griffith Asia Pacific
Research Institute (GAPRI) Griffith
University, Brisbane, Australia.)

WAY OF LIFE, *pp. 54–55*

CONSULTANT

Meng Yeh, *Rice University*

GRAPHICS

AT A GLANCE: FedStats: www.fedstats.
gov • www.shanghai.gov/cn; chinaview.
wordpress.com; U.S. Census Bureau.
CHINESE CUISINE: Hillman Quality
Publications, 2005.

TOURISM, *pp. 56–57*

CONSULTANT

Guangyu Zhang, *BEC Marketing
Consulting*

GENERAL REFERENCES

China National Tourism Agency: old.
cnta.gov.cn; United Nations World
Tourism Organization: www.world-
tourism.org; World Travel and Tourism
Council: www.wttc.org.

GRAPHICS

AT A GLANCE: *China: The 2006 Travel
and Tourism Economic Research*, World
Travel and Tourism Council. **VISITOR
ARRIVALS AND TOURISM RECEIPTS:**
China National Tourism Administra-
tion. **OUTBOUND TOURISM:** "China
Outbound Tourism: A Missed Op-
portunity for the U.S.?" Helen Marano,
Larry Yu, Brian Beall. **MAJOR TOURIST
SITES:** China Brief Introduction,
China Intercontinental Press, Beijing,
China. 2004; China Tourist Map, Na-
tional Tourism Administration of the
People's Republic of China.

ECONOMY, *pp. 58–59*

CONSULTANT

Clifton W. Pannell, *University
of Georgia (emeritus)*

GRAPHICS

AT A GLANCE: EconStats, Global Econ
Data: World Bank Development Data,
International Monetary Fund (IMF):
www.econstats.com. **UNEMPLOY-
MENT RATE:** International Monetary
Fund, World Economic Outlook Da-
tabase; National Bureau of Statistics
of China. **ECONOMIC OUTPUT:** Dr.
Dafang Zhuang, Chinese Academy
of Sciences.

TRADE, *pp. 60–61*

CONSULTANT

Daniel Griswold, *Center for Trade
Policy Studies, CATO Institute*

GENERAL REFERENCES

World Trade Organization (WTO):
International Trade Statistics, 2006.
www.stat.wto.org.

GRAPHICS

**MERCHANDISE TRADE BALANCE WITH
CHINA AND FOREIGN DIRECT INVEST-
MENT:** *World Investment Report, 2006*;
FDI statistics, UNCTAD, 2004: www.
unctad.org.

FOOD AND AGRICULTURE,
pp. 62–63

CONSULTANT

Liangzhi You, *The International Food
Policy Research Institute (IFPRI)*

GENERAL REFERENCES

*FAO Statistical Yearbook, Country
Profiles, 2005–2006.*

GRAPHICS

LIVESTOCK DENSITY: *Gridded
Livestock of the World.* Agriculture
Department Animal Production and
Health Division, Food and Agriculture
Organization of the United Nations:
www.fao.org/ag/AGAinfo/resources/
en/glw/default.html. **CROP PRODUC-
TION:** You, L., S. Wood, U. Wood-
Sichra. 2006. *Generating global crop
distribution maps: from census to grid.*
Selected paper at 2006 International
Agricultural Economists Association
(IAEA) Conference at Brisbane, Aus-
tralia. **AGRICULTURAL PRODUCTION
OVER TIME:** FAOSTAT, Production
statistics: faostat.fao.org. **AQUACUL-
TURE AND FISHING:** FishStat Plus:
www.fao.org.

ENERGY, *pp. 64–65*

CONSULTANT

David G. Fridley, *China Energy
Group, Lawrence Berkeley National
Laboratory*

GENERAL REFERENCES

China Energy Databook v. 6.0. Lawrence
Berkeley National Laboratory, June
2004; United States Energy Information Administration: www.eia.doe.gov.

GRAPHICS

AT A GLANCE: Energy Information
Administration: www.eia.doe.gov.
FUEL TRADE MAP: *Annual Report
to Congress: Military Power of the
People's Republic of China, 2006.*
Office of the Secretary of Defense. •
*Opening address to the Energy Security
in Asia Pacific Policy Forum.* Treasurer
of the Commonwealth of Australia.
GROWTH RATE: ENERGY vs. GDP:
Energy Information Administration:
www.eia.doe.gov/emeu/internation-
al/energyconsumption.html. Econ-
Stats: www.econstats.com. **MAIN
MAP:** *Energy Mineral Resources Map
of China and Adjacent Seas.* China
Geological Map Printing House,
1st Edition, 1992. • *International
Petroleum Encyclopedia, 2002.*
Pennwell Corporation.

TRANSPORTATION, *pp. 66–67*

CONSULTANTS

Christopher Bennett and **John
Scales,** *World Bank*

GENERAL REFERENCES

China: Transport Sector Brief. East Asia
and Pacific Region Transport Sector
Unit. World Bank (2004).

GRAPHICS

MAIN MAP: American Association of
Port Authorities, 2004: Port Industry
Statistics, World Port Ranking: www.
aapa-ports.org. • A-Z Index of China's
Major Airports: www.gov.cn.

POLITICS, *pp. 68–69*

CONSULTANT

Kenneth Lieberthal, *University of
Michigan*

GENERAL REFERENCES

U.S. State Department: www.state.
gov; China Today: www.chinatoday.
com; ASEAN+3 SME Network: www.
asean3.net.

MILITARY STRENGTH, *pp. 70–71*

CONSULTANT

David M. Finkelstein, *The CNA
Corporation*

GENERAL REFERENCES

*Annual Report to Congress: Military Power
of the People's Republic of China, 2006.*
(Figures 1, 2, 3, 6, 14) Office of the
Secretary of Defense, Department of
Defense, United States of America. *The
Military Balance: 2005–2006.* The Inter-
national Institute for Strategic Studies.

**TELECOMMUNICATIONS
AND CONNECTIVITY,** *pp. 72–73*

CONSULTANTS

Tim Kelly, *International
Telecommunication Union (ITU)*

Sarah Parkes, *Media Works Creative*

GENERAL REFERENCES

International Telecommunication Union
ICT Eye database: www.itu.int. • Statistical Survey Report on the Internet Development in China, January 2007, China
Internet Network Information Center:
www.cnnic.net.cn. • World Bank ICT at
a Glance tables from 2006 *Information
and Communications for Development:
Global Trends and Policies.*

GRAPHICS

TECHNOLOGICAL CONNECTIVITY:
2005–2006 Digital Opportunity Index,
International Telecommunication
Union. • TeleGeography: www.telege-
ography.com/products/map_cable.
CHINA'S TECH INDUSTRY: OECD Inter-
national Trade by Commodity Statistics
(ITCS) 2006. **TELEDENSITY:** Ministry of
Information Industry of the People's
Republic of China: www.mii.gov.cn.

History and Appendix

HISTORY TIME LINE, *pp. 102–105*

CONSULTANT

Robert Cliver, *Humboldt State
University*

FLAGS OF CHINA, *p. 109*

CONSULTANT

Whitney Smith, *Flag Research Center*

Photo and Imagery Credits

KEY: L=Left, R=Right, C=Center,
T=Top, B=Bottom

COVER (L TO R): O. Louis Mazzatenta;
Michael Wolf/laif/Redux Pictures; Paul
Chesley/NGS Image Collection; Rich-
ard Nowitz/NGS Image Collection.

BACK COVER (L TO R): Keren Su/Getty;
Keren Su/Getty; Pete Turner/Getty.

PREFACE: Fernando Moleres/Panos
Pictures.

CHINA SATELLITE (PP. 12-13): Robert
Stacey, WorldSat International Inc.;
Landsat 5; Landsat 7; NASA SRTM

COUNTRY THEMES: pp. 30-31 (L to R):
Art Wolfe/Getty; David Fairman/Getty;
Alessandro Digaetano/Polaris; Ed
Pritchard/Getty; Frank Rothe/Getty. pp.
32-33 (A-G): Bruce Dale; Galen Rowell/
CORBIS; Keren Su/Getty; Liu Liqun/
CORBIS; Ying Liu: Free Agents Lim-
ited/CORBIS; Michael S. Yamashita/
CORBIS. p. 33 (T): Michele Falzone/
JAI/ CORBIS. pp. 34-35 (A-E): Guang
Niu/Getty; Ric Ergenbright/CORBIS;
Keren Su/CORBIS; Keren Su/CORBIS;
Keren Su/CORBIS. p. 35 (T): China
Tourism Press/Getty. p. 37 (T to B):
Jerry Driendl/Getty; Liang Zhuoming/
CORBIS; Andrew K/epa/CORBIS. p.
38: Eugene Hoshiko, AP/Wide World
Photos. p. 39: Gavriel Jecan/CORBIS.
p. 40: (T), Ludovic Maisant/CORBIS;
(CL), Gerry Ellis/Getty; (CR), Byron
Jorjorian/Getty; (BL), Purestock/Getty;
(BR), Daniel J. Cox/Getty. p. 41 (L to
R): Keren Su/Getty; DLILLC/CORBIS;
Roger Tidman/CORBIS; Lynn M.
Stone/naturepl.com. pp. 42-43 (A-D):
Liu Liqun/CORBIS; Liu Liqun/COR-
BIS; Christophe Boisvieux/CORBIS;
Tibor Bognar/CORBIS. p. 43: (T), Liu
Liqun/CORBIS; (CL), Keren Su/Getty;
(CR), Chen Yan/china.org.cn. p. 44:
Peter Parks/AFP/Getty. p. 45 (T to
B): Bojan Brecelj/CORBIS; Michael
Reynolds/epa/CORBIS; Redlink/COR-
BIS. p. 46: Keren Su/Getty. p. 47:
James Nelson/Getty. p. 49: Xiaoyang
Liu/CORBIS. p. 51: (T), Martin Jones;
Ecoscene/CORBIS; (R), Justin Guari-
glia/CORBIS. p. 53: Peter Adams/Get-
ty. p. 54: (CL), Keren Su/Getty; (BL),
Louie Psihoyos/Getty; (TR), Michael
Prince/CORBIS; (CR), Artkey/COR-
BIS; (BR), Gareth Brown/CORBIS. p.
55: (T), Keren Su/Getty; (TL), Zhou
Guangli/Xinhua Press/CORBIS; (CL),
Free Agents Limited/CORBIS; (BL),
Photodisc/Getty; (CR), Jason Lee/Re-
uters/CORBIS; (BR), Art Wolfe/Getty.
p. 56: Courtesy EDSA. p. 57: (T), Louis
Laurent Grandadam/CORBIS; (A-J),
Keren Su/CORBIS; Keren Su/Getty;
Barry Yee/Getty; China Photos/Getty;
Liu Liqun/CORBIS; Keren Su/Getty;
Keren Su/CORBIS; Justin Guari-
glia/NGS Collection/Getty; Alissa
Crandall/CORBIS; TravelChinaGuide.
com. p. 58: Yann Layma/Getty. p. 59:
Wu Hong/epa/CORBIS. p. 60: Gary
Porter/*Milwaukee Journal Sentinel*. p.
61: Yang Liu/Getty. p. 62: Keren
Su/Getty. p. 63: *China Daily*/Reuters/
CORBIS. p. 64: Bob Sacha/CORBIS. p.
65 (T to B): Reed Kaestner/CORBIS;
Adrian Bradshaw/epa/CORBIS; Fritz
Hoffmann. p. 66: (L), Chogo/Xinhua
Press/CORBIS; (R), Dave Bartruff/

CORBIS. p. 67: (T), Claro Cortes IV/Reuters/CORBIS; (L), Jim Richardson/CORBIS; (C),Yann Layma/Getty; (R), IMAGEMORE Co., Ltd./Getty. p. 69: Jack Hollingsworth/Getty. p. 70: Guang Niu/Getty. p. 71 (T to B): Xinhua, Tao Ming, AP/Wide World Photos; Xinhua, Li Gang, AP/Wide World Photos; CHINA NEWSPHOTO/Reuters/CORBIS. p. 72: Aly Song/Reuters/CORBIS. p. 73: Gilles Sabrié.

CITIES: pp. 74-75 (L to R): Medioimages/Photodisc/Getty; Jerry Driendl/Getty; Jake Wyman/Getty; Jerry Driendl/Getty; Michael Prince/CORBIS. p. 76: David Noton/Getty. p. 80: Bohemian Nomad Picturemakers/CORBIS. p. 82: Tony Waltham/Robert Harding World Imagery/CORBIS. p. 84: Keith Macgregor/Getty. p. 86: Maria Stenzel. p. 88: David Frank/Polaris. p. 90: Martin Puddy/Getty. p. 94: Louie Psihoyos/Getty. p. 96: John Ruwitch/Reuters/CORBIS. p. 98: Jeremy Woodhouse/Getty.

HISTORY: pp. 100-101: China Tourism Press/Getty. p. 102: (T), Hulton Archive/Getty; (B), Topical Press Agency/Getty. p. 103: (T), AFP/Getty; (B), Keystone/Getty. p. 104: (T), Catherine Cabrol/Kipa/CORBIS; (BL), AFP/Getty; (BR), O. Louis Mazzatenta. p. 105 (T to B): By CNN via Getty; Keystone/Getty; Stephen Jaffe/AFP/Getty.

Key to Adminstrative Region Facts

The data presented in the Adminstrative Region Facts section are, unless otherwise noted, 2005 data from the following sources: For the provinces (excluding Taiwan), municipalities, and autonomous regions, data are from the *China Statistical Yearbook 2006*, published in the China Statistical Information Network of the National Bureau of Statistics of the People's Republic of China (www.stats.gov.cn); Hong Kong S.A.R. data are from the *Hong Kong Annual Digest of Statistics, 2006 ed.*, published by the Hong Kong Census and Statistics Department (www.censtatd.gov.hk); Macau S.A.R. data are from the Macau Statistics and Census Service (www.dsec.gov.mo/e_index.html); Taiwan data are from the National Statistics, Republic of China (Taiwan) webpage (eng.stat.gov.tw). NA indicates data are not available.

The total **Land area** is given in both square kilometers and square miles. **Population** is a rounded estimate of the 2005 year-end population for a given region. **Capital** city names are given followed by their 2007 city proper population estimates from World Gazetteer (www.world-gazetteer.com). **Population density**, population divided by area, provides the average number of people in one square kilometer. **Population growth 2000-05** is the percent change in total population from the year 2000 to 2005. **Life Expectancy** (2000 data) gives the average number of years a person (**M**ale or **F**emale) is expected to live. **Ethnic minorities** provides the percentage of all counties in a region that are designated as autonomous counties. Autonomous counties are counties with one or several designated ethnic minorities. These are analogous to autonomous regions at the province-level in that they provide county-level ethnic autonomy. **GDP per capita** is the Gross Regional Product divided by population. Gross Regional Product (or Gross Domestic Product for a specific region) is the total value, at current (2005) prices, of final products produced by all resident units during the year. The value in Chinese yuan, New Taiwan dollars (NT$), Macanese Patacas (MOP), or Hong Kong dollars (HK$) is followed by the same amount converted to U.S. dollars (US$). *China Statistical Yearbook 2006* provides provincial-level data on output of various agricultural and industrial products. For **Leading agriculture** and **Leading industry**, the products listed have outputs that rank the highest among China's provinces (excluding Taiwan), municipalities, and autonomous regions. Thus, the products listed may not have the greatest output (e.g., the most tons or cubic meters) but would be among the top when compared to the output of all other regions. Hong Kong S.A.R., Macau S.A.R., and Taiwan data are from the CIA World Factbook (www.cia.gov/library/publications/the-world-factbook/index.html). **Change in vehicles 2000-05** is the percent increase in the number of private vehicles from the year 2000 to 2005. **Water use per capita** is the total amount of water used in a region divided by the year-end population. Water use is defined as gross water use distributed to users, including loss during transportation, broken down with use by agriculture, industry, living consumption, and biological protection. **College students per 1,000 people** provides the number of students enrolled at regular institutions of higher education and adult institutions of higher education per every 1,000 people. **Foreign tourist visits** is the number of people from foreign countries coming to China for sightseeing, visits, tours, family reunions, vacations, study tours, conferences, and other activities of a business, scientific and technological, cultural, educational, or religious nature, and spending at least one night.

Published by the National Geographic Society

John M. Fahey, Jr.
President and Chief Executive Officer

Gilbert M. Grosvenor
Chairman of the Board

Nina D. Hoffman
Executive Vice President; President, Book Publishing Group

Prepared by the Book Division

Kevin Mulroy
Senior Vice President and Publisher

Marianne R. Koszorus
Director of Design

Staff for This Atlas

PROJECT EDITOR AND DIRECTOR OF MAPS
Carl Mehler

MAP EDITORS
Laura Exner, Thomas L. Gray, Nicholas P. Rosenbach

MAP RESEARCH
Matt Chwastyk, Steven D. Gardner, Gregory Ugiansky, and XNR Productions

MAP PRODUCTION MANAGER
Gregory Ugiansky

MAP PRODUCTION
John S. Ballay, Matt Chwastyk, Steven D. Gardner, Michael McNey, and XNR Productions

MAP RELIEF
Tibor G. Tóth

SENIOR GEOGRAPHER
David B. Miller

BOOK DESIGN
Marty Ittner

TEXT EDITORS
Judith Klein *Principal,* **Rebecca Lescaze, Victoria Garrett Jones**

PHOTO EDITOR
Jane Menyawi

PHOTO COORDINATOR
Meredith Wilcox

PHOTO ASSISSTANT
Jeremy M. Felson

MANAGING EDITOR
Jennifer A. Thornton

PRODUCTION DIRECTOR
Gary Colbert

Manufacturing and Quality Management

Christopher A. Liedel
Chief Financial Officer

Phillip L. Schlosser
Vice President

John T. Dunn
Technical Director

Chris Brown
Director

Reproduction by Quad/Graphics, Alexandria, Virginia

Printed and Bound by Mondadori S.p.A., Verona, Italy

Founded in 1888, the National Geographic Society is one of the largest nonprofit scientific and educational organizations in the world. It reaches more than 285 million people worldwide each month through its official journal, NATIONAL GEOGRAPHIC, and its four other magazines; the National Geographic Channel; television documentaries; radio programs; films; books; video and DVDs; maps; and interactive media. National Geographic has funded more than 8,000 scientific research projects and supports an education program combating geographic illiteracy.

For more information, please call 1-800-NGS LINE (647-5463) or write to the following address:

National Geographic Society
1145 17th Street N.W.
Washington, D.C. 20036-4688 U.S.A.

Visit us online at www.nationalgeographic.com/books

For information about special discounts for bulk purchases, please contact National Geographic Books Special Sales: ngspecsales@ngs.org

For rights or permissions inquiries, please contact National Geographic Books Subsidiary Rights: ngbookrights@ngs.org

ISBN: 978-1-4262-0136-3

Datong

Yungong Cave | Shanxi

Xuangong | province

Jinan - Shandong P.

China
中国